T0366187

The Wolf in the Sheep Pen 2

James Prince

Order this book online at www.trafford.com
or email orders@trafford.com

Most Trafford titles are also available at major online book retailers.

Print information available on the last page.

ISBN: 978-1-4907-9325-2 (sc)
ISBN: 978-1-4907-9326-9 (e)

Trafford rev. 01/29/2019

www.trafford.com

North America & international
toll-free: 1 888 232 4444 (USA & Canada)
fax: 812 355 4082

Preface and Warnings

Everything is not true, but there is the truth, and everything is not false, but there is the lie. Although, what is the most important I think, it is to believe yes, but to believe the truth.

There are in this book of mine very large quantities of truths against the lies and vice versa. This could most likely be very disturbing to the ones who still believe in the lies. But remember one thing; there is no truth in lies.

Jesus asked his disciples to teach everything he has commanded us to do and among his recommendations there is the warning to watch out for the false prophets, they are dressed in sheep's clothing, but they are there to mislead, because they are ferocious wolves.

Jesus said he came to bring us the truth and that his enemy, the devil came to bring us the weeds, the lies. Well, this is what I want you to see, the difference between the two of them and I don't count my hours anymore.

Then you'll be able to make your own mind and your own choices and the consequences will be yours as well. Don't forget though that you'll have to answer to the One who will judge everyone and everything. See God's own warning about this in;)

Deuteronomy 18, 17-19. 'The Lord said to me: (Moses) What they say is good. I will raise up for them a prophet like you (Moses, a man pure and simple) from among their brothers; (the Jews) I will put my words in his mouth and he will tell them everything I command him. If anyone does not listen to my words that the prophet speaks in my Name, I Myself will call him to account.'

(God is not like Satan, meaning He is neither a liar nor a cheater and if He wanted to say that He will come Himself among men; He would have simply say so. But this is not what He did. He said He will send a prophet like Moses, a descendant of David, a king He will put on David's throne in permanence, and this is what He did. It is God's word that came in the world, down from heaven, as He said it. Who dares to refute or to contradict Him?

We were told by some liars that everything that is in the Bible is nothing but the pure truth and all inspired by the Holy Spirit. Well, let me tell you that this is false and I will prove it to you and this from the truth that is written in the Holy Bible, because the lies, the contradictions to the word of God and the abominations are not inspired by the Holy Spirit.

Jesus, the Messiah, himself said it, that the lies and the truth will be together until the end time. So why are you contradicting him and don't you believe what he said and why are you saying the opposite of what is also written in the Holy Bible?

Don't you think that I am against the Bible or that I intent to take anything away from it, on the contrary, because it contains all the necessary proofs against God's enemies! It contains all the lies and the contradictions to the truth and this is most likely one of the reasons why the Messiah told his angels not to pull the weeds out of it.

But unfortunately and for a good reason, to see so many lies and contradictions in the book of the truth has most likely incited many atheists to become what they are. Their mistake is to blame God for what the devil did. I hope with my whole heart they will open their eyes before it is too late for them.

I read somewhere one day that three atheists wrote each a book about atheism and each of them sold more than ten millions copies of their books. This is to say that the work of the devil is following through, because his goal, as always, is to pull people away from God. But the truth opens the eyes of the ones who look for it and hopefully, they can see it in these books of mine, because all I am trying to do really is to distinguish the truth from the lies; so you too can see through the lies as I do.

Some people will say that all of this is out of line critics from my part, but I say this is rather denunciation of the ferocious wolf, denunciation of the Antichrist, denunciation of this wolf, who introduced himself in the sheep pen to contradict the Messiah and to make competition to the Jesus' sheep, to the Messiah' disciples.

All of this though that is written in this book of mine could very easily shock many people, especially if they strongly believe in the lies. But don't forget that Jesus, the Messiah, warned us long before I do, of all the abominations that cause the desolation. Read and be careful at what you read in;)

Matthew 24, 15. 'Therefore, when you see the abomination that causes desolation, which was spoken of through Daniel the prophet— standing in the holy place—(in the Bible) let the reader understand.'

(And if the reader should understand and be careful at what he reads; this is because the abomination that causes desolation is in the Holy Scriptures.

Some people, like my mom did, will ask me where in Daniel this is written. Well, this is in Daniel 11, 36-37.

To better understand everything that is written in this book of mine; I will put everything that is from the Bible inside quotation marks; 'like these,' and all of my commentaries in parenthesis; (like these.) I don't want you to be confused at all. I also hope that you will find my commentaries judicious and reasonable.

James Prince, a Jesus' disciple!

THE WOLF IN THE SHEEP PEN 2

I talked in my previous book about three different gospels and I found out that two of them are very questionable, but the one I am about to cultivate, meaning, to distinguish the weeds from the wheat, the truth from the lies, is in my opinion even more misleading than the other two questionable ones.

I can already read two lies or two deceits in only one verse and this one is in;)

John 1, 14. 'The word became flesh and made his dwelling among us. We have seen his glory, the glory of the One and only, (begotten of the Father) who came from the Father, full of grace and truth.'

(That the word of God that is to me the most powerful force in this whole world, because it is by the word of God that everything was created and that this most powerful force became flesh; flesh that the Messiah said it is weak; this doesn't only seems to me improbable, but also impossible.

This is not the Son of God who came down from heaven, coming from the Almighty, but it is the word of God and it came down from heaven to be in the mouth of the greatest prophet that Jesus is, and this to do everything that God has commanded him, and Jesus has fulfilled his mandate. See Deuteronomy 18, 18.

Jesus is not the only one who would have come from the Father, since Adam has also come from the Father. What about all the proud angels and Lucifer that God would have chased from the heavens to the earth? Didn't they all come down from heaven, from the Father?

Then to say that Jesus is the only one Son of God is also a huge lie. This is to say that all the other males on earth are the sons of the devil. I don't take this and it is my right to do so.

Everyone and all who do the will of the Father who is in heaven on earth are also sons and daughters of God. We are the sisters and the brothers of the Messiah. We are not the sisters and the brothers of God. We are God's children, if we do His will. See Matthew 12, 50.)

John 1, 17. 'For the Law was given through Moses; grace and truth came through Jesus Christ.'

(Would this author, this John, say that there was no truth in the Law? The truth Jesus said that not the least stroke of a pen will disappear from the Law. That's the truth.

The same lie is repeated here in John 1, 18, about the One and only Son. The truth is that Jesus, the

Messiah, has made God and the truth known to the world with the word of God, with his knowledge.)

John 1, 29. 'The next day John (the Baptist) saw Jesus coming toward him and said; "Look, the Lamb of God, who takes away the sins of the world!"'

(Do you see this abomination now? Not only the enemies of God succeeded in putting lies and abominations in the mouth of Peter and in the mouth of Jesus, but they also did this with John the Baptist. Jesus, the Messiah, didn't take anything away from the world, on the contrary; he brought to the world the word of God, his knowledge, and this is how he saves.

See Isaiah 53, 11. 'By his knowledge my righteous servant will justify many.'

(And it is with his knowledge that Jesus, the Messiah, told us how to get rid of our sins and this is how he took care of them. But this doesn't mean that he took them with him at all. See Matthew 4, 17.

And to say that John the Baptist would have said that Jesus is the Lamb of God, an animal; this too is a lie and an abomination put in the mouth of this John the Baptist and he has nothing to do with that. Though, this was the way of the John of Paul to do this kind of things, to say that Jesus and God are animals, some lambs as you will see many times in the Revelation of the John of Paul.

See another lie here put in the mouth of John the Baptist in;)

John 1, 31. 'I myself (John the Baptist) did not know him, (Jesus) but the reason I came baptizing with water was that he might be revealed to Israel.'

(What a bunch of fake news that is! I don't think that John the Baptist lied, but I do think that this author, the John of this gospel did it. And this is not surprising coming from one of Paul's disciples. And to put in the mouth of John the Baptist that he didn't know his cousin Jesus, who was almost of the same age and who lived just in the neighbouring community; this is an insult to people intelligence.

I don't think they were living far apart from one another either, because Mary, Jesus' mother walked all the way to her cousin Elisabeth, John the Baptist's mother, when both of them were pregnant of these two. This according to what is written in Luke 1, 39-40.

The same lie is repeated in;)

John 1, 33. 'I would not have known him, except that the One who sent me to baptize with water told me, 'The man on whom you see the Spirit come down and remain is he who will baptize with the <u>Holy Spirit</u>.'

(There is finally something true here in this gospel of John.)

See Matthew 3, 11. 'I (John the Baptist) baptize you with water for repentance. But after me will come one who is more powerful than I, whose sandals I am not fit to carry. He will baptize you with the <u>Holy Spirit</u> and with fire.'

(Jesus was not baptizing people with water, but with the Spirit of God, with the word of God, so with the truth, and if I had not received this baptism from Jesus; I could not do this work of mine, which is written to teach, to warn and to make disciples for Jesus out of all the nations. And if Jesus baptized with the Holy Spirit during all of his ministry; meaning, with all of the time he spent with his apostles and disciples; there was no reason at all then for them to wait for the Holy Spirit to come after the Messiah's departure. Then all of this story, this invention made by Jesus' enemies about the Holy Spirit who was to come, Who was not yet given, or not yet in the world, is simply a diabolic machination to introduce Paul in the picture. You can find references about this in John 14, 26, in John 15, 26, in John 16, 7 and in John 16, 13.

The insult and the disgrace is repeated here again in;)

John 1, 36. 'When he (John the Baptist) saw Jesus passing by, he said, "Look, the <u>Lamb</u> of God."'

(You do understand, of course, that John the Baptist has never said such a thing, such abomination, but that John, Paul's disciple, who is not without knowing what his master said in;)

Romans 6, 14. 'For sin shall not be your master, (sin have no power over you) because you are <u>not under Law</u>, (outlaw like Paul is) but under grace.'

(This is kind of strange that Paul didn't include himself in that statement, isn't it? But what kind of grace is he talking about, for Paul's disciples to say such disgraceful things, like saying that the Son of Man, the Son of God is a lamb, an animal; them who also say that Jesus is God? How could they say that sin has no power over them; they who also say that they all have sins?

From John 1, 37 to John 1, 51, this is nothing but fake news and a bunch of lies and all who know the truth about the first meeting between Jesus, the true Messiah, with his apostles will see that there are here in the gospel of this John a multitude of falseness.

Take for example what is written in;)

John 1, 39. 'So they went and they saw where he (Jesus) was staying, and spent that day with him.'

(Again here, the (he) that this John was talking about was maybe Paul, his master.

There are so many lies and so many contradictions in this gospel of this John! See rather what Jesus rather said to his disciples; something you can read in;)

Matthew 8, 20. 'Jesus replied, "Foxes have holes and birds of the air have nests, but the Son of Man has no place to rest his head."'

(When Jesus began his ministry to do everything that God has commanded of him; he left his family and his home also, and even his mother and brothers had to disturb the crowds to talk to him. Don't forget that the tree is recognized by its fruits and a liar by his lies and the gospel of this John is full of them.

The story of the wedding at Cana is in my opinion just as ridiculous as the story of Lazarus in Luke 16, 19, 31.)

John 2, 1-11. 'On the third day a wedding took place at Cana in Galilee. Jesus' mother was there, and Jesus and his disciples had also been invited to the wedding. When the wine was gone, Jesus' mother said to him, "They have no more wine."'

(Why would she say something like this to Jesus, since he hadn't made any miracle yet and he was known for carrying no money? And Jesus would have made from 120 to 180 gallons of the best wine for a crowd who had already too much to drink.)

'"Dear woman, why do you involve me?"'

(Do you believe that a son who is humble and gentle at heart would have answered his mother this way in those days; he, Jesus a son of the holy family? This was the equivalent of saying to his mother, 'mind your own business.' Jesus hasn't done that either.)

'"Mother, Jesus replied. "My time has not yet come."'

(In general when we speak about our time has come; we mean our last hour, not the time to make some of the best wine for a crowd that is already drunk.)

'His mother said to the servants, "Do whatever he tells you." Nearby stood six stone water jars, the kind used by the Jews for ceremonial washing, each holding from twenty to thirty gallons.'

(Would those jars be like some bathtubs of our days?)

'Jesus said to the servants, "Fill the jars with water"; so they filled them to the brim. Then he told them, "Now draw some out and take it to the master of the banquet." (In my opinion, this was an action done to be seen and appreciated by men; which is contrary to the true message of the true Messiah.) They did so, and the master of the banquet tasted the water that had been turned into wine. He did not realize where it had come from, though the servant who had drawn the water knew. Then he called the bridegroom aside and said, "Everyone brings out the choice wine first and then the cheaper wine after the guests have had too much to drink; but you have saved the best till now.'

(This means that they all had a lot to drink.)

'This, the first miraculous signs, Jesus performed at Cana in Galilee. He thus revealed his glory,'

(He who was still waiting to be glorified by the Father when he died.)

'And his disciples put their faith in him.'

(They would have told themselves, 'Of course, if this guy can make good wine as we want and need it and for free; he is our man.'

(It must have been something to see after this wedding. To believe such a story; it is not knowing very well neither Jesus nor Mary, his mother nor God. I don't doubt for a minute that Jesus had the power to make wine with water, but I sincerely doubt that he would have made good wine for a crowd that was already drunk and this under the eyes of his mother, and revealed his glory afterward.

I know a little story concerning this kind of miracles. 'There was this guy driving his car and couldn't keep it straight on the road. So he got caught and stopped by the police who asked him to open the lead of his trunk. When the officer saw three gallons of white wine; he asked this man, 'what is this?' The guy looked towards the skies and said,)

"Thank You Lord; You've done it again."'

(In that same story of this wedding at Cana in the French Bible; it is not written how many gallons of wine Jesus would have made for this drunken crowd, so some people asked me where I got that. I tell them then that this is what is written in the English Bible. They took it off in the French Bible, and this most likely because someone realized that this makes no sense at all that Jesus would have made more wine for someone already drunk.

I don't invent anything concerning the word of God, but I write the information to the best of my knowledge, and this is to help you to see the truth.

There was manipulation of the truth in the Scriptures here too in what is next.)

John 2, 14-17. 'In the <u>temple court</u> he (this Jesus) found.'

(Here in the New International Bible, this happened in the temple court, but in my French Bible and in the King

James Bible, this happened inside the temple and this is manipulation of the Holy Scriptures again.)

'Men selling cattle, sheep and doves, and others selling at tables exchanging money. So he (Jesus) made a <u>whip</u> out of cords,'

(The true Jesus, who is humble and gentle at heart and came to call the sinners.)

'And <u>drove all</u> from the temple area,'

(Jesus who came to call sinners here was chasing them away.) 'Both sheep and cattle; he scattered the coins of the money changers and overturned their tables. To those who sold doves he said,'

(How could he? He drove them all out already.) "Get those out of here! How dare you turn <u>my Father's house</u> into a market?" His disciples remembered that it is written: "Zeal for your house will consume Me."'

(As if Jesus, the true Messiah, would have had this kind of zeal for violence, he who is humble and gentle in heart. At first, this false Christ said they were in the temple court and then he talked about a market <u>in</u> his Father's house. Besides, the true Messiah knew that no one can put God in a box made by men.

Like I have already said it, if Jesus would have done all of this, the Romans wouldn't have had to crucify him; these farmers would have stoned him in the temple court. This was rather Paul who was travelling from one of his church to another with his whip and his little army where all were waiting for him or his disciples with fear and trembling.)

See 2 Corinthians 7, 15. 'And his affection for you is all the greater when he remembers that you were all obedient, receiving him with <u>fear</u> and <u>trembling</u>.'

(The same story elsewhere only mentioned men selling doves, so no cattle and no sheep, and there is no mentioning of a whip made out of cords either. And who can say without lying that Jesus, and again, the true Messiah, would be capable of such violence and such strength, enough to chase strong men, for they were farmers and also capable to chase cattle and sheep and also to overturn tables? This was not Jesus who had an army of soldiers to defend and to protect him. And again, Jesus, the true one, was not without knowing that the temple was not his Father's house; he who always said, 'My Father who is in heaven.' And, 'My heavenly Father.'

Elsewhere, Jesus would have mentioned a den of robbers and here it is a market. Who is the one who's telling the truth, or who lied?

I rather think again that this story was written only to try to make people believe that Jesus was not that gentle after all, but believe it; this defamation was not written by one of Jesus' disciples, but by one of his enemies.

I don't think that this John and Luke agreed with one another about what is written in the next verse.)

John 2, 22. 'After he was raised from the dead, his disciples recalled what he had said, then they believed the Scriptures and the words that Jesus had spoken.'

(See now;)

Luke 24, 25. 'He (this) Jesus said to them, (Jesus' apostles) "How foolish are you, and how slow of heart to believe all that the prophets have spoken!'

(They contradict one another, but they both have lied. One has to wonder which one has lied the most.

Neither this John nor his false Christ knew the difference between the kingdom of God and the kingdom of heaven.)

See John 3, 3. 'In reply (this) Jesus declared, "I tell you the truth, no one can see the kingdom of God unless he is born again."'

(The true Jesus was preaching the kingdom of heaven, his kingdom. See now how this is written in the French Bible and in the King James. "Verily, Verily, I say to you." But this is not the way Jesus was speaking at all. There is a false Christ who came under Jesus' name in Mark, in Luke and also here in this John. He is an imposter.

There is a lot of fake news again here from this John in the story of Nicodemus, from John 3, 1 to John 3, 21. There is here among other things a say that make Jesus a liar, but you will see that a lot of times in John's gospel, so brace yourselves.)

John 3, 13. 'No one has ever gone into heaven except the one who came from heaven—the Son of Man.'

(What about Moses and Elijah? What about Lucifer and his angels that the Almighty chased out of the heavens?

The Son of Man came to this world like all the other men. What came down from heaven is the word of God that God put in the mouth of the Messiah.

We will see later on in this John's gospel that this John contradicted himself and even made Jesus to be a liar.)

See John 20, 17. 'Do not hold on to me, for I have not yet returned to the Father.'

(Then here we can see one of the worse and biggest lie in what is following in;)

John 3, 14-15. 'Just as Moses lifted up the snake in the desert, (I think this was done in town before Pharaoh) so the Son of Man must be lifted up, that everyone who <u>believes</u> in him shall not perish but may have eternal life.'

(There are millions of Christians who believe in Jesus, but don't listen to him, not to say maybe billions. There are thousands of mafia people, who live in crimes, murderers and thieves who are living out of corruption all the days of their lives and also believe in Jesus. The demons and even Satan also believe in the Messiah. Do you really believe they will inherit eternal life just because they believe in him? Jesus, the Messiah, told us how to enter life, and this was not to believe in him, but something else that is written in;)

Matthew 19, 17. 'But if you want to enter into life, keep the commandments.'

('You shall not kill,' and all the rest. See Exodus 20, 1-17. Not much is simpler than this, but the Jesus' enemies will tell you that it is impossible to obey all of the God's commandments, and that this is why He sent his Son on earth. Jesus told us that everything is possible to God. I say that this is greatly possible too, but for this, one has to love God with all his heart, with all of his mind and with all of his soul, and I say too that to obtain eternal life; this is largely worth it. All of those who tell you that this is impossible should read with you what is written in;)

Luke 1, 6. 'Both of them (Zechariah and his wife Elizabeth) were upright in the sight of God, observing all the Lord's commandments and regulations blamelessly.'

(It is possible to obey all of the God's commandments, but for this we have to love God with all of our heart, mind and soul, and this is why I can. It is most likely why the demons can't and why they invented a different fake way, faith and grace without deeds.

A bit earlier I mentioned what I think is the biggest lie in the New Testament. Now I must tell you what I think is the worse abomination in the Holy Scriptures. I also think it is the most popular of them all, and it is written in;)

John 3, 16. 'So God so loved the world,'

(That He wanted to destroy it a couple of times and by his word put in the mouth of the Messiah; He asked us to withdraw from the world, because the world is the kingdom of the devil.)

'That He <u>gave his one and only Son</u>, that <u>whoever believes</u> in him shall not perish but have eternal life.'

(What an abomination this one is! First of all, God didn't give his Son and his Son is still with God. Secondly, Jesus is not God's only Son. To say that Jesus is God's only Son is to say that all the other men are the sons of the devil, and this is a lie and I don't take it. Thirdly, to sacrifice or to give his first born Son for what ever or for whomever; this is something that God Himself called an abomination; this is something that God Himself condemned. God could not do and He didn't do something that He Himself has condemned.)

See Deuteronomy 18, 10-12. 'Let no one be found among you (Israelites) who <u>sacrifices</u> (give) his son or daughter in the fire, (kill in fire or any other ways) who practices divination or sorcery, interprets omens, engages in witchcraft, or casts spells, or is a medium or spiritist or who consults the dead. (Whoever prays somebody else than God.) Anyone who does these things is detestable (abominations) to the Lord, and because of these detestable practices (abominations) the Lord your God will drive out those nations before you.' (Israel!

See also 2, Kings 16, 3. I don't really know if this number has inspired this John or not, but this is the number of John 3, 16 backward.)

2 Kings 16, 3. 'He walked in the ways of the kings of Israel and even sacrificed his son in fire, following the detestable ways (abominations) of the nations the Lord had driven out before the Israelites.'

(God almighty cannot say that offering in sacrifice his son is an abomination and committed it Himself, this is impossible and even to say that He did is another abomination.

And to say that God the Father gave his one and only Son in sacrifice, when it is also written this here from one of the greatest prophets in whom God has confided a lot of messages is also unlikely, see;)

Isaiah 53, 12. 'Because he poured out his life unto death.'

(The same lie is also repeated here in;)

John 3, 18. 'Whoever believes in him,'

(In Jesus, like Satan and the demons do.)

'Is not condemned, but whoever does not believe stands condemned already because he has not believed in the name of God's one and only Son.'

(They are judged and condemned by whom and what for, since the judgement will only take place at the end of the ages? Jesus, the Messiah, said it himself that he didn't come to judge the world, but to save it. But Paul, Jesus' enemy and his disciples, on the contrary, didn't wait till the end to start judging others, and condemning them and handing people over to Satan. All of this without being sat on a throne. We will see more of that a bit farther. As for saying that God's one and only Son; let's go read something else also written in the Holy Scriptures, in;)

Luke 3, 38. 'The son of Enosh, the son of Seth, the son of Adam, the son of God.'

(Let's see also something about God's one and only Son, about God's first born in;)

Exodus 4, 22. 'And thou shall say unto Pharaoh, thus saith the Lord, Israel is <u>my first son</u>, even my <u>firstborn</u>; and I say unto thee, let my son go, that he may serve Me; <u>and if thou refuse</u>,'

('But you refused.' As written in the New International Bible.)

'To let him go, behold, I will slay thy son, even thy firstborn.'

(You have most likely noticed that this last verse was taken out of the King James Bible and I had a good reason for that; this is because the four words underlined above were not written in the New International Bible and neither in the Gideons' Bible.

This is why I chose a version that tells the truth as it is written in my French Bible, because I love the truth.

Not according to me, but according to what is written in the Bible; to say that Jesus is the only one Son of God is lying and there are many out there who are not shy at all to do just that.

Not only they have lied, but they have also made God to be a liar; which is also a terrible abomination.

There are also many places in the Bible where the sons and the daughters of God are mentioned. See Genesis 6, 2, Deuteronomy 32, 19 and many more.)

John 3, 22. 'After this, Jesus and his disciples went out into the Judean countryside, where he spent some time with them, and baptized.'

(Just remember this last word underlined above.

John, 3, 36. 'Whoever believes in the Son has eternal life, but whoever rejects the Son will not see life, for God's wrath remains on him.'

(We have already seen that this is false, because as I have already said it, even Satan and the demons believe in Jesus, and even maybe more than anyone.

Believing and accepting is different from believing and rejecting also. It would be good to read this again;)

See James 2, 19-20. 'You believe that there is one God. Good! Even the demons (like Paul) believe that—and shudder. You foolish man, (Paul) do you want evidence that faith without deeds is worthless?'

They shudder mainly because they truly and firmly believe in Jesus, in the Son of Man, in the Messiah.

John 4, 2. 'Although in fact it was not Jesus who baptized, but his disciples.'

(Who is telling the truth, since the same John said earlier that Jesus baptized and now he says he was not baptizing?

The truth is that Jesus was not baptizing with water and neither did his disciples, but was and still is baptizing with the truth, with the word of God, with the Holy Spirit. But the John, Jesus' apostle knew this and obviously this John of Paul here of this gospel of John didn't know that and he lied just as much as his master Paul did.

According to John the Baptist, Jesus was not baptizing with water, but he was baptizing with the Holy Spirit, with word of God, with the truth. See again;)

Matthew 3, 11. 'He will baptize you with the Holy Spirit and with fire.'

(The liars get very often caught in their lies and it is by their lies that we recognize the liars. This is what happened with this liar here in his gospel and as we will see it farther, not only he lied, but he has also put lies in the mouth of Jesus. Just like his companions and his master did. And this is what I call the abomination.

But make sure to understand something here; this liar in the gospel of John is not the John, the Jesus' apostle nor Jesus' brother John nor John the Baptist, but he is the John, Paul's disciple and he lied just as much as his master did. It has crossed my mind too that the gospel of John was written by Paul and I think he wrote the book of Revelation as well. This won't surprise me at all if this was the case.)

John 4, 4-5. 'Now he (this Jesus) had to go through Samaria. So he came to a town in Samaria called Sychar, near the plot of ground Jacob had given to his son Joseph.'

(It seems to me very unlikely that Jesus, the true Messiah could have told his apostles not to enter the towns of Samaria and to enter it himself with his disciples.

I think there are to me two things that might have happened and maybe more. Either this Jesus here in this gospel of John is not the true Messiah, or this false Christ tried to make Jesus a liar. In both cases there is swindling.

You can believe if you want to the rest of that story, but I don't believe in lies that are this obvious. Just read again;)

Matthew 10, 5-6. 'Do not go among the Gentiles or enter any town of the Samaritans. Go rather to the lost sheep of Israel.'

(See also what Jesus himself would have said in;)

Matthew 15, 24. '"I was sent only to the lost sheep of Israel."'

(But the way it is written in French and in the King James Bible; it is a bit confusing, enough not to be sure if Jesus said; 'I was sent,' or, 'I was not sent only to the lost sheep of Israel. See the King James version of;)

Matthew 15, 24. 'I am not sent but unto the lost sheep of the house of Israel.'

John 4, 27. 'Just then his, (Jesus') disciples returned,'

(From the town of the Samaritans where Jesus told them not to enter.)

'And were surprised to find him talking with a woman.'

(This was not the true Jesus who said it was best for a man not to touch a woman. This was Paul and this made me think that maybe those were Paul's disciples here and this false Christ was Paul, because this was his territory.

It is a good thing to know that Paul too had a disciple called Jesus. See;)

Colossians 4, 10-11. 'My fellow prisoner <u>Aristarchus</u> sends you his greetings, as does <u>Mark</u>, the cousin of Barnabas. You have received instructions (orders) about him; if he comes to you, welcome him. Jesus, who is call <u>Justus</u>, (just us) also sends greetings. These are the <u>only Jews</u> (two) among my fellow workers for the kingdom of God.'

(So we have to believe here that God has protected his people of Israel as He promised He will and He protected his Law too against this mercenary of Paul. If we have to believe what Paul said here; all of the roads he went through, all of his entries in the Jewish synagogues to mislead the Jews were in vain. We can also see that Mark, as I was saying was one of Paul's disciples. This also means that Mark, Luke, this John and all the other of Paul's disciples were Gentiles. This is just as I was saying.

When I speak about Paul pulling all the strings of his churches; we can see another proof of that here again, because even when he was a prisoner, he could give his orders to his disciples, but this was not the way that the true Messiah was running his Church.

From John 4, 28 to John 5, 23, there is a lot of unnecessary and complicated fake news and this was Paul's ways to write.

John 5, 3-4. 'In these lay a multitude of those who were sick, blind, lame, and withered waiting for the moving of the waters; for an angel of the Lord went down from time to time into the pool and stirred up the waters;'

(When the faith of a person is fragile and sees such a stupid story and doesn't know and doesn't understand the stratagems of Satan; this is enough for that person to become atheist. This would explain why there are so many of them now in the world.)

'Whoever then first, after the stirring up of the waters, stepped in was made well from whatever disease with which he was afflicted.'

(This took an angel to think such a stupidity, yes, but a hell angel. This must have been quite a show, to see all those sick people, those blinds, those lame and withered racing up against one another to get down there first and risk their lives, risking to be drowned on top of all. But to say that an angel of the Lord was involved in this kind of orgy is to say another abomination. This would be worthy of an angel alright, but from a Satan's angel. Don't believe in such abomination; this has never happened, especially not before Jesus, the true Messiah. There is more to retain about that story. There were many sick people, but Jesus would have cured only one of them.????? This too is very questionable.)

John, 5. 6. 'When Jesus saw him lying there and learned that he had been in this condition for a long time, he asked him, "Do you want to get well?"'

(What a stupid question! This is too stupid really to be from the true Messiah.

See another stupidity here in;)

John 5, 14-19. 'Later (this) Jesus found him at the temple and said to him, "See, you are well again. <u>Stop</u> sinning or something <u>worse</u> may happen to you." The man went away and told the Jews that it was Jesus who had made him well. (Was that a sin?) So because Jesus was doing these things on the Sabbath, <u>the Jews</u> persecuted him. Jesus said to them, "My Father is always at his work to this very day, and I, too, am working.'

(So, there is no resting day for God or for Jesus, according to this one.)

'For this reason <u>the Jews</u> tried all the harder to kill him;'

(But this Jesus was arguing with them in the temple,) not only was he breaking the Sabbath, but he was calling God his own Father, making himself equal with God.'

(I don't know how it is for you, but I have never though myself being equal to my father because I am his son, and you? There is more yet; which prince or princess in this low world would think or would say being equal with the king or the queen? He or she would be brought quickly to reality.)

'Jesus gave them this answer: "I tell you the truth,'

(This is how it is written here in the New International Bible, but see how it is written in the King James, 'Verily, verily, I say to you.' In the Gideons it is, 'Truly, truly, I say to you.' And in the French Bible it is, 'En vérité, en vérité.' which is the same than in the King James Bible. All of this is proving that there are more manipulations of the Scriptures.)

'The Son can do nothing by himself; he can do only what he sees his Father doing, because whatever the Father does, the Son also does.'

(What a bunch of fake news all of this is. And if all who sin would receive worse than this man has, who was sick for more than thirty-eight years, there would not be too many people healthy on this earth. According to Paul, all have sin.

Besides, it was not what the true Jesus saw that made him act, but what he heard. See Deuteronomy 18, 18.

This John wrote that the Jews wanted to kill Jesus because he said about himself being the Son of God, but see what the same John wrote about the same Jews in;)

John 8, 41. '"We are not illegitimate children," they (the Jews) protested. "The only Father we have is God Himself."'

(We will see in this same gospel of John that this Jesus contradicts himself more than once and this is not very brilliant. But just as I said it earlier, the true Jesus, the true Messiah, has nothing to do with this, but his enemies have.)

See John 9, 1-3. 'As he (Jesus) went along, he saw a man blind from birth. His disciples asked him, "Rabbi, who sinned, this man or his parents, that he was born blind?" "Neither this man nor his parents sinned," said Jesus.'

(Let's see now where this John took this story of the sickness relate to sins, by reading Paul, his master in;)

1 Corinthians 11, 29-30. 'For anyone who eats or drinks without recognizing the body of the Lord eats and drinks judgement on himself. This is why many among you are weak and sick, and a number of you have fallen asleep.'

(This is Paul, who said that all have sin. This would means that according to him, who had a few infirmities, what he called a thorn or two in his flesh, by the way; we should all have at least a sickness, an infirmity, or else been dead.

It was him, Paul, the sickliest man of all, who needed the word of God, just like the publicans who sat with Matthew and Jesus to listen to him and just like everybody does. But Paul and his disciples have preferred to use the word of God to mislead people. Just like the serpent did it in the Garden of Eden with Adam and Eve and his stratagem is continuing to this very day.

John 5, 19. 'Jesus gave them this answer, "I tell you the truth,'

(These last five words are copied from Jesus who is in Matthew. The Jesus in the gospel of John has not spoken this way at all in the other English Bibles, nor in the gospel of John in the French Bible, and this John has not written this way either. This is cheating, always some cheating.)

'The Son can do nothing by himself; he can do only what he sees his Father doing, because whatever the Father does the Son also does.'

(More fake news and what a lie this is again! Did the Son have seen the Father being crucified? Did the Son have seen the Father create the world and has he done as much and all the same? The truth, the truth is that the Father has put his word in the mouth of a prophet and this man is the Messiah. This man is Jesus and he has done everything the Father has commanded from him. This was to give us the word of God truly; not like this liar of John and his false Christ have done it here in this fake and lying gospel. In turn, the world who didn't want to hear anything from him managed to kill him. This is the truth and there is no point to look for the truth somewhere else or to listen to these liars.)

John 5, 24. '"I tell you the truth,'

(This is cheating here again, trying to look like the true Jesus who is in Matthew and worse yet, to make Jesus look like he is a liar.)

'Whoever hears my word and believes (like Satan and his demons) him who sent me has eternal life and will not be condemned; he has crossed from death to life."'

(The author of this gospel of John preached faith without deeds, just like Paul has done it and this is antichrist. I do believe that the one who sent this false Christ is Satan, because God couldn't have sent someone to lie this way about his word. This is impossible.

There is another thing here. In the entire gospel of Matthew, an apostle that I am sure have spent much time closely with Jesus, the Messiah, a man of truth who wrote about the life and the activities of Jesus, but according to Matthew; Jesus, the Messiah, has never repeated, 'Verily, verily,' as the Jesus of the gospel of John has done it. See Jesus in;)

Matthew 10, 15. 'I tell you the truth.'

(This is not the same Jesus at all who speaks in both gospel and one of them is an impostor, a false Christ.

This John has lied too much to speak about the true Messiah. The copy that is in Luke 4, 25 is more credible.

It is not all who believe in God that are the brothers, the sisters and the mothers of Jesus, so God's children, but all who do the will of the Father who is in heaven. They are the ones who will have eternal life. Remember, 'Faith without deeds is dead, worthless and useless.' It is the same than to believe without acting, without obeying the Laws of God.

See another lie here from this false Christ and written by this John in;)

John 5, 27. 'And He (God) has given him (the Messiah) authority to judge because he is the Son of Man.'

(This is Paul who gave himself the power to judge others and to hand them over to Satan, but the true Jesus didn't do this and he even told us not to judge. See rather what the true Messiah declared in;)

Matthew 19, 28. 'Jesus said to them, (his apostles) "I tell you the truth, at the renewal of all things (at the end time, not before) when the Son of Man sits on his glorious throne, you (Jesus' apostles) who have followed me (the Messiah) will also sit on twelve thrones, judging the twelve tribes of Israel."'

(We'll see shortly that this false Christ is contradicting himself in this same gospel.

John 5, 29. 'Those who have done good will rise to life and those who have done evil will rise to be condemned.'

(And we all have done evil at one point or another in our life and all without exception will have to face the judgement of God. Take a look at Matthew 25, 31-45, to see how the Messiah will proceed at the judgement.

All of those who have sincerely repented for their sins will pass quickly to the right side with God's sheep and all of the others will go cry on the left side, but this will be too late to change anything about their condition. Maybe you have mocked God down here on the earth, but you won't be able to mock Him at that time. Though, for as long as there is life, there is hope, and always remember that the least room in the kingdom of God will be much better than the nicest place in hell.)

John 5, 30. 'By myself I can do nothing; I (this false Christ) judge only as I hear.'

(Didn't he say earlier that he was acting as he sees? This is just a little change that I noticed.

'And my judgement is just, for I seek not to please myself but him (the devil) who sent me.'

(The demons too are out to please the one who sent them and I do think this is the case of this false Christ here.

This Jesus who is in the gospel of John judges here, but this same false Christ contradicted himself in;)

John 12, 47. 'As for the person who hears my words but does not keep them, I do not judge him. For I did not come to judge the world, but to save it.'

(He is confusing the man. He reminds me of the girl who plays with the flower, you know the marguerite, 'He loves me, he loves me not. He loves me, he loves me not.' 'I judge, I don't judge. I judge, I don't judge.'

We should all know by now too that this was Paul who allowed himself to judge others and to hand them over to Satan.

From John 6, 17 to John 6, 21, this John spoke about Jesus walking on the agitated sea. He also talked about the fear of the other disciples, but he didn't mention at all that Peter too did walked on the water, just a little maybe, but he did, and I do think this deserved to be mentioned, especially by a companion who spent everyday together with him and for the same cause. The John, the Jesus' apostle, Peter's companion would have done it.)

John 6, 28-29. 'Then they asked him, (Jesus) "What must we do to do the works God requires?" Jesus answered, "The work of God is this; to <u>believe</u> in the one he has sent."'

(This was to preach for his oneself. There is a difference between believing in someone and listening to someone. The true Messiah also said something about the works required from God, when he said this here in;)

Matthew 19, 16-17. 'Now a man came up to Jesus (the true one) and asked, "Teacher, what good thing I must do to get eternal life?" "Why do you ask me about what is good?" Jesus replied. "There is only One who is good. If you want to enter life, obey the commandments."'

(This is a little more than just believe. This false Christ in this John's gospel preached like Paul, which is faith without deeds, which is useless, as you now know.

(There is only One who is good, but how come there are so many saints in those false churches? Will they say that the Messiah lied or his enemies did it?

Satan and his demons also believe in the one that God sent and they believe in him so much that they deployed all kind of practices, lies and contradictions to confuse the truth. These are the weeds that have over grown the wheat.

There is also a lying answer here from this false Christ in John 6, 28-29, and again, the answer is in harmony with Paul's policy and his disciples who preached faith in, 'Christ,' without observing the Law of God. To observe the Law is necessary, according to the Messiah, to obtain eternal life, contrary to what Paul said.

There are always more lies and more deceits that come from Paul and from his disciples. See what the Lord Himself said about his work concerning the Messiah and it is written in;)

Matthew 17, 5. 'While he was still speaking, a bright cloud enveloped them, and a voice from the cloud said, "This is my Son, whom I love; with him I am well pleased. Listen to him."'

(Again, there in a huge difference between believing in God's commandments and obeying them just as there is a big difference between believing in Jesus and listening to him.

Listening to the Messiah is to obey the commandments, to obey the Law of God. Listening to Paul, listening to the Antichrist is to believe in the Messiah; have faith in him without observing the Law.

John 6, 32. '(This) Jesus said to them, I tell you the truth, (Verily, verily,) it is not Moses who has given you the bread from heaven, but it is my Father who gives you the true bread from heaven.'

(To say that Moses didn't tell the word of God, the truth to his people, is in my opinion a huge lie and to my knowledge, only Paul dared mocked Moses that way and this is worthy of the devil. To read so many lies in the Holy Bible makes me bring up and truly this is disgusting.

Never Jesus, the true Messiah, has spoken a single word against Moses or against any other of God's prophets, on the contrary. What this false Christ just said here in John 6, 32, is completely diabolic.)

John 6, 38. 'For I have come down from heaven not to do my will but to do the will of him who sent me.'

(One more verse, one more lie! Yes, we know, Satan came down, chased out of heaven by God with his proud angels to do the will of his father, Lucifer.

How could someone pretend being Jesus, the saviour, and lie this much as this false Christ did here in this gospel of John? This is diabolic again. It is not Jesus as a child or as a man who came down from heaven, but the word of God that took place in the mouth of a man named Jesus. And this was not to lie this way, but to do everything God has commanded him. And this was not to say such stupidities or to lie this much.

The same lie is repeated here again in;)

John 6, 47. 'I tell you the truth, he who believes has everlasting life.'

(We have seen it already. This is totally false, because Satan too believes in the Messiah and he will not get everlasting life.

Again here for the last time I mention it, but, 'I tell you the truth,' here in John is not the true translation of John's writing, but, 'Verily, verily, or truly, truly is and I have seen it twenty times in the French Bible and in the King James Bible. But this John has used the true Jesus way of speaking to lie again about everlasting life and about faith. No one else than this John has reported Jesus' messages this way. This is kind of strange, isn't it?

Then comes one of the biggest promotion of cannibalism of the story of this false Christ here in the

Scriptures and I don't think it is that holy. But believe it; the true Jesus has never taught this way and if he did, none of the Jews would have followed him and neither would I.)

John 6, 48-59. 'I am the bread of life. Your forefathers ate the manna in the desert, yet they died.'

(Jesus' apostle ate the bread of life, the word of God and they died too. This is a very bad example to give to anyone.)

'But here is the bread that comes down from heaven, which a man may eat and not die. I am the living bread that came down from heaven. If anyone eats of this bread, he will live forever. This is my flesh, which I will give for the life of the world.'

(If this false Christ went in one of these countries where cannibalism was practiced and in the middle of the cannibals instead of in Israel; I don't think his ministry wouldn't have last very long. I don't even think he would have the time to finish his speech. I can imagine him too going to speak like this, saying those stupidities in a homosexual club.)

'Then the Jews began to argue sharply among themselves, "How can this man give us his flesh to eat?" Jesus said to them, "I tell you the truth, unless you eat the flesh of the Son of Man and drink his blood,'

(These poor Jews who heard these foolish words, they who were not even allowed to eat meat with its blood in it were scandalized and with a good reason too, but the true Messiah didn't do this, he didn't teach this way, to push away and to scandalize his disciples, on the contrary.)

'You have no life in you. Whoever eats my flesh and drinks my blood has eternal life, and I will raise him up at the last day.'

(It is a bit ironic and contradictory to resurrect someone who could never die and has eternal life, isn't it?)

'For my flesh is real food and my blood is real drink.'

(I would say so too, but for the cannibals and for the vampires.)

'Whoever eats my flesh and drinks my blood remains in me, and I in him.'

(Yes, the time it takes for the stomach to digest everything, and for the intestines to evacuate, just like any other food and liquid, and we know where this ends and how.)

'Just as the living Father sent me and I live because of the Father,'

(And why not use the influence of God, the Father who is in heaven to make people swallow this terrible venom?)

'So the one who feeds on me will live because of me. This is the bread that came down from heaven. Your forefathers ate manna and died,'

(They might have died, but they are not all condemned, especially not Moses and many others. This false Christ here in John was speaking as if he could prevent people from dying if they would eat his flesh and drink his blood, but the Jews are intelligent people and they didn't believe this imposter.)

'But he who feeds on this bread will live forever." He said this while teaching in Capernaum.'

(In all the other Bibles I read, it is mentioned that this Jesus was teaching in the synagogues, but not here. This was Paul who was going from one synagogue to another just about everywhere, trying to mislead the Jews, who didn't believe him anyway. While the true Jesus, the true Messiah, spent most of his time teaching his apostles outside of these places, where he said this was dangerous for them to go.

(Unlike this Jesus here in John, the true Messiah in Matthew, taught his disciples with his parables; here in this gospel of John we see none of that and we don't learn anything about the kingdom of heaven either. This John, Paul's disciple, has not even mentioned the kingdom of heaven. All of us can understand that the demons, Satan's disciples, were not to promote, to speak for the kingdom of the Messiah, or to promote God's word in there world.

The one who could write that Jesus would have preached this way in the gospel of John is no one else than his enemy. Jesus, the true Messiah, the good shepherd, was gathering his lost sheep; he didn't disperse them like this false Christ did it in the gospel of John. The true Jesus was not preaching and teaching in a way to send his disciples away from him, away from the truth, on the contrary.

Yes, I can eat the truth, the bread that comes down from heaven and I eat it every day, but I will not eat this false teaching from this false Christ and neither did the Jews. Good for them! God has protected his people from the teaching of this false Christ and He still does.)

John 6, 60-62. 'On hearing it, many of his disciples said, "This is a hard teaching. Who can accept it? Aware that his disciples were grumbling about this, (this) Jesus said to them, "Does this offend you? What if you see the Son of Man ascend to where he was before?'

(I think that the highest point Jesus ascent before while he was alive, is the Mount of Olives. Jesus was born like everybody and he grew up like everybody. He studied the Scriptures, because he knew them. He went up and down the Mont of Olives many times, but he didn't come down from heaven or he would have died when touching the ground. Jesus also went up to his Father only after his resurrection.

Like I said it before; it is the word of God that came down from heaven and the word of God is the bread of life; not the flesh and the blood of whomever. The Jews of that time didn't take such a teaching, his disciples didn't take it either. They were scandalized because this was scandalous. But Jesus, the true Messiah, didn't teach that way; that I am sure of at one hundred per cent.

It seems to me that from the beginning of this gospel of John, this Jesus spent more time arguing with the Jews in their synagogues, just like Paul did it in his so-called ministry, than to teach his disciples. In one synagogue Jesus was teaching the people and, according to Luke; they wanted to kill him, to push him down a cliff. But this was more privately that the true Jesus taught his apostles. This is something that this false Christ didn't seem to have done at all in this gospel of this John. The true Messiah was also teaching the crowds at times, but that too happened outside the synagogues.

This Jesus in John preached the exact opposite of the Jesus who is in Matthew and some times contrary to himself.)

John 6, 65. 'He went on to say, "This is why I told you that no one can come to me unless the Father has enabled him.'

(This would also mean that if a person doesn't come to Jesus; this is God's fault; which would be a complete stupidity and would also be worthy of the devil. And if this was true again; Jesus wouldn't have had to go through all the roads he went through and all he would have had to do is waiting in the temple that God gives them or sends the people to him.)

John 6, 65. 'He (this false Christ) went on to say, "This is why I told you that no one can come to me unless the Father has enabled him.'

See now the exact opposite in;)

John 14, 6. '(This) Jesus answered, "I am the way and the truth and the life. No one comes to the Father except through me.'

(In fact, the truth that should have been written here is, 'No one comes to the Father except through the word of God.' Nevertheless, this false Christ is saying the opposite from one verse to another and this in the same gospel and by the same writer. This is something though that Paul, Mark and Luke have done and many of times.)

John 14, 7. 'If you really knew me, you would know my father as well. From now on, you know him and have seen him.'

(Know that the son of the devil could have said the very same thing and this is most likely what we have just seen.

This was to pretend to be God; which the true Jesus, the true Messiah, has never done. Though, this is something that Paul has often done, especially by allowing himself to judge others and to hand them over to Satan. No wonder the Jews are refusing to believe in Jesus and in our Bible. They didn't want to believe Jesus was the <u>begotten</u> Son of God; how can they believe he is God?)

Now today, on the 3rd of April 2018, and this after seeing it and reading it many times before; I discover for the first time a different and important aspect of the verse 7 of Psalm 2. This is that the day when the Almighty has begotten his Son, said to be the one and only, was long before his day of birth and not in the belly of his mother, like the liars said it again and again.)

See Psalm 2, 7. 'I will proclaim the decree of the Lord: He said to me, (to his son) "You are my Son; to day I have become your Father."'

(Today is not yesterday or any time before or after; this was that day. And if the Almighty told him personally; this is because he was big enough to understand this. Now, who would dare to continue to make God a liar and continue to contradict Him, by saying that the Holy Spirit had put his seed in the womb of Mary?

The Jews understood and so did I, that this whole story with Mary and the Holy Spirit is a devilish machination to make people believe in the lies.

I have discovered a lot of things in the Bible, as you can tell now, but this one is one of the most important to this day to show people how the devil works.

In John 6, 16-21, this John talked about Jesus walking on the water, but he didn't mention at all the walk of Peter that happened in the same event according to Matthew. The true John, Jesus' apostle, Peter's every day companion would have mentioned it; that is for sure.

From John 6, 23 to 6, 71, this Jesus, this false Christ too has a lot of fake news, a big stew for cats and he has mixed up some discussions he would have had with the crowd of Jews and other discussions with his disciples, but the truth is that the true Messiah was speaking to them separately; at least most of the time.

And here is the number of the beast, the 666, and it looks like it did chase Jesus' disciples away.)

John 6, 66. 'From this time many of his disciples turned back and no longer followed him.'

(Thank You Lord! But the true Jesus would have left the twelve apostles, like a good shepherd that he is. He would have left the 99 to go get the one that got lost, but this false Christ here in John has done nothing like that. On the contrary; he said all he wanted to say without any explanation and this was not the way of the true Messiah to teach at all.

There is one testimony though that is telling us this was the way of Paul that we can read in;)

2 Peter 3, 16. 'He (Paul) writes the same way in all his letters, speaking in them of these matters. His letters contain some things that are hard to understand.'

(But the true Jesus is gentle at heart, humble and I am sure too, he is easy to understand. These are Jesus' enemies, the God's enemies, who came to make the Scriptures complicated with their lies and contradictions; just as Jesus told us in his parable of the weeds and Jesus also told us that this was done by the devil.)

John 6, 69. 'We believe and know that you are the Holy One of God.'

(Remember that the demons have said the very same thing in;)

See Mark 1, 23-24. 'Just then a man in their synagogue who was possessed by an evil spirit cried out. "What do you have with us, Jesus of Nazareth? Have you come to destroy us? I know who you are—the Holy One of God!'

(Curiously, these last four words written this way, are only found in Mark 1, 34, in Luke 4, 34 and in this John 6, 69. All three are Paul's disciples.)

John 6, 70. 'Then this Jesus replied, "Have I not chosen you, the Twelve? Yet one of you is a devil!'

(For once that this Jesus talked to his apostles; he did it to lie to them. The true Messiah didn't mentioned anything about the traitor until the last supper and this for a very good reason; if he did it before, it would have been a mess among his apostles all along his ministry, and frankly; Jesus had no time to play the mother of the family, to play the mother hen with them to settle their disputes.

I have a warning for you now about what is following, because there is a lot of anti-Semitism, a lot of disparagement against the Jews. What we have seen here in this gospel of this John is quite deplorable.)

John 7, 1. 'After this, Jesus went around in Galilee, purposely staying away from Judea because the Jews there were waiting to take his life.'

(It is kind of strange, isn't it, that Luke, Mark, this John of Paul and Paul have hardly said anything against the Romans, maybe nothing at all, yet the Romans were dominating over the whole territory? But yet none of them were shy to speak against the Jews. But they deployed a lot of efforts to make Jesus look like a liar and for a man who contradicted himself and who was not too sure of what he was talking about. Is that surprising that the Jews don't like our Bible too much? Is that surprising that so many people became atheists? The people of Israel, the Jews are intelligent people.

Let me show you a small detail, but one that is quite important.)

John 7, 2. 'But when the Jewish Feast of Tabernacles was near.'

(The John of Jesus, his apostle was a Jew and the John of Jesus wouldn't have spoken disparagement against the Jews like the John of Paul did and neither would the true Jesus. The John of Jesus would have rather said here, "Our Feast of Tabernacles was near."

(I don't think the John of the gospel of John was a Jew, but a Roman, just like Paul.

Talking about someone who talks through his hat; what is next is a good example of that.)

John 7, 18. 'He who speaks of his own does so to gain honour for himself, but he who works for the honour of the one who sent him is a man of truth; there is nothing false about him.'

(Did you see the poisoned BS? What about the sons of the devil sent in the world to mislead people and Judas sent to betray Jesus, are they men of truth? Would you still say there is nothing false in them? But again I say; it is not from the mouth of the true Messiah that such a stupidity came out, but from someone who has an interest to make Jesus look like an idiot. And who those can be, if not the sons of the devil?)

John 7, 19. '"Has not Moses given you the Law? Yet not one of you keeps the Law. Why are you trying to kill me?"'

(Not other people on earth are observing the Law of Moses as much as the Jewish people, the people of Israel do. I would rather say it is because this Jesus in the gospel of John was preaching cannibalism and this was a good reason enough to get rid of him. I would also say that the Jews of those days and those of nowadays are obsessed by the Law, especially about the day of rest, the seventh day of the week, the Sabbath day. The Jews seem to know that the Sabbath day is the last day of the week and that we have to take a break from working as much as possible that day and this seems to be something the Christians don't know and don't give a (S) about it and are acting as if this Law doesn't exist at all.)

John 7, 22. 'Yet, because Moses gave you circumcision, though actually it did not come from Moses, but from the patriarchs, you circumcise a child on the Sabbath.'

(The circumcision didn't come from the patriarchs, but from God, because it is an everlasting covenant the Almighty made between Him and his male children, and Jesus, the true Messiah, knows this very well. This false Christ here in John has clearly lied about this. At least the one who wrote this has again made Jesus to be a liar in his gospel. See Genesis 17, 9-14, to know the true story about the circumcision.

To my knowledge, Jesus, the true Messiah, who is in Matthew has never spoke again circumcision or against the Law of God or the Law of Moses. On the contrary, he told us to observe everything the scribes and the Pharisees are telling us to do. See Matthew 23, 1-3. Though, one that has made his mouth going against the Law of God and the Law of Moses and against circumcision is Paul and this John of Paul. This is another proof; I think that the John of the gospel of John is the John, a disciple of Paul or Paul himself.)

John 7, 24. 'Stop judging by mere appearances, and <u>make</u> a right judgement.'

(Contrary to the true Messiah; this false Christ here is telling people to judge. See again the true Jesus, the true Messiah in;)

Matthew 7, 1. 'Do not judge, or you will be judged.'

(See now the one who not only was judging others, but has also taught his disciples to judge others. See Paul in;)

1 Corinthians 6, 2-3. 'Or do you not know that the saints will judge the world? If the world is judge by you, are you not competent to constitute the smallest law courts? Do you not know that we will judge the angels? How much more matters of this life?'

(Paul has made all kinds of efforts to preach the exact opposite of the Messiah's teaching and Paul's disciples have done the very same things. Not only I say this, but the writings are there in the Holy Bible to prove it.)

John 7, 28. 'Then Jesus, still teaching in the <u>temple courts</u>,'

(Here in the French Bible and in the King James Bible; this Jesus is not in the temple court, but in the temple. This is just to say there were more manipulations.)

'<u>Cried out</u>, "<u>Yet you know me</u>, and you know where I am from. I am not on my own, but he who sent me is true. <u>You do not know him</u>.'

(It seems to me that he said the exact opposite somewhere else. Let's go look at;)

John 8, 19. 'Then they asked him, "Where is your father?" "<u>You do not know me</u> or my father." (This) Jesus replied. "If you knew me, you would know my father also."'

(The Jews might have known his father too, if this Jesus had something else to say than his father sent him. This false Christ has done everything possible to make people believe he is God and this is what caused confusion to a big number of Christians and readers.

Once I heard a woman say on the air that Jesus was an impostor. I can't remember if this was on TV, or on the radio, but I remember what she said. The impostor is not the true Messiah, but rather this author of this gospel of John, who made Jesus looks like an impostor and a liar.

We always have to come back to that message from the true Jesus. 'We will recognize the tree by its fruits.' We will recognize the liar by his lies, but for this; we have to know the truth.

Also, this was not Jesus who had such a bad temper, but this was Paul. We will see this a bit farther and according to a great prophet, the true Jesus, the true Messiah, wouldn't yell or cry out like Paul did.)

See Isaiah 42, 1-2. 'Here is my <u>servant</u>, whom I uphold, my <u>chosen one</u> in whom I delight; (this was not Paul, but the true Jesus) I will put my Spirit on him and he will bring justice to the nations. He will <u>not shout</u> or <u>cry out</u>, or <u>raise his voice</u> in the streets.'

(So, who is this impostor who cried out in the temple courts? I think this was Paul; the one who entered all the synagogues on his way and where he had no business at all. This was Paul, who was supposed to teach only to the Gentiles. This was Paul, who was telling the Jews that they were not under the Law of God anymore. This was a false Christ anyway.

Here in the New International Bible, this false Christ cried out in the temple courts, but in the King James Bible and in my French Bible, this was inside the temple. So there have been manipulations of the Scriptures about that too. The Jews wanted to get rid of Paul and they had a lot of good reasons for that too, but the Romans were dominating over the Jews of Israel in those days and they were powerless against a Roman and his army.

Here in John 7, 37, this one, no matter who he is, he is an impostor, but certainly not the true prophet Jesus, because he is yelling again.)

John 7, 37. 'On the last and greatest day of the feast, (this) Jesus stood and said in a <u>loud voice</u>, (this is yelling) "If anyone is thirsty, let him come to me and drink.'

(Go to him to drink his blood, no thanks. This is what all of true Jesus' disciples, all the Jews and I will tell him. After all, he was not a cow and neither a goat.

Here in John 7, 39, this John, if this is not Paul himself, started to prepare the entry of Paul in the picture; to prepare the entry of the one who knows and sees everyone and everything and this without even being present.)

John 7, 39. 'By this he meant the Spirit whom those who believe in him were later to receive. Up to that time the Spirit (who got Mary pregnant) had not been given, since Jesus had not yet been glorified.'

(See now the spirit that this John is talking about here, or yet the spirit that this John made his false Christ speak about and there are many more. See Paul in;)

1 Corinthians 5, 3. 'Even though I am not physically present, I am with you in spirit. And I have already passed judgement on the one who did this, just as if I was present.'

(Only the one who puts himself in the place of God dares judging others this way, and even Jesus, the Messiah didn't dare doing this.

Besides, if the disciples of this false Christ didn't receive the Holy Spirit yet; this is because he is the false Christ, because the true Jesus' apostles received the Holy Spirit as the Messiah was talking to them. The Messiah was baptizing them with the Holy Spirit. See again Matthew 3, 11.

I, myself, began receiving the Holy Spirit as I began receiving and accepting the Jesus' messages. This was true for the Jesus' disciples and this is true for all of those who truly listen to him and follow him. For all of the others, I think they are at a huge risk to be lost, because none go to the Father in heaven but through the word of God.)

John 7, 42. '"Does not the Scriptures say that the Christ will come from David's family and from Bethlehem, the town where David lived?"'

(Well then, why did you, false Christ, tell the Jews that Jesus came down from heaven? The Jews had maybe many faults and their wrong doing, but one thing works in their favour, they knew and they know the Scriptures very well and this is why that neither Paul or the false Christ could convince them that the Law of Moses and the Law of God was an old code of the letter and was ready to disappear.

It is a fact that Jesus, the Messiah, is coming down from the line and the family of David and it is not Jesus who would deny it. The word of God is coming from God and it is it that came down from heaven to light up the world. In any cases, the Jews in that gospel of John seem to know the truth better than this false Christ. But Jesus, the true Messiah, prevented us against the false prophets and the false Christs who will come under his name.)

See Matthew 24, 4-5. 'Jesus answered: "Watch out that no one deceives you. For many will come in (here in my French Bible it is not in my name, but under my name) my name, claiming, 'I am the Christ,'

(To claim being the Christ is to come under Jesus' name.)

'And will deceive many.'

(And again this was a good prediction from the Messiah, because there are many who are deceived by this false Christ and by this false apostle, who pretended being the John of Jesus. And no one can say that this false Christ didn't say he was the Christ, because he repeated it at least forty times that he was sent by his father and this always without saying where is father is from. But the Jesus in Matthew only said it twice that he was sent by his Father. As far as I am concerned, if this false Christ in the gospel of John has never said where his father is from, this is because his father is in hell and to tell this to the people; that wouldn't have helped them building their diabolic empire.

To come, to speak or to teach in someone's name and to come, to speak or to teach under someone's name are the very distinct things. All of the true Jesus' disciples were and are speaking and teaching in Jesus' name and so do I. The ones who speak and teach under the true Jesus' name and are not the Messiah are false Christs and are impostors.

John 8, 2-8. 'At dawn he (this Jesus) appeared again in the <u>temple courts</u>,'

(Here again in the French Bible and in the King James, it is in the temple, not outside, so these are more manipulations. Not only that, in the temple, this was a place where they wanted to arrest him. So here they try to make him look like an idiot who threw himself in the mouth of the wolves.)

'Where all the people gathered around him, (a million and a half Jews) and he sat down to teach them. The teachers of the Law and the Pharisees brought in a woman caught in adultery. They made her stand before the group and said to Jesus, "Teacher, this woman was caught in the act of adultery. In the Law Moses commanded us to stone such women. Now what do you say?" They were using this question as a trap,' (This is more disparagement against the Jews.) 'In order to have a basis for accusing him. But Jesus bent down and started to write on the ground with his finger.'

(Who would believe that the temple that took forty-six years to build had no floor? I rather think the floor was made of solid and heavy stones and not a hard-packed surface. The temple was not a barn.)

'When they kept questioning him, he straightened up and said to them, "If anyone of you is without sin, let him be the first to throw a stone at her."'

(There are a couple of things out of line here. First, no one, not a Jew would have stoned anyone inside the temple. Second, the true Jesus knew this and according to what it was said about the true Messiah and what this one here in John said, he would have been the one to throw the stone at her, because the true Messiah was without sin. Besides, the true Messiah would have not said anything against the Law of God or against Moses or against any of God's prophets and to be sure of that; go read again Matthew 5, 17.

Even if the Jews wanted Paul dead and had many good reasons for that; they didn't stone him in the temple, but they dragged him outside.)

See again Acts 21, 30. 'The whole city was aroused, and the people came running from all directions. Seizing Paul; they dragged him from the temple, and immediately the gates were shut.')

'Again he stooped down and wrote on the ground.'

(Not satisfied for lying once about the flooring of the temple; they repeated that lie again, just in case you have missed it the first time.

So in my opinion, this whole story was invented and written to make Jesus look like a liar and an idiot and this is worthy of the devil, Jesus' enemy.)

John 8, 9. 'At this, those who heard began to go away one at the time, the older ones first, until <u>only Jesus</u> was left, with the woman still standing there.'

(This is unlikely and not very credible and the proof is in what is following.)

See John 8, 12. 'When Jesus spoke again to the people,'

(To whom was he saying this, since they were all gone and this false Christ was left alone with the woman?)

'He said, "I am the light of the world. Who ever follows me will never walk in the darkness, but will have the light of life.'

(If this one is the light of the world; his world must be very small, because he doesn't seem to see any farther than the tip of his nose.)

John 8, 15-16. 'You judge by human standards; I pass judgement on no one. But if I do judge (like Paul did) my decisions (other Bibles say, 'my judgements,') are right, because I am not alone. I stand with the Father, who sent me.'

(But where is his father? Paul has done that a lot, saying one thing and contradicting himself in the same phrase. 'I pass judgement on no one. But if I do judge.')

John 8, 21. 'Once more (this) Jesus said to them, "I am going away, and you will look for me, and you will die in your sin. Where I go, you cannot come."'

(I'd like to say this is a good thing. Who wants to go to the devil in hell? What this Jesus, this false Christ did in this gospel of John was to judge and to condemn. This is something Paul did a lot, but this is also something that Jesus, the true Messiah, didn't do at all and this in the whole gospel of Matthew.

Knowing what some people could do with the manipulations of the Holy Scriptures; I better make sure I have a copy of my books safely hidden.

John 8, 26. 'I have much to say in judgement of you.'

(See the same false Christ in;)

John 12, 47. '"As for the person who hears my words, but does not keep them, I do not judge him. For I did not come to judge the world, but to save it."'

(No comment is needed here. We have to remember too that the John, Jesus' apostle, was without any education; so he could not write these stupidities of this gospel.)

John, 8, 39-44. '"Abraham is our father," they (the Jews) answered. "If you were Abraham's children," said (this) Jesus, "then you would do the things Abraham did. As it is, you are determined to kill me, a man who told you the truth that I heard from God'

(Here, the true Jesus would have said, 'I heard from my Father who is in heaven.')

'Abraham did not do such things.'

(Abraham too would have done the impossible to get rid of the devil and his sons.)

'You are doing the things your own father does." "We are not illegitimate children," they protested. "the only Father we have is God Himself."

(They just said that Abraham was their father, but the Jews are not responsible for that; the author of this gospel of John is. Certain Jews have accused Jesus of blasphemy for saying the very same thing.)

See John 5, 18. 'For this reason the Jews tried all the harder to kill him; (Jesus) not only was he breaking the Sabbath, but he was calling God his own Father, making himself equal with God.'

See also John 19, 7. 'The Jews insisted, "We have a Law, and according to that Law he must die, because he claimed to be the Son of God."'

(This is just the same thing the Jews would have done in John 8, 41. I personally call this, 'disparagement against the Jews.'

See also Matthew 26, 65. 'Then the high priest tore his clothes and said, "He has spoken blasphemy! Why do we need any more witnesses? Look, now you have heard the blasphemy.')

(This) Jesus said to them, "If God were your Father, you would love me, for I came from God and now am here.'

(Then Satan must be his god and he worked hard enough to make people believe he is and also to take His place.)

'I did not come on my own; but he sent me. Why is my language not clear to you? Because you are unable to hear what I say. You belong to your father, the devil, and you want to carry out your father's desire. He was a murderer from the beginning, not holding to the truth, for there is no truth in him. When he lies, he speaks his native language, for he is a liar and the father of lies."'

(A murderer, a liar and the father of lies; this is to me the exact description of Paul.

That this one here, who pretended to be Jesus, the 'Christ,' in this gospel of John, and the one who wrote those abominations; this author saying that God's people, his first born, has the devil as a father, and that all the Christians of this world are venerating, have accepted and have called him, 'saint,' this is beyond the imaginable. I even wonder if there is something in the Bible more diabolic than that. But this is not all. Let's go see a little farther what this false Christ said in;)

John 8, 56. 'Your father Abraham rejoiced at the thought of seeing my day; he saw it and was glad.'

(For this false Christ to say that Abraham is the father of the Jews and at the same time to say that their father is the devil; this is more or less to say that God, the Father, is the devil and this is to say a terrible abomination.

We have to know as well that it was God who sent, who has chased Satan and his angels out of heaven, and apparently Satan too was sent on earth. So, he too came down from God. So, Satan too has knowledge of what happened in heaven.

My question is how it is then that billions and billions of people who read the book the most sold in the world didn't see all of those abominations in this Holy place, in the Bible? The only answer that comes to my mind is written in;)

Daniel 12, 9. 'Go your way, Daniel, because the words are closed up and sealed until the time of the end.'

(This means, to me anyway, that the time of the end has really arrived, because those things are now revealed to me and this even without me looking for them. The voice that told me in a dream one night that I will discover the identity of the beast and of the Antichrist and that it will be revealed to me in an obvious way has not mistaken, because I see.

Jesus, the Messiah, the true one, who spoke about the day when we'll see the abomination of desolation in the Holy place, in the Holy Bible, and that we'll have to be careful as we read, has said and seen right also. But he also said that the end will be near, at the door. It is clear to me then that everything is in line for the victory of the true Jesus over evil, over his enemies is about to arrive.)

John 8, 58-59. '"I tell you the truth," (this) Jesus answered, "before Abraham was born, I am!"

(The true Jesus, the true Messiah has never pretended to be God like this one just did. What is written about the Antichrist?

See again 2 Thessalonians 2, 4. 'He will oppose and he will exalt himself over everything that is called God or is worshipped, so that he sets himself in God's temple, proclaiming himself to be God.'

(Well then, this is exactly what this Jesus in this John's gospel has just done and this false disciple, this John, is the accomplice of this fraud. In this John's gospel we can see one abomination after another and I cannot blame anyone for not seeing them, because even though I read the Bible many times and this for many years, there are a lot of abominations I didn't see until lately.

I also think that we cannot see them until we are ready to accept the truth and I also believe this is why many members of my family don't see them and don't want to see them either.

Only God with the help of the Messiah can open our eyes and it is a miracle each time.)

'At this they (the Jews) picked up stones to stone him, but Jesus hid himself, slipping away from the temple grounds.'

(This is false again; this is another lie, because the Jews wouldn't stone anyone inside the temple. And where were these stones from? There were certainly not stored inside the temple.

There were manipulations here again, because it is not from the temple grounds that this Jesus slipped away from, but from the temple and this in the King James Bible and in the French Bible as well.

He also said, "Verily, verily," and not, "I tell you the truth," like it is here in the New International Version. So they put in the mouth of this false Christ some words that belong to the true Messiah and this is what I call cheating, manipulation. This is not honest for something written in the book of the truth.)

John 9, 35. 'Jesus heard that they (the Pharisees) had thrown him out, (the cured blind man) and when he (this Jesus) found him, he said, "Do you believe in the Son of Man?"'

(There are more manipulations here again, because in the French and in the King James Bibles; he didn't say, "The Son of Man," but he said, "the Son of God."

Anyone who does the will of the Father in heaven is a son or the daughter of God, but not necessarily a prophet, which the Son of Man is, one of God's prophet.

The true Jesus in Matthew was saying about God that He is his Father, but about himself; he was saying he is the Son of Man, which really means he is one of God's prophet, but born of man. And the true Jesus wasn't lying when he called himself, 'Son of Man.'

This is not saying he is the Son of the Holy Spirit. And if you really need a proof about what I am saying, just read;)

Ezekiel 2, 1. 'He (God) said to me, "Son of man, stand up on your feet and I will speak to you.'

See also Ezekiel 2, 4-5. 'The people to whom I am sending you are obstinate and stubborn. Say to them, 'This is what the Sovereign Lord says.' And whether they listen or fail to listen—for they are a rebellious house—they will know that a prophet has been among them.'

(I don't really know if the people to whom my writing is destined will know or not if a Jesus' disciple have talked to them, but this message in Ezekiel is the exact same I received from a voice in one of my dreams, but adding, "The people to whom you talked to won't be able to blame Me for not sending them someone." And this message to this very day is to me the most comforting I received from Him.

There are also many more references about the Son of Man. See Job 16, 21, Psalm 11, 4 and 80, 17, Isaiah 56, 2 and many more.

The first one to talk about Jesus as being the Son of God in Matthew is Satan. He is also the first one in the New Testament to do it.

See Matthew 4, 3. 'The tempter came to him (Jesus) and said, "If you are the <u>Son of God</u>, tell these stones to become bread."'

(Then the true Jesus said;)

See Matthew 5, 9. 'Blessed are the peacekeepers, for they will be called sons of God.'

(Just like Jesus! This is far from saying that Jesus is God's only Son. The apostles also said it.)

See Matthew 14, 33. 'Then those who were in the boat worshipped him, saying, "Truly, you are the Son of God."'

(The high priests asked Jesus;)

See Matthew 26, 63-64. 'The high priest said to him, "I charge you under oath by the living God: (But Jesus didn't swear at all) Tell us if you are the Christ, the Son of God." "Yes, it is as you say," Jesus replied.'

(Jesus said it. The high priests, the scribes and the elders also said that Jesus said.)

See Matthew 27, 43. 'For he (Jesus) said, "I am the Son of God."'

(If the Romans would have to crucify all the people who say being children of God today, they might just run out of wood to make crosses.

And finally, the centurion too said it after the death of Jesus.)

See Matthew 27, 54. 'When the centurion and those with him who were guarding Jesus saw the earthquake and all that had happened, they were terrified, and exclaimed, "Surely he was the Son of God."'

(As far as I am concerned, Jesus still is the Son of God. All of those who do the will of the Father who is in heaven are Jesus' brothers, sisters and mothers, so they are the sons and daughters of God too. The others are his enemies. But as I have already said it, Jesus in Matthew, contrary to what is happening in John, was mostly saying about himself being the Son of Man; which certainly doesn't mean being born from the Holy Spirit, but from a man. Being born again means being born from God and for God, but this could happen to everyone and this is not the same thing at all. The Son of Man is mentioned 28 times in Matthew.)

John 9, 39. '(This) Jesus said, "For judgement I have come into this world, so that the blind will see and those who see will become blind."'

(What a stupidity this is! I can see this coming out of Paul's mouth, but not from the true Messiah. The true Messiah is opening the eyes of the blind and this not only physically, but also spiritually. The one who blinds people is Satan. See Paul in;)

Acts 13, 11. 'Now the hand of the Lord is against you. You are going to be blind.'

(When the true Lord put his hand on someone, this is not to make him blind, on the contrary. I even think that Paul here recounted his own story, the way he became blind himself. See Acts 9, 8.)

John 9, 41. '(This) Jesus said, "If you were blind, you would not be guilty of sin, but now that you claim you can see, your guilt remains."'

(What a stupidity this is again! This false Christ didn't succeed to blind those Jews, even though they could see. But he just said that he will make blind those who can see. Let me show you a very similar phrase from Paul, meaning a phrase where the speaker says one thing and its contradiction in the same phrase. See Paul in;)

1 Corinthians 3, 10-11. 'By the grace God has given me, I (Paul) laid a foundation as an expert builder and someone else is building on it. For no one can lay any foundation other than the one already laid, which is Jesus Christ.

(Do you see this contradiction? At the same time Paul said that no one can build another foundation than the one Jesus Christ has made, and he also said he, himself, laid one foundation as an expert builder. Did he pretend being the Christ, like the false Christ who is in John?

I won't be surprised one of these days to hear that Paul and the false Christ who is in the gospel of John are one and the same man. They both certainly have something in common, because they both wanted to sit themselves in the temple and they both succeeded to install themselves in the heart of people, but Jesus, the Messiah, has predicted that. There is also the fact that both of them have judged and condemned others.

See Matthew 24, 11. 'And many false prophets will appear and deceive many people.'

(This is something like two point four billions Christians and this just for these days and this beside the J....witnesses. These are a lot of people indeed. These are one third of the actual world population. And, apparently, the Koran is very similar to the Bible and there are just as many Moslems than Christians, which would add up to around five billions people. These are a lot of people alright.

There are apparently 1, 25 billions Catholics in the world of nowadays. These are a lot of blinds and they are blind by whom? They are blinded by Paul and company and their successors. Jesus had many enemies, but don't try to count mine, for they are too many. But Jesus said it long before me.)

See Matthew 10, 22. 'All men will hate you because of me, but he who stands firm to the end will be saved.'

(And believe me, this is my intention. But this is also what I expect. I am though determined to go to the end despite the threats and the danger and this is what I wish to all who will follow me on this road to the kingdom of heaven, to the wonderful kingdom of Jesus, the King of the Jews.)

John 10, 1. '<u>I tell you the truth</u>'

(This again is copied and pasted from the true Jesus, just like I mentioned before. Never in the French or in the

King James Bibles and in the gospel of John, this false Christ has spoken this way, but he said, 'Truly, truly, or verily, verily.' There were definitely manipulations of the Holy Scriptures to make people believe in this false Christ and this is not only a terrible sin, but it is also a crime.)

'The man who does not enter the sheep pen by the gate, but climbs in some other way, is a thief and a robber.'

(He is also a liar. This is all this book of mine is about. This is about the false prophets, the false apostle who entered the sheep pen from a different gate than the true apostles did, by a different way than the other apostles whom Jesus, the true Messiah, has chosen with care. These Jesus' apostles whom Jesus chose with care and his disciples were aware of the false prophets and they didn't like the voice or the way of Paul, and this even after fourteen year of Paul's false ministry. Paul introduced himself in the sheep pen with his fake story of Jesus blinding him and to believe Jesus could have done that to Paul or to anyone; this is not knowing the true Jesus very well. It is true that the sheep recognize the voice of their shepherd, but none of Jesus' apostles liked the voice or the way of Paul.)

See Acts 9, 26. 'When he (Paul) came to Jerusalem, he tried to join the disciples, but they were all afraid of him, not believing that he really was a disciple.'

(This last message should have been enough by itself to tell us that Paul was the enemy, because all the apostles and the Jesus' disciples were warned about the false prophets and the ferocious wolves. They were all warned men inspired by the Holy Spirit and I am sure they didn't let themselves believe and his lies. There is another message that demonstrates this truth.)

See Acts 21, 22-24, where James, Jesus' brother and the Jesus' apostles, inspired by the Holy Spirit, managed to get rid of Paul definitely, and this is how and why Paul found himself in Rome, where he could operate securely under the protection of Caesar.

The Jesus' apostles saw him coming, this Paul, this lawless one with his lies and his contradictions and with all his stories that don't make any sense.)

John 10, 8. 'All who ever came before me where <u>thieves</u> and <u>robbers</u>, but the sheep did not listen to them.'

(Aren't thieves and robbers the same? This was said by the false Christ. Now, this is true only if it is the Antichrist who spoke here and this was a very good thing if the sheep didn't listen to them. I suppose then that if all of those who came before this false Christ were thieves and robbers, then they were demons.

But this is a very big lie if this was said by the Messiah. This was said to make Jesus, the true Messiah, look like a liar, because John the Baptist came before Jesus and the sheep listened and believed him. So were many other prophets like Ezekiel, Daniel, Isaiah, Zachariah and many more who came before the Messiah. They were not thieves or robbers and the sheep have listened to them. Besides, the true Jesus said this here in;)

Matthew 5, 17. "'Do not think that I have come to abolish the Law or the prophets; (who came before the Messiah) I have not come to abolish them but to fulfill them.'"

(He or she who believes in such a liar; this false Christ who is in this John's gospel after reading this book of mine is worthy of him and deserves to be in the same camp, but this is certainly not in the kingdom of heaven, in Jesus' kingdom. Neither Jesus nor his disciples lied this way. And if the sheep didn't listen to the false prophets, why worrying about them?

The Jesus' apostle John has heard the same instructions, the same recommendations, the same warnings and the same teaching than Matthew and he would have written about the same things. But this John here, this false apostle in his gospel has reported a totally different Jesus; one who kept arguing against the Jews, Just like Paul has done in all the synagogues on his way.

The true Jesus, the Messiah, who is in Matthew, began his ministry by choosing his disciples and he started to teach them right from the beginning. This is not at all what we see here in this gospel of John.)

John 10, 17-18. 'The reason my Father loves me is that I lay down my life only to take it up again. No one takes it from me, but I lay it down on my own accord. I have authority to lay it down and authority to take it up again. This command I received from my Father.'

(I mentioned this once before; the capital, 'F,' for father doesn't really mean the person talks about the true God. If this is the only reason his father loves this one; there must be a lot of reasons not to be loved.

To my knowledge, I think it is the first time where I read that God gave an order to Jesus. On the other hand, as we saw it before; I read many of times where Paul gave orders to his disciples. See for examples Colossians 4, 10 and Acts 17, 15.

I really think that this false Christ said no one takes his life to exculpate the Romans; the ones who have literally killed Jesus. This false Christ is not a Jew, like the true Jesus, the true Christ is and he doesn't miss an occasion to blame the Jews and to spear the Romans.

There is something else in there. The life on earth has a lot of value only because it is unique and if someone could take his life back any time he wants to; he could even give it away every day without fear to loose it. Then his life would be a lot less important.)

John 10, 22-23. 'Then came the Feast of Dedication at Jerusalem. It was winter, and (this) Jesus was in the temple area walking in Solomon's colonnade.'

(There where the Jews wanted to cease and kill him.?????? Here this Jesus was walking in the temple area, (temple court) but in the French Bible and in the King

James; he was inside the temple. So many manipulations of the Holy Scriptures; isn't this a crime punishable by the laws of men on top of the Laws of God?

John 10, 30-33. 'I (this false Christ) and the Father are one.'

(Here this false Christ is not saying being the Son of God, but he is saying being God and the Jews would have been right in wanting to stone him.)

'Again the Jews picked up stones to stone him, but (this) Jesus said to them:'

(Before a crowd of people holding stones in their hands to stone you, would you say something else to piss them off even more or just run away from the danger as the true Jesus advised us to do and has he did it himself?)

See Matthew 10, 23. 'When you are persecuted in one place, flee to another.'

See also the true Jesus in;)

Matthew 12, 14-15. 'But the Pharisees went out and plotted how they might kill him. Aware of this, Jesus withdrew from that place.'

(So the true Messiah didn't stay in front of those who wanted to kill him and he didn't stay to argue with them either.

It seems that this false Christ who is in the gospel of John didn't learn to listen to the good advices from the true Messiah and he kept annoying the Jews, just like Paul did it in every synagogue on his way.)

'I have shown you <u>many great miracles</u> from the Father. For which of these do you stone me?" "We are not stoning you for any of these," replied the Jews, "but for blasphemy, because you, a mere man, claim to be God."'

(It is true that this false Christ claimed to be God. But there are two more things here. This last attempt to stone him was done in the temple, according to that story and this is totally unlikely and this false Christ also said having made many miracles to them, but the true Messiah said this in;)

Matthew 16, 4. 'A wicked and adulterous generation looks for a miraculous sign, but none will be given it except the sign of Jonah.'

(So, it is also false to say that the Messiah showed them many miracles. This false Christ in this gospel of John is a liar and so is the author of this gospel.

These are this false Christ and Paul and maybe the two of them are the one and the same man, who pretended haven made many miracles and great signs to seduce the Jews.

If the Jews had stones in the temple to stone whoever; they would have stoned Paul and this even before dragging him outside. This would have been the end of him before the roman army took him away from the Jews.)

See again Acts 21, 30. 'The whole city was aroused, and the people came running from all directions. Seizing

Paul; they dragged him from the temple, and immediately the gates were shut.'

(I do think though that the whole city was aroused, and the people came running from all directions, after Paul was dragged outside the temple, not before.)

John 11, 2. 'This Mary, whose brother Lazarus <u>now lay sick</u>, was the same one who poured perfume on the Lord and wiped his feet with her hair.'

(Here this John said that this Mary poured perfume on Jesus' feet and she wiped them with her hairs, but according to himself, this happened a lot later. And according to Matthew; this happened much later yet, just before Jesus' persecution and in a much different way.)

See John 12, 3. 'Then Mary took about a pint of pure nard, an expensive perfume, she poured it on Jesus' feet and wiped his feet with her hair.'

(Some people will say this John was a prophet who predicted what was to come, but I'd say he is a liar, because he said the thing was done, when it was to come. I mean in his story.

There is a lot to say to re-establish Jesus' reputation concerning this Mary. In Luke this same Mary was a sinner, but there is no mention of it in this John.)

See Luke 7, 36-39. 'Now one of the Pharisees invited Jesus to have diner with him, so he went to the Pharisee's house and reclined at the table. When a woman who had lived a sinful life in that town learned that Jesus was eating at the Pharisee's house, she brought an alabaster jar of perfume, and as she stood behind him at his feet weeping, she began to wet his feet with her tears. Then she wiped them with her hair, kissing them and poured perfume on them.'

(Apparently this perfume was worth more than a year salary for a labour in those days. Would this be the same Mary, who was the sister of the poor Lazarus in Luke 16, 19-31; who was longing to eat what fell from the rich man's table, and who died and was carried to Abraham's side without being resurrected?

Would have she let her brother die from hunger; her who had such an expensive perfume? Could she remain an appreciated friend of Jesus after such ignorance?)

'When the Pharisee who had invited him saw this, he said to himself, "If this man were a prophet, he would know who is touching him and what kind of woman she is—that she is a sinner.'

(If God and Jesus were not touching the sinners with the word of God; might as well saying that no sinner and nobody would be saved.

This word of God that I propagate has highly cured a man who was deeply distressed lately, and I really mean highly, not entirely.

In Matthew there is question of this woman too. This Mary is mentioned as one who will be remembered everywhere where the kingdom of heaven will be preached.

It is question that this happened in the house of Simon the Leper, but no one said he was a Pharisee. It was written in Matthew that this perfume was poured on Jesus' head, not on his feet. There is no question in Matthew about her wiping Jesus' feet with her hairs and her name is not mentioned either. It is not mentioned either that she was a sinner. In Matthew this happened just before his death when elsewhere; it happened a lot sooner.)

John 11, 3-5. 'So the sisters sent word to (this) Jesus, "Lord the one you love is sick." When he heard this, Jesus said, "This sickness will not end in death. No, it is for God's glory so that God's Son may be glorified through it." Jesus loved Martha and her sister (Mary) and Lazarus.'

(Jesus loves all the sinners, because he came to call them all, but he was not in love with any particular man, like this John has tried to make people believe and as we'll see a bit farther in the gospel of this John and many times.)

See John 19, 26. 'When Jesus saw his mother there, and the disciple whom he loved.'

(Maybe Jesus loved Mary the Magdalene in a different way. Her name was apparently written on Jesus tomb. This would be one of the last discoveries about him. But what do we really know and where is the truth about this?

Jesus said that God is his Father and I too say this. I say this not only about Jesus, but I say this also about myself. But when Jesus was talking about himself; he said being the Son of Man. I say I am one of his disciples and I follow him.)

John 11, 12-16. 'His disciples replied, "Lord, if he sleeps, he will get better." Jesus had been speaking of his death, but his disciples thought he meant his natural sleep.'

(This is as good as another a way to make Jesus' disciples look like dummies, and this too is disparagement against them, but you should believe it, the true Jesus has not done this to his followers.)

'So then he told them plainly, "Lazarus is dead, and for your sake I am glad I was not there, so that you may believe. But let us go to him. Then Tomas, called Didymus, said to the rest of the disciples, "Let us also go, that we may die with him.'

(What a bunch of BS. This story tells that Jesus' disciples were with him, but there is no mentioning of Peter, John and James, who were following Jesus everywhere except when Jesus was praying privately his Father who is in heaven. And if that story was true, Matthew too would have mentioned it. To me this means it has never happened, because Lazarus is not mentioned at all in the gospel of Matthew.)

John 11, 43-44. 'When he had said this, Jesus called in a loud voice,'

(To my knowledge, yelling is always in a loud voice, otherwise this is not yelling, and it has never waked up the dead and it was said about the true Jesus that he will not shout.)

"Lazarus, come out!" The dead man came out his hand and feet wrapped with strips of linen, and a cloth around his face.'

(If he was resurrected and came out, this was no longer a dead man who came out, but a man alive. Did you ever see a person walked with his feet wrapped up? And one more time, as it was said about the true Messiah, "He will not shout," like this imposter, this false Christ did it in this gospel of John.)

John 11, 52. 'And not only for that nation but also for the scattered children of God, to bring them together and make them one.'

(This last quotation is directly related to the lying one from Paul in;)

Ephesians 2, 15. 'By abolishing in his flesh the Law with its commandments and regulations. His purpose was to create in himself one new man out of the two, thus making peace.'

(Jesus, the true Messiah, has abolished nothing at all from the Law of God or from the Law of Moses, not even the least stroke of a pen and not the smallest letter, either by his flesh or by any other way. And the true Messiah said it himself that he didn't come to bring peace on earth, but the sword that causes division. And I would add to this; it is the division between those who love the truth and those who don't; those who believe in it and those who don't. See again Matthew 10, 34.

Here is another lie and the proof is seen all along this gospel of this John that they had planned to stone the Messiah long before that day.)

John 11, 53. 'So from that day on they plotted to take his life.'

John 11, 54. 'Therefore Jesus no longer moved about publicly among the Jews.'

(He who said he was sent only to the lost sheep of Israel.)

'Instead he withdrew to a region near the desert, to a village called Ephraim, where he stayed with his disciples.'

(Wouldn't the true John, Jesus' apostle had rather said, "with us, his disciples?" Besides, Jesus, the true Messiah declared having no place to rest his head. As far as I am concerned, this false Christ should have been stoned right from the beginning. And didn't Jesus, the Messiah, move about publicly among the Jews when he entered Jerusalem before he was assassinated by the Romans?

Chapter 2

John 12, 4-6. 'But one of his disciples, Judas Iscariot, who was later to betray him objected, "Why wasn't this perfume sold and the money given to the poor? It was worth a year's wages." He did not say this because he cared for the poor but because he was a thief; as keeper of the money bag. He used to help himself to what was put into it.'

(If they knew he was a thief; why they let him hold the money bag in the first place? And again; this was not mentioned at all in the gospel of Matthew. Also, here the year' wages is mentioned, but not of it is mentioned in the French Bible and neither it is in the King James.

John 12, 7. '"Leave her alone," (this) Jesus replied. "It was intended that she should save this perfume for the day of my burial."'

(Here in the French Bible, in the same gospel and by the same John, this Jesus rather said, "Let her keep this perfume for the day of my burial." And this was said when it was already poured on his feet. No big deal, right? And according to what this John said so far here at this point in his gospel; there is still a long way to Jesus' burial, because he didn't even start to teach his disciples yet with his parables.)

John 12, 8. 'You will always have the poor among you, but you will not always have me.'

(The Messiah has rather said the exact opposite in;)

Matthew 28, 20. 'And surely I am with you always, to the very end of the age.'

John 12, 14. 'Jesus found a young donkey and sat upon it, as it is written.'

(Here, just like a thief, this Jesus found a donkey and made it his, as if there was nothing to it. Not only were they happy to make Jesus a liar; they also made him to be a thief. There are a lot of abominations in the holy place.)

John 12, 16. 'At first his disciples did not understand all this.'

(These were dummies according to this John.)

'Only after Jesus was glorified did they realize that these things had been written about him and that they had done these things with him.'

(This again is disparagement against the true Jesus and against his disciples, pretending they didn't understand anything at all. What a liar he is! But again, this was also what Paul was saying and doing.

We have passed more than half of this gospel of John and this Jesus hasn't started to teach his apostles yet and we didn't see one of his parables yet either; as we have seen in the gospel of Matthew. We are certainly not reading about the same Jesus and not dealing with the true John, Jesus' apostle either.)

John 12, 28. '"Father, glorify your name!" Then a voice came from heaven, "I have glorified it, and I will glorify it again."'

(But no one of the Jesus' disciples has ever mentioned this in the Scriptures. The true Jesus, who is humble in heart, was not telling God what to do either. The true Messiah wouldn't have told such a thing either, because he already knew that God's Name is and was glorified. It is good to invent things some times, but please, don't go tell others they are holy stories.

John 12, 36. '"Put your trust in the light while you have it, so you may become sons of light, Jesus left and hid himself from them."'

(And if he hid himself from them, this is because and again; he was not talking to his disciples, but to the Pharisees. This Jesus didn't show himself to the Jews anymore, according to this John, as we have read earlier in John 11, 54, but here he was still talking to them.

The true Jesus, the true Messiah, was not saying that the light will turn off after he left, on the contrary, and see here what he said to his apostles.)

See Matthew 5, 14. 'You are the light of the world.'

(This was far from saying the Jesus' disciples didn't understand anything. The true Messiah didn't waste all of his time arguing with the scribes and the Pharisees. He has instructed his apostles and he has transmitted his light to them, his knowledge, and this in a way that the truth, the word of God could make it up to us. And this despite all of the crafty ways, lies and contradictions of Satan and his disciples.

Fortunately for us, there is a true Messiah, because this false Christ here in this gospel of John is miserable and despicable, and to follow him would be to find oneself in darkness, far away from the Jesus' light, far from the truth.)

John 12, 44-45. 'Then Jesus cried out, (again) "When a man believes in me, he does not believe in me only, but in the <u>one</u> who sent me.'

(This could be interpreted in different ways, because I believe that Satan too has sent his sons and his demons in the world. I believe also that many believe in Satan and in his sons.

And if this is not to pretend to be God Himself; then tell me what else it is. But according to the Word, no one can see God with his human eyes and survive!)

See 2 Thessalonians 2, 4. 'He will oppose and he will exalt himself over everything that is called God or is worshipped, so that he sets himself in God's temple, proclaiming himself to be God.'

(This is what we have just seen in John 12, 44-45. I didn't put a capital O to the <u>one</u> underlined above, who sent this one, only because I thing the one who sent him is Paul. Paul is the one who, as an imitator of God, has became the father of many, and this without even touching a woman whom he saw as dirt, someone impure.

This false Christ was sent by Satan and this was only to mislead people, as usual. There was a reason why this false Christ has never said who is father is and where he is from. And be sure of something else; these were not and they are not Satan and his angels, who worship God and love whatever is from God.)

John 12, 47. 'As for the person who hears my words and does not keep them, <u>I do not judge him</u>. For I didn't not come to judge the world, but to save it.'

(But this one allowed himself to judge people anyway, just like Paul has done. See again;)

John 5, 30. 'By myself I can do nothing; <u>I judge only</u> as I hear and my judgement is just, for I seek not to please myself but him who sent me.'

(This one said he didn't come to judge, but he did it anyway. And I think the one who sent this one here is Paul. Paul is the one who has pretended to be the father of many and who also was judging others, handing them over to Satan, and to do so is to pretend to be God. This was taking God's place.)

John 12, 50. 'So what ever I say is just what the Father has told me to say.'

(But who is and where is the father that he is talking about? The true Jesus, the true Messiah, was often saying: "My Father who is in heaven." We know that Paul, contrary to the true Jesus; was calling his disciples his children. Up until now, this false Christ hasn't say a single time; 'My Father who is in heaven,' while the Jesus who is in Matthew said it at least eight times and this beside speaking about the heavenly Father many of times.????? Question and answer!

Isaiah 7, 14, among others, is contradicted by what is written in;)

John 13, 3. '(This) Jesus (here) knew that the Father had put all things under his power, and that he had come from God and was returning to God.'

(According to the true Messiah who is in Matthew 28, 18, it is only after Jesus' resurrection that all power was given to him.

Where did Satan come from? We know that Satan came from God, just like all things and everyone, but Satan was chased away from heaven with all of the revolutionary bad and proud angels, apparently one third of them! To see where Jesus really came from; we have to read;)

Isaiah 7, 14-15. 'Therefore the Lord Himself will give you a sign: The virgin (here in my French Bible, it is; 'Young girl,') will be with child and will give birth to a son and will call him Immanuel. He will eat curds and honey when (until) he knows enough to reject the wrong (evil) and choose the right.'

(This last declaration is confirming in one way that Jesus, the Messiah, was born, just like everybody else, he grew up, just like everybody else, but he listened to God, and this, not like everybody else. It is not Jesus as a child or as a man who came down from heaven, but this is the word of God that did it and this by the will of God. Jesus, the true Messiah, did not lie to anyone about where he is from, or about anything else, like this false Christ did it in this gospel of John. The Messiah said he was, 'The Son of <u>Man</u>.'

See what this false Christ was capable of, and this is a scene that you will find no where else than in this gospel of John, simply because Jesus, the true Messiah, would have never got naked before his apostles. This was not Jesus, the true one, who was perverse and we will see more of this before the end of this gospel of John.)

John 13, 4-5. 'So he (Jesus) got up from the meal, took off his <u>outer clothing</u>,'

(Oups, there were manipulations of the Scriptures here too. See how it is written in the King James Bible.) "He riseth from supper, and laid aside <u>his garments</u>."

(Remember that he had only two. In the French Bible he took off his clothes also.)

'And wrapped a towel around his waist.'

(The towel was to hide something.)

'After that, he poured water into a basin and began to wash his disciples' feet, drying them with the towel that was wrapped around him.'

(Now, just try to do this without showing your parts to anyone. Of course, this is a story that makes no sense at all. That Jesus, the Son of Man, who is a Son of God, and that someone says he is God, would have gotten completely naked in front of his men, at the time of the most important supper time of his life; when we know that Canaan was cursed and handed over to slavery, because his father Cham has seen the nakedness of his father Noah.???? Come on people!

Please take a second of your time to think about this, would you? Jesus was a very humble man, this is a sure thing, but he was not a pervert man.

A just and decent man could hardly get completely naked to make babies in those days and this was still the way less than one hundred years ago.

But nevertheless, we can see that the manipulations of the Scriptures exist and I believe there will be more of them after my books are known to the world.

John 13, 4. 'So he (Jesus) got up from the meal, took off his <u>outer clothing</u> and wrapped a towel around his waist.'

(We already saw that this was changed from the original writing. I do think that someone like me has mentioned this to some leaders of the church and someone else thought that this didn't make any sense at all. So they changed, "His garments," for, "Outer clothing." They were smart enough to change this stupidity in John 13, 4, but not smart enough to dress him properly in;)

John 13, 12. 'When he had finished washing their feet, he put on <u>his clothes</u> and returned to his place.'

(The entire scene was only an intermission. Ho yes; they replaced his garments for his outer clothing in John 13, 4, but they didn't do it in John 13, 12. They were not too brilliant, these members of the church. They are not as crafty as their master Paul was. But still, millions of people have swallowed their venom and still millions others are still swallowing it and I did too for way too long. I do not anymore though; now I see, but it is very desolating to see all of this corruption. There are some out there who are way more of traitors than Judas was.

For once that this false Christ spent time with his disciples in this gospel of John; there is some disparagement against them, by making people think that Peter didn't understand anything at all.)

See John 13, 6-7. 'He (this Jesus) came to Peter, who said to him, "Lord, are you going to wash my feet?"

Jesus replied, "You do not realize now what I am doing, but later you will understand."'

(Luckily!)

John 13, 8. '"No," Peter said, "you shall never wash my feet." Jesus answered, "Unless I wash you, you have no part with me."'

(What a bunch of BS! But truly, it would be very good for Peter and for anyone to have no part with this false Christ and Peter had nothing to do with him either. Peter was led by the Holy Spirit and he has never spoke about this ridicule scene either, and I am sure of it; it was all invented by one of Jesus' enemies. This is actually a scene that someone could find in a gay party, where every one of them loves each other, but not quite in the way the Lord Jesus was talking about.

There is also quite a bit of BS, here in;)

John 13, 10. 'Jesus answered, "A person who has had a bath needs only to wash his feet; his whole body is clean. And you are clean, though not every one of you."'

(That had to smell dirty feet pretty bad in this party, for this John to invent such a laughable and stupid story.)

John 13, 19. 'I am telling you now before it happens, so that when it does happen you will believe that I am He.'

(This again is to pretend to be God, and this is something the true Jesus, the true Messiah, has not done. Paul did it. It is also very ridiculous to say such a thing, because all of the Jesus' apostles believed in the true Messiah, and this long before the last supper; otherwise, not too many of them would have followed him to this point.

Get ready for worse, because this party of this perverse false Christ is not over just yet.

John 13, 21-26. 'After he had said this, (this) Jesus was troubled in spirit and testified, "I tell you the truth,'

(Here again, in the King James Bible it is written, "Verily, verily, I say unto you." In the International Bible, this false Christ tried to imitate the true Messiah the best way he could.)

'One of you is going to betray me." His disciples stared at one another, (with reasons) at a loss to know which of them he meant.'

(Here is more disparagement against the Jesus' apostles and also and at the same time, this is to make the Messiah look like a traitor. This author is saying that the Jesus' apostles were too stupid to understand what this false Christ was telling them.

They all seemed to be surprised to hear that here, but this false Christ told them all already in this same gospel that there was a demon among them.

See John 6, 70. 'Have I not chosen you, the twelve? Yet one of you is a devil.'

(So, there was no reason really for them to be surprised, at least here in this gospel.)

One of them, the disciple whom Jesus loved,'

(Here, what this writer said is nothing less than trying to make people believe that Jesus had a lover among his apostles, and the true Jesus said this is an abomination in the holy place, and this is what I say too. Also, by the way; this was written by the one who said that Jesus loved him.)

'Was reclining next to him.'

(There was manipulations of the Scriptures here again and this was to reduce the importance of this gesture, but see how it is written in the King James Bible, "Now there was leaning on Jesus' bosom one of his disciples, whom Jesus loved."

(Can you imagine the scene; this John leaning on this Jesus' bosom, who had just got undressed completely, just a few minutes earlier to wash his disciples' feet? To be next to someone and to be on someone are truly two different gestures, two different actions and also two very different meanings.)

'Simon Peter.'

(Who was never shy to ask Jesus whatsoever.)

'Motioned to this disciple and said, "Ask him which one he means."'

(They were all in the same room and at the same supper; so Jesus could very well hear the question as well, since this John was close enough, since he was leaning on him.)

'Leaning back against Jesus, he asked him, "Lord, who is it?"

(There were manipulations of the Scriptures here again. See how it is written in the King James Bible.)

"He then lying on Jesus' breast, saith unto him, Lord, who is it?')

(This) 'Jesus answered, "It is the one to whom I will give this piece of bread when I have dipped it in the dish. Then, dipping the piece of bread; he gave it to Judas Iscariot, son of Simon.'

(And this is a gesture he just couldn't do in a way that none of the other apostles could see, because they were all present at this supper. Unless, of course; he put them all to sleep. And this Jesus could do all of this with a man leaning on his chest.?????????

This is not all; in Matthew, the true Jesus told his apostles that the one who has dipped the piece of bread with him in the dish is the traitor. This was done in a way that only the traitor and the Messiah knew it. Who has dipped is pass, who will is coming. Then in John, this meant; 'Watch and you will see.'

But in the gospel of this John, this false Christ told his disciples before he did it, how to know who is the traitor; which would make this false Christ a traitor just as bad as Judas and maybe worse. It is true that this false Christ could do unbelievable miracles.

I just wonder if this Jesus was more troubled in spirit because of Judas' treason or by the fact the disciple he loved was leaning on his bosom in front of all the other disciples and at the time of the supper.

I hope that you still don't think this is a holy story, because to me; it is a perverse abomination and it is rather diabolic.)

John 13, 27. 'As soon as Judas took the bread, Satan entered into him.'

(This was totally unnecessary, according to the John of this gospel, because Judas was already a demon.)

See again John 6, 70. 'Then this Jesus replied, "Have I not chosen you, the Twelve? Yet one of you is a devil!'

(If the true Jesus would have told his apostles that there was a traitor among his apostles at any time before that supper or at any other time of his ministry; there would have been at least some squabbles and at least a serious discussion among them at one time or at another. And if the true Jesus would have told them there was a demon among them; as it is written in John 6, 70, none of them would have had a reason to question to know who he was. They would have known it for a long time, because we cannot have a demon among us without knowing who he is; especially if we are inspired by the Holy Spirit as the Jesus' apostles were. And frankly, if this was the case, Matthew too would have talked about it.

When the Messiah was talking about recognizing the tree by its fruits; let me tell you that there are some in this gospel of John that are quite juicy.

There is disparagement against Jesus' apostles here again in;)

John 13, 28. 'But no one at the meal understood why Jesus said this to him.'

(But this Jesus had just told them that one of them will betray him and he even showed them how to find out who he was. There was no reason then for them not to understand what was going on. What is understandable in this whole story is that; if they all knew there was a traitor among themselves for a long time and that he was a demon; why then they didn't do anything to stop him? The answer is very simple; none of them knew it, except Jesus and Judas maybe.

But again, if they were all at the table; where were they leaning on one another? I mean this John whom this Jesus loved leaning on this Jesus' bosom. Was that on the floor? This was a very strange party, but this was not the kind of reunions the true Jesus was gathering his disciples for.

At the last supper of Jesus with his apostles; there was the celebration of the bread and the wine, but no washing of the feet and no orgy of this kind.

There is a delirium language as the way Paul did here again in;)

John 13, 31-32. 'When he (Judas) was gone, Jesus said, "Now is the Son of Man <u>glorified</u>.'

(This means it's done and this before the ultimate sacrifice.)

'And God is glorified in him.'

(The Messiah would have said here, "My Father who is in heaven.")

'If God is glorified in him, God will glorify the Son in himself, and will glorify him at once.'

(This is just a foolish language again, since he already said he is glorified, and this before the ultimate sacrifice. And he also said this is to come. This is talking through one self's hat; saying something that means nothing at all. Paul was very good at that, he was a specialist in making contradictory phrases. Either he was glorified or he will be, but not both. Paul most likely thought these were parables, or he wanted you to believe they were.

Here is another point on which Paul was very strong; this was to pretend to be the father of all his disciples.)

John 13, 33. 'My children,'

(This too was to pretend to be God; which the true Messiah has not done.)

'I will be with you only a little longer. You will look for me, and just as I told the Jews, so I tell you now: Where I am going, you cannot come.'

(And I think this one was going to hell and it is just a good thing if the Jews and the Jesus' disciples couldn't go. Jesus, the true Messiah, asked his disciples to follow him, and the true Messiah could not tell them also that they couldn't enter his beautiful kingdom of heaven.

The Jesus, who is in Matthew, has never pretended being the father of his disciples, not even once in the gospel of Matthew.

But we can see these words in 1 John 2, 1. 'My little children.' See also 1 John 2, 12, 1 John 2, 13, 1 John 2, 18, 1 John 3, 7, 1 John 3, 18, 1 John 4, 4, and 1 John 5, 21.

Jesus, the true Messiah, said not to call anyone, 'father,' on earth, but there are many, especially in Paul's camp, who pretend to be the fathers of many and this without touching women.)

John 13, 34. '"A new command I give you: Love one another. As I loved you, so you must love one another.'

(We just saw how these perverts were loving each other in this gospel; by getting naked and by leaning on one another, as if there were not enough homosexuals in this corrupted world. What a lie this one is again from the mouth of this false Christ! And what is this new command that existed already for a couple of thousand years? The whole Law of God gave to the world through Moses are commandments that ask us to love one another; to love God more than anything and more than anyone and to love our neighbour as ourselves. So what is that new command about? Is it for men to love each other among themselves without touching women? See what Jesus, the true Messiah, said about this.)

Matthew 22, 37-40. 'Love the Lord your God with all your heart and with all your soul and with all your mind. This is the greatest commandment. And the second one is like it; love your neighbour as yourself. All the Law and the Prophets hang on these two commandments.'

(But this, my dear friends, it is not to undress and be completely naked before other men, and it is not either to let a man lay on another man's breast, like this false Christ did it in this gospel of John.

No wonder why the congregations of nuns, friars and priests have preferred following Paul, not to touch women, not to touch the opposite sex, to stay single and to love each other among themselves. Hundreds, if not thousands of scandals have brook out in the open, but this seems not to be enough to open people eyes. Blindness is blind, especially for those who don't want to see.)

John 14, 7. 'If you really knew me, you would know my Father as well. From now on, you do know him and you have seen him.'

(This declaration in itself is contradictory, just like Paul was very good at it. It is most likely from this declaration that came the expression; 'Like father like son.' But I am not like my father and my son is not like me at all. This false Christ has insisted so hard to be believed he is God that he seemed to be believed by no one. But I sincerely believe that his father, the one who sent this one is Satan himself, and in this particular case; those who have seen this false Christ have seen Satan. In any cases, I see evil and lies in this gospel of John.

Even Moses couldn't see God; otherwise, he too couldn't survive. And Jesus, the true Messiah, didn't have to insist this way to be believed by his apostles, and after the last supper; he didn't have time to bullshit his disciples the way this false Christ did it here with his poisoned stew in this gospel of John.

Here is another proof that this false Christ has pretended to be God in;)

John 14, 8-9. 'Phillip said, "Lord, show us the Father and that will be enough for us." Jesus answered: "Don't you know me, Philip, even after I have been among you such a long time? Anyone who has seen me has seen the Father. How can you say, show us the Father?"'

(But all of this brings us back again to;)

2 Thessalonians 2, 4. 'He will oppose and he will exalt himself over everything that is called God or is worshipped, so that he sets himself in God's temple, proclaiming himself to be God.'

(And this is exactly what this false Christ has done again here in the gospel of this John, Paul's disciple.

Jesus, the true Messiah, was praying God, and this is something God doesn't have to do.

There is more insistence from this false Christ here, but don't be fooled by this impostor, because all of this, on top of pretending to be God, is to make people believe that Jesus' apostles and disciples had no faith in Jesus, which is completely false and if they didn't believe in this false Christ; this is just a good thing. See here in;)

John 14, 10-11. 'Don't you believe that I am in the Father, and that the Father is in me? The words I say to you are not just my own. Rather, it is the Father, living in me, who is doing his work. Believe me when I say I am in the Father and the Father is in me, or at least believe on the evidence of the miracles themselves.'

(To believe only after seeing some miracles; this is not what I would call having faith. The Jesus, who is in Matthew, didn't have to insist this way for his apostles or for his disciples to believe in him, and certainly not after the last supper. Satan, who is also the father of many, is in his children and his children are in him too and I think this is what this false Christ tried to tell them.

To my knowledge, this was Paul, who had to insist this way with his disciples for them to believe in him and with the Jews in the synagogues and with all the others who didn't want to believe that the Law was abolished with Jesus dying on the cross. See for reference Ephesians 2, 15.)

John 14, 12. 'I tell you the truth, (here in the French Bible and in the King James, it is written, "Verily, verily,") everyone who has faith in me (like Satan, his angels and his demons) will do what I have been doing. He will do even greater things than these, because I am going to the Father.'

(This false Christ, who is saying being God and said that others will do greater things than he has done; this is dementia, impure and simple. And we'll see the proof of that soon. This is because he is preparing the coming of Paul in the picture; the very same way John the Baptist has prepared the coming of the Messiah in the world. This is no less than a diabolic imitation.

This false Christ pretended to be God here again in;)

John 14, 13-14. 'And I will do whatever you ask in my name, so that the Son may bring glory to the Father. You may ask me for anything in my name, and I will do it.'

(If this is not pretending being God, then tell me what else it is. I just wonder how many people asked this one for millions of dollars. Anything is anything, isn't it? Now, what is the true message of the true Messiah?)

See Matthew 21, 22. 'If you believe, you will receive whatever you ask for in prayer.'

(Here Jesus didn't say that whatever was coming from him.)

See also Matthew 6, 6. 'But when you pray, go into your room, close the door and pray to your Father, who is unseen. Then your Father, who sees what is done in secret, will reward you.'

(Jesus didn't involve himself in these two messages as to know who is rewarding whoever. This is the one who tells the truth. So, free to you to believe the lies, but you will have a better chance to be rewarded if you believe in the truth from the true Messiah.

It is in John 14, 16 that this false Christ and this John, this false apostle, started to announce the coming of the one who will come after this Jesus' departure.)

See John 14, 16. 'And I will ask the Father, and he will give you another Counsellor to be with you forever.'

(And who made his entry in the picture just after Jesus was gone? Well, this was Paul, who made his entry by a different door than all the other Jesus' apostles have taken. This is the one who knows all and sees all without being present and beside all this; he allowed himself to swear and to judge others. So, according to the testimony of this false Christ; Jesus, the Messiah, would have sent someone to do the exact opposite of what he taught his own apostles.

See again Paul in 1 Corinthians 5, 3. 'Even though I am not physically present, I am with you in spirit. And I have already passed judgement on the one who did this, just as if I was present.'

(This last message in itself is proving that Paul is not a true Jesus' disciple and that he doesn't teach what the Messiah has prescribed. Although, this is the Paul, this supposedly spirit of the truth that this false Christ in this John sent as being the comforter. I would rather say that he is the spirit of lies, but there are still thousands and millions and even maybe billions who are still following him. Yet, it is written, "Many are called, but few are elected.")

John 14, 17. 'The Spirit of truth. The world cannot accept him, because it neither sees him nor knows him. But you know him, for he lives with you and he will be in you.'

(So, if he lives in them, why does he have to send them another one? The fact is that the true Messiah in Matthew has never mentioned another comforter.)

John 14, 26. 'But the Counsellor, the Holy Spirit, whom the Father will send in my name, will teach you all things and will remind you of everything I have said to you.'

(As if the Jesus' disciples had poor memory and that everything that Jesus taught them was easy to forget. Besides, Jesus, the true Messiah, told them he will be with them every day to the end of the ages.

So much BS, in this gospel of this John gives me headaches. And what this false Christ in this John taught his disciples? That he is himself God and that he will give them everything they want.

There is more of this rubbish here in;)

John 14, 29. 'I have told you now before it happens, so when it does happen you will believe.'

(If the Jesus' disciples didn't believe him; they wouldn't have followed him this far and this long.

See now some multiple repetitions with a few differences.)

John 15, 7. 'If you remain in me and my words remain in you, ask whatever you wish, and it will be given to you.'

(What a pile of rubbishes this is again. Sure, I want a million of dollars to publish and to promote my books, and this, no later than tomorrow. Some people will tell me; "You won't get it because you don't believe it." And I will tell them that I prefer, and this by far, to believe the truth from the true Messiah.)

John 15, 12. 'My command is this; Love each other as I have loved you.'

(We have already seen how this false Christ has promoted the way his disciples should love each other among themselves in John 13, 25.)

See also John 15, 16. 'Then the Father will give you whatever you ask in my name.'

John 15, 17. 'This in my command: Love each other.'

(To love men the way this false Christ did it, no thanks; this is not for me.

See what the true Jesus said in;)

Matthew 5, 46. 'If you love those who love you, what reward will you get? Are not the tax collectors doing that?'

(And all the demons are doing this also. This is something that all the sinners and all the demons can do too. I can also say that all the homosexuals love their neighbours more than themselves.

According to the Messiah and to the God's commandments; we have to love God, the Father, with all of our heart, with all of our soul and with all of our thoughts. But just like Paul; this false Christ could not say it and neither do it. Which makes me think that this false Christ could very well be Paul himself, because each one of them has spent his time arguing with the Jews in the temple and in the synagogues, on top of despising them, disparaging them and irritating them? And this is understandable too coming from the devil and his people, because the Jews are the people of God, his first born. To better understand this go read;)

Exodus 4, 22. 'Then say to Pharaoh, "This is what the Lord says: Israel is my first born.'

(So, those who said and those who say that Jesus is God's only Son have lied and continue to lie.)

See also Exodus 8, 1. 'Then the Lord said to Moses; "Go to Pharaoh and say to him, 'This is what the Lord says: Let my people go, so that they may worship me."'

Let's go see now how Paul said we should love in;)

Galatians 5, 14. '"The entire Law is summed up in a single command: "Love your neighbour as yourself."'

(This is false and it is the same new command told by the false Christ, who is in the gospel of John. And if you don't know that this is a lie; this is because you don't know the truth, the word of God, or you don't want to recognize it.

I like to direct people to the beginning of the Bible, especially for them to see exactly how the devil is operating and how he contradicts God and everything that is coming from God by manipulating the truth. Read carefully Genesis 3, 1-5.

The same way God said it is not good for a man to be alone and give him a woman to be his suitable companion, but the devil one more time said it is not good for a man to touch a woman and to love each other among themselves. The very same thing happened about the Law of God.

The true Jesus, the true Messiah, said differently than Paul about the Law of God too. See Jesus in;)

Matthew 22, 36-40. 'One of them, an expert in the Law, tested Jesus with this question: 'Teacher, which is the greatest commandment in the Law?' Jesus replied; 'Love the Lord your God with all your heart and with all your soul and with all your mind. This is the greatest commandment. And the second one is like it; love your neighbour as yourself. All the Law and the Prophets hang on these two commandments."

(But then, why neither Paul nor this false Christ, who is in the gospel of John couldn't say that the greatest commandment is to love God first? To ask the question is kind of answering it.

There must be many people who don't love themselves very mush, if they love their neighbour as themselves.)

John 15, 19. 'If you belonged to the world, it would love you as its own. As it is, you don't belong to the world.'

(When we were children in my family, playing very hard in the house and being very noisy in our childhood; this is what our mom was saying; that we were not from this world; meaning that we were little devils. But she was not talking to us in parables, and if this was one; we understood it. I also often heard her say to me: "Ha my little apostle, I'm going to disembowel you." But she didn't know in those days that I will become a Jesus' disciple later on in my life and neither did I.

Here is another stupidity in;)

John 15, 22. 'If I had not come and spoken to them, they would not be guilty of sin. Now, however, they have no excuse for their sin.'

(Do you see this? besides judging them, this false Christ is condemning them. But didn't this false Christ said that he came to save the world? He, who knows everything, should have refrained from going and talking to them, if he really wanted to save them. But we already know the devil wants to condemn all the Jews, mainly because they are the people of God. Jesus, the true Messiah, didn't come to judge the world and neither to condemn it, but he came to make the Father known to us and to save us with his knowledge. This is what the word of God, the truth does.)

John 15, 24. 'If I had not done among them (the Jews) what no one else did, they would not be guilty of sin. But now they have seen these miracles, and yet they have hated both me and my Father.'

(If the Jews have hated this false Christ and his father, the devil and their lies, this is nothing else than good news. I also think that it would have been a lot better for the Jews if this false Christ had refrained from doing his deeds among them. But this false Christ is also misinformed, because the true Jesus said that the scribes and the Pharisees wouldn't see another miracle than the one of Jonah in the big fish.

See Matthew 16, 4. 'A wicked and adulterous generation looks for a miraculous sign, but none will be given it except the sign of Jonah.'

(Then, what are those miracles this false Christ has done among the Jews? I know though that Paul gave them a lot of troubles, more than anyone else, and who doesn't know why? Paul is against everything that is coming from God. He is against God's Law, against God's creation and reproduction, against Jesus' apostles and disciples, against God's people, the Jews, against circumcision and mainly against the truth, the word of God. Then, the people of God, the people of Israel, the Jews, God's first born didn't escape the persecution from this devil.)

Here in John 15, 25, this false Christ is excluding himself from the Jew people.)

John 15, 25. 'But this is to fulfill what is written in <u>their</u> Law; 'They hated me without reason.'

(If this false Christ was a Jew, he would have said; "In our Law." Paul was a Roman, so an enemy of the Jews and so was this John. The two of them despised the people of God, despised the Jews. See Paul in;)

1 Thessalonians 2, 15. 'From the Jews, who killed the Lord Jesus and the prophets and drove us out.'

(This is not only despising and gossiping against the Jews, but it is also a huge lie. The Jews have accused Jesus of blasphemy, which was a crime deserving death, according to their Laws, but they didn't kill him. Jesus was actually killed by some Romans like Paul. The Romans were killing by crucifixion, not the Jews. The Jews were killing by stoning and we can see many examples of this. Then Jesus, the true Messiah, said he will be crucified by some Gentiles and these Gentiles were roman soldiers. See Jesus in;)

Matthew 20, 18-19. 'We are going up to Jerusalem, and the Son of Man will be betrayed to the chief priest and the teachers of the Law. They will condemn him to death and will turn him to the <u>Gentiles</u> to be mocked and flogged and <u>crucified</u>.'

(Then the introduction of Paul in the picture continued from this John and his false Christ here in;)

John 15, 26-27. 'When the Counsellor comes, whom I will send to you from the Father, he will testify about me. And you also must testify, for you have been with me from the beginning.'

(Well, my dear friends, the Spirit of truth that comes from the Father, that comes from God, to be more precise, doesn't let Itself be sent away by anyone but by God the true Father and certainly not by this false Christ. The Spirit of truth doesn't need to be sent by anyone either, because It was already with the true Jesus, and this was with this Holy Spirit that Jesus was teaching and baptizing. See one more time;)

Matthew 3, 11. 'I (John the Baptist) baptize you with water for repentance. But after me will come one who is more powerful than I, whose sandals I am not fit to carry. He will baptize you with the Holy Spirit and with fire.'

(It was with the Holy Spirit that Jesus was teaching his apostles and his disciples and he didn't have to wait for anyone to send the Holy Spirit over to him. The Holy Spirit was with Jesus and he was also with all of Jesus' disciples, Judas put aside maybe. To be sure of that read again;)

Isaiah 42, 1-2. 'Here is my servant, whom I uphold, my chosen one in whom I delight; I will put my Spirit on him and he will bring justice to the nations. He will not shout or cry out, or raise his voice in the streets.'

(To show you one more time how the manipulations were done in the Holy Scriptures of the New International Bible Version; I would like for you to see this. In Isaiah 42,

1-2, the Lord would have said: 'I will put my Spirit on him.' Meaning this is to come and according to the false Christ; this will be done once he is gone. But then, in the French Bible and in the King James Bible, it is not the same.

See Isaiah 42, 1, from the King James Bible. 'Behold my servant, whom I uphold; mine elect, in whom my soul delighteth, I have put my Spirit upon him.'

(This means it was done back then, and not it will be done like the liars said. You could certainly admit that this is not the same thing. According to this false Christ; the Spirit of God will come only after he is gone and that he is the one who will send Him. And if he said so; this is because he pretended to be God.

I know and everyone should know that Jesus couldn't have done everything he did, if the Spirit of God was not on him. Not more than I could say everything I write without the Spirit of God being with me.

Will you argue the words that directly came out from God's mouth, and replace them by the words of a false Christ, like the manipulators have done?

(The testimony that Matthew made about Jesus is true; contrary to this one from this John, this impostor, who introduced this false Christ in the Holy Scriptures. What a shame! What a scandal! What abominations these are! But the true Jesus warned us about this phenomena in;)

Matthew 24, 15. 'Therefore, when you see the abomination that causes desolation, which was spoken of through Daniel the prophet— standing in the holy place—(in the Bible) let the reader understand.'

(Yes, may the reader be careful when he reads, as it is written in the French Bible. This in one advice and a teaching from the Messiah that way too many people have ignored and still do. And if this was for the readers; this means then that the abomination that causes desolation is in the Scriptures, in the Holy Scriptures. This is what I am talking about in this book of mine, and I also talk about those who have committed these abominations.

This brings us back to the parable of the weeds, the lies among the truth and there are many of them. This of course is if we want to see them. You are not obligated to believe me or to listen to me, but this would be beneficial to you to listen to the true Messiah, because he is the one who leads us to God, to the salvation, to eternal life.)

John 16, 5. 'Now I am going to him who sent me, yet none of you asks me, "Where are you going?

(This false Christ repeated at least forty times that he was sent by his father, and this is about all he had to say about him. This is not what I would call making his father or his will known to the world. If I know the spiritual Father of Jesus now, if I know God, the Almighty and his will; I learned it from the Messiah who is in the gospel of Matthew and from the God's prophets who are in the Old Testament.

In any cases, the lost sheep of the house of Israel didn't seem to recognize the voice of this false Christ, and this false Christ didn't seem to know the message of the true Messiah; saying we have to shake off the dust off our feet when someone doesn't listen to our words that are coming from God. The Jews didn't seem to listen to this one, but he didn't stop arguing with them, just as Paul did it.

But this is it, the gospel of this John is not from God and neither is the false Christ that he has invented, and the Jews didn't let themselves being fooled by him.

On the other hand, millions of pagans who let themselves being involved, being brainwashed by those pagan religions and by these ferocious wolves are duped and not just a little.)

John 16, 7. 'But I tell you the truth: It is for your good that I am going away.'

(What's this? Is this something true in that gospel of this John for a change?)

'Unless I go away, the Counsellor will not come to you; but if I go, I will send him to you.'

(And this false Christ has pretended being God here again. God has never needed anyone to put his Spirit on anyone, and as always; He still doesn't need anyone to put his Spirit on whomever.

I am persuaded that this false Christ is talking about Paul as being the Counsellor; but all of Jesus' apostles inspired by the Holy Spirit didn't want him, they didn't receive him and they didn't listen to him, because he was breathing out murderous threats against the apostles and always lying through his teeth. Murderer one day, murderer always!)

See again Acts 9, 1. 'Meanwhile, Saul (Paul) was still breathing out murderous threats against the Lord's disciples.'

(And it is most likely this false Christ who sent Paul in the picture to give the Jews and the Jesus' disciples so much trouble.

John 16, 8. 'When he comes, (this comforter) he will convict the world of guilt in regard of sin and righteousness and judgement.'

(And it was by Paul that all of the diabolic religions were founded and with them came the confession, the communion and the repeated prayers to the saints that are not and the fabricated images that created the biggest club of idolaters in the world and more.)

John 16, 10. 'In regard to righteousness, because I am going to the Father, where <u>you can see me no longer</u>.'

(But didn't he say the exact opposite earlier? See what is written in;)

John 14, 18-19. 'I will not leave you as orphans; I will come to you. Before long, the world will not see me anymore, but <u>you will see me</u>. Because I live, you also will live.'

(Would he be the one who thinned out the leaves of the marguerite? You know; "You will see me, you will not see me, you will see me, you will not see me.'

Here again in John 16, 12, this impostor is saying the apostles are not intelligent enough to understand what he has to tell them, but the true Jesus didn't do such a thing.)

John 16, 12. 'I have much more to say to you, more than you can now bare.'

(I think he should hurry a little more, because the true Messiah didn't live this much longer after the last supper. In fact, the true Jesus didn't have time to say everything, all these lies this false Christ said to his disciples in John.

Then come more promotions for the false spirit that sees everything without being present.)

John 16, 13. 'But when he, the Spirit of truth, comes, he will guide you into all truth. He will not speak on his own, he will speak only what he hears, and he will tell what is yet to come.'

(Isn't it exactly what the Messiah did with his apostles? See for example what he told them in;)

Matthew 24, 37-39. 'As it was in the days of Noah, so it will be at the coming of the Son of Man. (The end of this actual world) For in the days before the flood, people were eating and drinking, marrying and giving in marriage,'

(This was pedophilia, abominations and corruptions to no end.)

'Up to the day Noah entered the ark; and they knew nothing about what would happen.'

(This was because they didn't want to listen to the one who was talking to them about God and his will.)

'Until the flood came and took <u>them all</u> (evildoers) away. That is how it will be at the coming of the Son of Man.'

(With what is happening in the world nowadays, all the marriages and gay parades, the abortions, and for a while now, the murders and suicides of the sick people to end their life before time; it won't be long before the wrath of God will be manifested again. But I believe this time this will be the end of this perverted world. The difference, I thing, for this last time; it will be that more than half of the people of the world will be frozen, considering the legalization by the governments of the drugs on the market.

Here in John 16, 23, this John has put in the mouth of his false Christ the same thing but a bit differently than the other times. But this is repetition again.)

John 16, 23. 'In that day <u>you will no longer ask</u> me anything. I tell you the truth, my Father will give you <u>whatever you ask</u> in my name.'

(Sometimes he says it is his father that will give whatever and some other times he says he himself will do this. But many of times he wants people to believe he is God. The Jews, from whom salvation comes from, didn't want to believe that Jesus was the Son of God. I am pretty sure they will believe even less he is God.)

John 16, 25. 'Though I have been speaking to you figuratively.'

(In the French Bible the word used is parables, but these repetitions and these contradictory phrases are not parables at all. And the true Jesus was not talking figuratively to his apostles. He spoke to them clearly and if not; he was explaining the parables to them. This kind of tells me that this false Christ didn't really know what a parable is; contrary to the true Messiah, who was using them continually. The true Jesus did it especially with the crowds. This false Christ should have read the gospel of Matthew completely before pretending being the truth Christ or God, and so should have done this John, this impostor, this liar, who has not known the true Jesus.

Then come some more rubbishes, more repetitions and the marguerite game again here in John 16, 14 to 16, 33.

From John 17, 1 to John 17, 26, this is again more rubbishes and endless repetitions; something the true Messiah has not done at all. Those who know the true Jesus, as I do; know very well that the true Jesus was retrieving himself to pray the Father who is in heaven, and most of the time this was on the top of a mountain.

The true Messiah told us where his Father is, but the false Christ didn't do that. It is a sure thing that telling his disciples or anyone that his father is in hell wouldn't have helped them attracting billions of people as the Christian churches have done it; especially in those days. It is much different today; this world is almost just as bad as it was at the time of Noah.

Shortly after the last supper, the true Jesus retrieved himself from his apostles to pray and he didn't have time for all of this serenade, this poisoned stew, as this false Christ had in this gospel of John.)

See Matthew 26, 36. 'Then Jesus went with his disciples to a place called Gethsemane, and he said to them, "Sit here while I go <u>over there and pray</u>."'

(Then, in the next few verses; Jesus took Peter and the two sons of Zebedee, James and his brother John, the true Jesus' apostle, to go with him. After walking away for a bit, Jesus fell with his face on the ground and prayed, but none of the apostles saw this, because they were sleeping. But the John of this gospel didn't mention any of this, and if he didn't; this is because he is just an impostor and a liar and has seen nothing about the true Messiah.

The story of the arrest of Jesus is also completely different in this John than it is in the gospel of Matthew. The reason is very simple; what is in the gospel of John is a tissue of lies and diabolic inventions.

In Matthew there is the kiss of Judas. There is none of that in the gospel of John.

In Matthew Jesus' prayer is completely different than the one who is in John.

In Matthew, there is no question at all about Jesus asking whoever to spare his disciples, as it is in John. And why would he ask that, knowing they will all flee the scene?

In Matthew, Jesus spoke to the crowd; in John he questioned the officials.

In Matthew Jesus said to the one who drew the sword: "Put your sword in its place; for all who draw the sword will die by the sword." In John he said; "Put your sword away! Shall I not drink the cup the Father has given me?"

(In Matthew Jesus mentioned twelve legions of angels. There is nothing about that in John.

In Matthew Jesus told them he was every day in the temple. There is nothing about this in John at that moment.

In Matthew, there is no mentioning of the whole crowd falling on their ass because he would have said; I am he. Yet, I think this would have been very important. This is because it has never happened. It is all invented by this John, by this impostor.

In Matthew all of the apostles fled the scene. There is nothing mentioned about that in the gospel of this John. Yet, this too would have been important to mention.

In Matthew the officials seized Jesus without binding him, but they did so in John.

In Matthew they brought Jesus first to Caiaphas. In John this was to Annas.

In Matthew Peter followed Jesus at a distance up to the courtyard of the high priest by himself.

In John Peter was accompanied by this John, but the truth is that the John, Jesus' apostle has fled the scene with all the others.

There is no mentioning of Caiaphas in Matthew, who would have advised the Jews, like we see in this John.

There is no mentioning of this John in Matthew, who would have followed Peter to the courtyard and opened the door for him.

In Matthew the high priests were looking for witnesses against Jesus. There is nothing about that in John.

In Matthew Jesus kept silence for his defense. In John he kept arguing, exactly like Paul did it at his trial.

In Matthew Jesus said to the crowd: "Am I leading a rebellion, that you have come out with swords and clubs to capture me? But these words are not mentioned at all in John.

In Matthew we have the discussion between Jesus and Peter about the denial, but nothing about that in John.

In Matthew we can read about the regrets of Peter for his denial. There is nothing about that in John, and yet; this John was supposedly with Peter.

In Matthew we have the discussion about the deal Judas would have made with the high priests for the betrayal of Jesus, but we have none of that in John.

In Matthew we have the repentance and the hanging of Judas. There is none of that in John.

In Matthew Jesus talked about the lost soul of Judas. There is none of that in John.

In Matthew there is question of the potter's field bought with the betrayal's money, for the burial of the foreigners, but there is nothing about that in John.

In John they have made a fire in the courtyard to warm up, and this is not mentioned in Matthew.

Here is another falsified story in;)

John 18, 15-17. 'Simon Peter <u>and another disciple</u> were following Jesus. Because this disciple was known to the high priest, (like Paul was) he went with Jesus into the high priest's courtyard, but Peter had to wait outside at the door. The other disciple, who was known to the high priest, came back, spoke to the girl on duty there and brought Peter in. "You are not one of his disciples, are you?" The girl at the door asked Peter.'

(In that unlikely story, they would have questioned Peter three times, but they wouldn't have questioned this John, yet he would be the one who entered the courtyard with Jesus, and was known to the high priest.????

And if he was known to the high priest; this high priest would not have been without knowing the true

John was with Jesus. Which means the very life of John would definitely have been in danger, but this was not the case for this impostor.

There is a very simple explanation for this; Jesus' John, his apostle, had fled the scene with all the other apostles and stayed away from that scene. The John, who was known to the high priest, is surely an impostor. He is the John, Paul's disciple and he is just as much of a liar. We know too that Paul was known to all the high priests, for he was working for them.)

See now Matthew 26, 58. 'But Peter followed him (Jesus) at a distance, right to the courtyard of the high priest. (By himself) He entered (with no help from anyone) and sat down with the guards to see the outcome.'

(There is no girl on duty here to question Peter.

Let's see now the one who, in reality, was not supposed to open his mouth, to defend himself, this said.)

John 18, 20. '"I have spoken openly to the world," (this) Jesus replied. "I always taught in synagogues or at the temple, (this is false; Paul did that) where all the Jews come together. I said nothing in secret.'

(This is false too, at least according to the true Jesus. But the true Jesus didn't open his mouth, for his defense, this is. See Jesus in;)

Matthew 10, 27. 'What I tell you <u>in the dark</u>, (in secret) speak in the daylight; what is whispered <u>in your ear</u>, proclaim from the roofs.'

(Yes, the true Jesus, the true Messiah, has kept silence before those who persecuted him; just like the ancients prophets have predicted it, but this in not the case for this false Christ, who is in the gospel of this John.

This is another proof that proves my theory that the gospel of this John is just an imposture. It is in fact only trickery coming from the ferocious wolves. Some wolves that entered by a different door than the one taken by the true apostles to enter the sheep pen. They have seduced millions of people and unfortunately; they continue to do so.

Maybe it will be a good thing at this moment to read this again here in;)

Isaiah 53, 7. 'He (the Messiah) was oppressed and afflicted, yet he did not open his mouth; he was led <u>like a lamb</u> (this is not being a lamb) to the slaughter, and as a sheep before her shearers is silent, so <u>he did not open his mouth</u>.'

(For his defence that is.)

See also John 18, 21. 'Why question me? Ask those who heard me. Surely they know what I said.'

(If this one meant to tell Caiaphas to ask the high priests; they already told him about Jesus and judged him, and if he meant to tell Caiaphas to ask his disciples; the governor couldn't reach them, because most of them had fled already. If he meant for the governor to ask Jesus' disciples about what he told them; this would have been treason just as bad as Judas did. The true Messiah surely didn't do this, and he couldn't do this either, because he knew they were all gone by then, except for Peter.

John 18, 22. 'When Jesus said this, one of the officials nearby struck him in the face. "Is this the way you answer the high priest?" He demanded.'

(It seems to me that I have seen this kind of trial before, and this is in the story of Paul's trial that we can read in;)

Acts 23, 2-5. 'At this the high priest Ananias ordered those standing near Paul to strike him on the mouth. Then Paul said to him, (to the judge) 'God is going to strike you whitewashed wall! You sit there to judge me according to the law, yet you yourself violate the law (Roman law) by commanding that I be struck! Those who were standing near Paul said, "You dare to insult God's high priest?" Paul replied, "<u>Brothers</u>, I did not realize that he was the high priest; for it is written: 'Do not speak evil about the ruler of your people."'

(It seems to me that when a liar is lacking imagination; he repeats the same lies.)

John 18, 23. '"If I said something wrong," (this) Jesus replied, "testify as to what is wrong. But if I spoke the truth, why did you strike me?"

(All of this, no doubt, resemble a lot more of Paul's trial than Jesus' trial; he, who didn't open his mouth for his defense. Not like this false Christ here in this John did it, and he did it a lot.)

John 18, 24. 'Then Annas sent him, still bound, to Caiaphas the high priest.'

(But we have absolutely nothing about this interrogation of Jesus by Annas in Matthew, contrary to all of it here in John. On the other hand; in John, we have absolutely nothing of the interrogation of Jesus by Caiaphas.)

See Matthew 26, 57. 'Those who had arrested Jesus took him (directly) to Caiaphas, the high priest, where the teachers of the Law and the elders had assembled.'

(There is no mentioning of Annas at all here in Matthew, and contrary to what is in John; we have the interrogation of Jesus by Caiaphas that we can read from Matthew 26, 62 to 26, 68.

You will see in these few verses that Jesus didn't open his mouth for his defense; contrary to this false Christ who is in the gospel of John.

The true Jesus who is in Matthew is not at all the same one than the one who is in John, and he didn't preach the same thing and he didn't preach the same way either.

The questions from Pilate to Jesus and the Jesus' answers are also different from one gospel to the other. See first Jesus in;)

Matthew 27, 11-12. 'Meanwhile Jesus stood before the governor, and the governor asked him, "Are you the King of the Jews?" "Yes, it is as you say." Jesus replied.

When he was accused by the chief priest and the elders, he gave no answer.'

(Here in Matthew, Jesus answered simply and with the truth to a question he was asked, but he didn't open his mouth for his defense when comes to the accusations from the high priests. See now what happened in the John's gospel with the false Christ.)

John 18, 33-34. 'Pilate then went back inside the palace, summoned Jesus and asked him, "Are you the king of the Jews?" "Is that your own idea," (This) Jesus asked, "or did others talk to you about me?"'

(This is being arrogant the way Paul was, but Jesus was and is gentile and humble in heart. And this arrogant did open his mouth again and way more than someone who was supposed not to do so. See the big difference there is with the Jesus who is in;)

Matthew 27, 13. 'Then Pilate asked him, "Don't you hear the testimony they are bringing against you?" But Jesus made no reply, not even to a single charge—to the great amazement of the governor."

(And this is how ended the interrogation of Jesus by Pilate in Matthew, but in the gospel of this John; it continued a bit longer and this false Christ has continued to open his mouth again and way more than he was supposed to.)

John 18, 35. "Am I a Jew?" Pilate replied.'

(This too is completely different than what is in Matthew.)

'"It was your people and your chief priest who handed you over to me. What it is you have done?"'

(This demonstrates clearly that the governor was not a Jew but a roman, and one has to remember also that Paul, according to himself, was a Jew too, a treacherous Jew and a Roman.

The true Messiah said that we cannot serve two masters.)

See Matthew 6, 24. 'No one can serve two masters. Either he will <u>hate</u> the one and love the other, or he will <u>be devoted to the one</u> and <u>despise the other</u>. You cannot serve both God and money.'

(Paul could not serve Israel and Rome, so he hated Israel and he loved Rome. He was devoted to Rome and he despised Israel and the Jews. We cannot serve God and serve a religion that collects money either and they all do just that.

Then this false Christ riposted by opening his mouth again and to lie above all.)

See John 18, 36-37. '(This Jesus) said, "My kingdom is not of this world. If it were, my servants would fight to prevent my arrest by the <u>Jews</u>.'

(How would they do that, if he is already arrested?)

'But now my kingdom is from another place."'

(Here in the French Bible, he rather said: "My kingdom is not down here on earth and this is a lie.")

'"You are a king, then!" Said Pilate. Jesus answered, "You are right in saying I am a king. In fact, for this reason I was born, and for this I came into the world, to testify to the truth. Everyone on the side of truth listens to me."'

(Not too bad for someone who kept his mouth shut, isn't it? And apparently, Pilate was listening to him too.

Well, Jesus is the king of the Jews, as this was demonstrated in this writing and the Jews are in this world too and they are on earth as well. The kingdom of heaven is also on earth and the Messiah is the king of it. Everything will be different in the kingdom of God.)

John 19, 4-5. 'Once more Pilate came out and said to the Jews, "Look, I am bringing him out to you to let you know that I find no basis for a charge against him.'

(And all of this, of course, is to make people believe that a roman governor was more compassionate with the Messiah than the bad Jews. But in reality, the Romans were more afraid of the King of the Jews than any Jew. The fact is that the Romans have even tried to kill this King before he was out of his cradle. They even went as far as killing all the baby boys of his region with the only goal to eliminate him. There is no question in my mind as to know who Jesus worse enemies were and are. To know who those murderers are from the beginning, read;)

'When (this) Jesus came out wearing the crown of thorns and the purple robe, Pilate said to them, "Here is the man!"'

See now Matthew 27, 26. 'Then he (Pilate) released Barabbas to them. (The Jews) But he had Jesus flogged, and handed him over to be crucified.' (By the roman soldiers.

Remember now that this Jesus is outside.

John 19, 8-9. 'When Pilate heard this, he was even more afraid and he went back inside the palace. "Where do you come from?" He asked (this) Jesus, but this Jesus gave him no answer.'

(Of course this Jesus couldn't answer him inside, he was outside and he couldn't even hear the question.

And Pilate continued to speak by himself like a dummy. See again him in;)

John 19, 10-11. 'Do you refuse to speak to me?"'

(Of course, Pilate is in the palace and this Jesus is still outside.)

'Pilate said. "Don't you realize I have power either to free you or to crucify you?"

(This is kind of proving that the responsibility in the death of the Messiah was only and completely on the shoulders of Pilate. He is the one who decided he will die and he delivered Jesus to his soldiers to be crucified. Contrary to what happened to Paul; the Romans didn't protect Jesus, a Jew.

(This) Jesus answered, "You would have no power over me if it were not given to you from above.'

(Isn't this a way to blame God for the death of the Messiah?)

'Therefore the one who handed me over to you is guilty of a greater sin.'

(And these last words are there, in some ways, to exculpate the governor, because he was roman and to blame only the Jews for the death of the Messiah. According to this false Christ; it is worse to condemn someone than to kill someone. One has to note also that when this author spoke about the soldiers; he didn't mention they were Romans and if they were Jews; he would have mentioned their nationality. As a result, this roman false Christ has preferred saying that those (the Jews) who condemned the Messiah are way worse than the Romans who killed him. And of course, a Roman like Paul, who was chasing and killing the Jesus' disciples, has done nothing wrong, since he said it himself that his conscience was clear, that he felt guilty of nothing.

Even the inscription at the top of Jesus' cross is not the same in both versions of this whole story of the persecution of the Messiah. In Matthew 27, 37, we can read, "THIS IS JESUS, THE KING OF THE JEWS."

In John 19, 19, we can read; "JESUS OF NAZARETH, THE KING OF THE JEWS."

(They didn't go to the same school.)

Matthew 27, 32-33. 'As they were going out, they met a man from Cyrene, named Simon, and they forced him to carry the cross. They came to a place called Golgotha, which means, 'The place of the Skull."

(But there is no mentioning of this Simon at all in John's version of this story.)

John 19, 17. 'Carrying his own cross, he went out to the place of the skull; which in Aramaic is called Golgotha.'

(Who has told the truth? It is a sure thing that those who don't know the true story of Jesus, or don't know that the devil, his angels and his demons, those who don't know that the ferocious wolves have entered the sheep pen; have entered the Holy Scriptures can be very confused.

My mother is almost ninety five years old, but when she was only a little child; a catholic priest told her father not to let his children read the Bible, that this might drive them crazy. It is a sure thing too that for a young child or for anyone to discover so many lies, contradictions and abominations in the Bible, in the Holy Scriptures, the book of the absolute truth; this can be very disturbing. Especially for he or she who doesn't understand the parable of the weeds from Jesus that we can read in Matthew 13, 36-43.

There are a lot more of those contradictions and lies. Here is another good or bad one in;)

John 19, 25. 'Near the cross of Jesus stood his mother, his mother's sister, Mary the wife of Clopas, and Mary Magdalene.'

(See now what has really happened near the cross of Jesus or far from it in;)

Matthew 27, 55-56. 'Many women were there watching from a distance. They had followed Jesus from Galilee to care for his needs. Among them were Mary Magdalene, Mary the mother of James and Joses, and the mother of Zebedee's sons.'

(Then, there was no mother of Jesus near the cross of Jesus, and Mary Magdalene, even if she was called, 'a saint,' she couldn't have been at two different places at the same time. And because that all of the Jesus' apostles had to flee to avoid persecution, and that it was way too dangerous for any close ones of Jesus to be near him at that time; I am persuaded that if they watched what was happening; they did it from a distance, just as it is written in Matthew. The story of Peter's denial proves the danger that was there for all of them, and this includes Mary, Jesus' mother and all of Jesus' brothers and friends.

More lies here again and just an unlikely statement in;)

John 19, 26-27. 'When Jesus saw his mother there, and the disciple whom he loved,'

(This was the one who was lining on Jesus' breast during the last supper, but this John wasn't there near the cross in the previous verse. This was Jesus who was so broken down that he couldn't carry his cross anymore.)

'Standing nearby, he said to his mother, "Dear woman, here is your son," and to the disciple, "Here is your mother." From that time on, this disciple took her into his home.'

(Jesus was well guarded by the roman soldiers and if Jesus' mother would have been near Jesus' cross at any time and if Jesus would have talked to her; he would have put her in danger of death and his disciple too. And believe it, all of the Jesus' apostles had fled the scene, they have listened to our Master and they went to Galilee, as they were told. There was maybe someone called John near Jesus' cross, but this was certainly not John, Jesus' apostle and neither John, his brother.

I think this is the invented lying story that made people believe that Mary, Jesus' mother became God's mother, the Queen of heavens. This is nothing else than swindle.

Mary, Jesus' mother, had at least three other sons who could take care of her, and believe me, in those days; the children could take care of their parents, especially in the holy family.

Even the burial of Jesus is different from one version to the other. Let's see first how it was done in;)

Matthew 27, 57-60. 'As evening approached, there came a rich man from Arimathea, named Joseph, who had himself become a disciple of Jesus. (So, it is possible for a rich man too.) Going to Pilate, he asked for

Jesus' body, and Pilate ordered that it be given to him. Joseph (by himself) took the body, wrapped it in a clean linen cloth, and placed it in his own new tomb that he had cut out of the rock. He rolled a big stone in front of the entrance to the tomb and went away.'

(See the difference now in;)

John 19, 38-42. 'Later, Joseph of Arimathea, asked Pilate for the body of Jesus. Now Joseph was a disciple of Jesus, but secretly because he feared the Jews. With Pilate's permission he came and took the body away. He was accompanied by Nicodemus, the man who earlier had visited Jesus at night. Nicodemus brought a mixture of myrrh and aloes, about seventy-five pounds.'

(In the French Bible, he had one hundred pounds, but this is a very small detail. Though, carrying one hundred pounds of what so ever in an addition of a dead corps; this could make a difference.)

'Taking Jesus' body, the <u>two of them</u> wrapped it, with the spices, in strips of linen. This was in accordance with Jewish burial customs. At the place where Jesus was crucified, there was a garden, and in the garden a new tomb, in which no one had ever been laid. Because it was the Jewish day of Preparation and since the tomb was nearby, <u>they</u> laid Jesus there.'

(Here in John, there is no mention of a big stone rolled if front of the entrance of the tomb, and according to the story in Matthew; Jesus had already received the perfume for his burial from the historical woman, but of course, she didn't have seventy-five pounds of it. She had some of a value enough to pay the salary of a labour for more than one year. How much was worth seventy-five pounds? I think that Nicodemus, who didn't speak up for Jesus' defense at his trial, wouldn't have spent this much on Jesus' body. On the contrary, he is the one who said it would be better if Jesus dies instead of many Jews.

There is also confusion about the number of women who went to Jesus' tomb.)

Matthew 27, 61. 'Mary Magdalene and the other Mary were sitting there opposite the tomb.'

John 20, 1. 'Early on the first of the week, while it was still dark, Mary Magdalene (alone) went to the tomb and saw that the stone had been removed from the entrance.'

See also Matthew 28, 1-2. 'After the Sabbath, at down on the first of the week, (Sunday morning) Mary Magdalene and the other Mary went to look at the tomb. There was a violent earthquake, for an angel of the Lord came down from heaven and, going to the tomb, rolled back the stone and sat on it.'

(A violent earthquake and the vision of an angel from heaven are not things easily forgotten.

And if Jesus died Friday afternoon, the day before the Sabbath, and that he spent three days and three nights in the heart of the earth; there is no way that he could have been resurrected on the first day of the week, the day following the Sabbath. Someone lied and cheated and this is not Jesus and neither Matthew. This is someone else who manipulated the truth and I truly believe this was done by the religions, for a monetary reward, and if they sold their soul to the devil; there is nothing there for them to sell one little detail like one day off for Jesus to be in the heart of the earth. They most likely told themselves that no one will notice, and that no matter what; this wont make any difference to the fact that the Messiah died and resurrected.

(See what the true Jesus' apostles did just after the crucifixion of their Master in;)

Matthew 28, 16. 'Then the eleven disciples went to Galilee, to the mountain where Jesus had told them to go.'

(But in the gospel of John, there are again a load of rubbishes about the occupations of the Jesus' apostles after his death.)

See John 20, 2-5. 'So she (Mary Magdalene) came running to Simon Peter and the other disciple, the one Jesus loved, and said. "They have taken the Lord out of the tomb, and we don't know where they have put him. So Peter and the other disciple started for the tomb. Both where running, but the other disciple outran Peter and reached the tomb first. He bent over and looked in at the strips of linen there but did not go in.'

(Personally I doubt he could see the strips of linen without getting inside the tomb, but anyway; the true

John, Jesus' apostle, was already on his way to Galilee with the other ten and Peter too.)

John 20, 8-10. 'Finally the other disciple, who had reached the tomb first, also went inside. He saw and believed. (And like some idiots) They still did not understand from Scriptures that Jesus had to rise from the dead. Then the disciples went back to their homes.'

(And this author, this impostor, this John made Mary Magdalene look like a simple idiot also here in;)

John 20, 14-15. 'At this, she turned around and saw Jesus standing there, but she did not realize that it was Jesus.'

(And this even after he talked to her.)

"Women," he said, "why are you crying? Who is it you are looking for? "Thinking he was the gardener, she said.'

(Mary Magdalene, who was near Jesus' cross; this according to this author, could very well see in what condition he was just before he was put in his tomb. But she didn't recognize him or his voice. And this, again according to this same author, not even a day and a half after his death. This is enough to wonder if this was really Jesus. What the sons of the devil wouldn't do to create doubts in people's mind?

John 20, 17. '(This) Jesus said, "Do not hold on to me, for I have not yet returned to the Father.'

(When I say that we can recognize the liars by their lies; here is one more. Just look one more time at what this one would have said a few days earlier in;)

Luke 23, 39-43. 'One of the criminals who hung there hurled insults at him: (Jesus) "Are you the Christ? Save yourself and us!" But they other criminal rebuked him. "Don't you fear God," he said, "since you are under the same sentence? We are punished justly, for we are getting what our deeds deserve. But this man has done nothing wrong." Then he said, "Jesus, remember me when you come into your kingdom." (This) Jesus answered him. "I tell you the truth, today you will be with me in paradise."'

(This was the day he died. And don't you go think that Jesus' Father, our Father, is not in paradise.

Then, this false Christ, pretending to be the Messiah, would have told Thomas to touch him, and this too before he went to his father. It is true that Paul was afraid to be defiled by a woman if he touches her, or if she touches him.)

See John 20, 27. 'Then he said to Thomas, "Put your finger here; see my hands. Reach out your hand and put it into my side. Stop doubting and believe.'

(As far as his hands are concerned, the two criminals crucified at the same time, also had holes in their hands. A woman couldn't touch this one, but a man could. This whole thing resembles more and more to the stories of

Paul and this is why I say this John is Paul's John or Paul himself.)

See 1 Corinthians 7, 1. 'Now concerning the things about which you wrote, it is good for a man not to touch a woman.'

(I said it before; it is good to believe, but to believe the truth, not in those lies and in these liars. If this really happened, Matthew too would have spoken about it. But all of these lies are in there to make the Holy Scriptures lose some credibility, and this too, is Satan's goal.

There is another big lie in this next story;)

See John 20, 19. 'On the evening of that first day of the week, when the disciples were together, with the doors locked <u>for fear of the Jew</u>, (this) Jesus came and stood among them and said. "Peace be with you!"'

(First thing first; it is not in a house that the first meeting between Jesus and his apostles happened after his resurrection, and this was not in Jerusalem either, but in Galilee, on a mountain where he told them to go.

Secondly, the Jesus' apostles could not fear the Jews, and at the same time spend all of their time at the temple, there where the Jews could have put their hands on them at any time. But see what the other liar said about them in;)

Luke 24, 52-53. 'Then they (the apostles) <u>worshipped him</u> (this is another lie. In the French Bible it says; 'bowed down before him,') and returned to Jerusalem with great joy. And they stayed continually at the temple, praising God.'

See now Matthew 28, 16. 'Then the eleven disciples went to Galilee, to the mountain where Jesus had told them to go.'

(And I believe that the confession and the confessional box were invented in;)

John 20, 22-23. 'And with that he breathed on them and said, "Received the Holy Spirit.'

(This, according to himself, to this false Christ in John, was supposed to be done only once he reached his father, but according to this lying story; it is not done yet.)

'If you forgive anyone his sins, they are forgiven; if you do not forgive them, they are not forgiven."'

(What a pile of rubbishes this is! The true Messiah told his disciples not to judge, which is the exact opposite of what this false Christ did. And since that time, I suppose, all of those, who make people call them, 'father,' and this despite the Messiah's interdiction to do so, are pretending having the power to forgive people's sins to those who call them, 'father.' And this too is done by them despite Jesus' interdiction.

What the true Messiah said about that to his disciples is written here in;)

Matthew 16, 18-19. 'And I (Jesus) tell you that you are Peter and on this rock I will build my Church, (only one) and the gates of Hades will not overcome it. I will give you the keys of the kingdom of heaven; whatever you bind on earth will be bound in heaven, and whatever you loose on earth will be loosed in heaven.'

(This was told to Peter by Jesus. This was told to Peter by the true Messiah and this in a much different occasion and long before he was resurrected.

This was told to the ones who follow Jesus. The ones who follow the true Messiah received this power, not the sons of the devil, who ignore the messages coming from God, and make people call them, 'father.' See this here to refresh your memory in;)

Matthew 23, 8-9. 'But you (my disciples) are not to be called 'Rabbi,' for you have only one Master and you are all brothers. And do not call anyone on earth 'father,' for you have one Father, and He is in heaven.'

(Besides, this false Christ said in this same gospel, here in John that he had to go to his father before his disciples could receive the Holy Spirit, but he pretended here being able to give it to them before he leaves. There is a big pile of rubbishes here again in this gospel of John, but by doing so; he has accomplished his goal; which his making people pulling away from God; those who don't want to believe the truth anymore, and this is because of all of these rubbishes of lies.

Though, I still believe that those who don't believe in God anymore are closer to Him than all of those who believe in lies. I also think they will accept the truth one day and this easier than those who have received the brain washing from the religions and have accepted the lies and the contradictions as if they were true.)

John 21, 4. 'Early in the morning, Jesus stood on the shore, but the disciples did not realize that it was Jesus.'

(They just saw him and talked to him a couple of days earlier, according to this same author, but they couldn't recognize him again. A nice bunch of idiots those were, isn't it?

John 21, 5. 'He called out to them, "Friends,'

(In my French Bible and in the King James; it is not, 'Friends,' here but, 'Children.' This means there were more manipulations of the Holy Scriptures here about that, and this is most likely because some people told them that the true Messiah didn't call his disciples, 'my children'. Paul has done just that. What will they do when people tell them everything I found and denounced?)

'Haven't you any fish?" "No," they answered.'

(In the entire gospel of Matthew, never Jesus has pretended to be the father of his disciples or treated them as little children. This is something Paul did a lot though.

John 21, 6. 'He said, "Throw your net on the right side of the boat and you will find some." When they did, they were unable to haul the net in because of the large number of fish.'

(No wonder so many fishermen are exaggerating their fishing stories. This false Christ had just remembered that there was a miraculous fishing story during Jesus' ministry. Only one thing though; he is at least three years too late. Remember too now that there are seven men in the boat, which means it was quite big, and they couldn't haul the net because of the big number of fish. And to fill the net this much; they had to be in deep enough water.)

John 21, 7. 'Then the disciple whom Jesus loved,'

(This was enough to make the other apostles a bit jealous.)

'Said to Peter, "It is the Lord!" As soon as Simon Peter heard him say, "It is the Lord," he wrapped his outer garment around him, for he had taken it off, and jumped into the water.'

(There was a very by manipulation of the Holy Scriptures here too. See how it is written in the French Bible and in the King James Bible.)

John 21, 7. 'Therefore that disciple whom Jesus loved saith unto Peter. It is the Lord. Now when Simon Peter heard that it was the Lord, he girt his fishers' coat unto him, for he was naked, and did cast himself into the sea.'

(The difference is quite obvious, isn't it? And apparently, the only one to recognize this Jesus among the seven of them, is the John who was loved by him and this even after hearing his voice. This was only a few days after all of them saw him. This is quite strange too.

But there is something more unlikely yet in that story. To say that Peter was naked in front of his companions, early in the morning and on the sea; there where it is much colder than in the city, where they had to make a fire to warm up because it was cold, just a few days earlier.)

See John 18, 18. 'It was cold, and the servants and officials stood around a fire they had made to keep warm. Peter also was standing there with them, warming himself.'

(Besides, in those days, an honest and just man could hardly undress to make babies. So, to say that Peter was naked in front of his companions is no less than dementia. I strongly believe that this John liked the nakedness of men, since he has already undressed his Jesus, the one who loved him, at his last supper. And if he could undress his lover during a supper, why not undress the most considerate of all the apostles; the one who was holding the keys of the kingdom of heaven? Does someone still dare telling me that this is a holy story?

If someone is telling a lie, why not telling such a big one that no one dare not to believe it. Isn't it Hitler, another insane man, who said something like: 'The biggest a lie is, the easier it is to believe it.' Hitler learned from his master, from Paul and from this John. How could someone think the Jews could believe such stupidities? Why so many pagans believed these lies? Is it because they are written in the Holy Bible?

Then Peter, who didn't know how to swim, would have put his coat on to jump into the sea. It seems to me that the other way around would have been a bit more appropriate, don't you think? See Peter with Jesus in;)

Matthew 14, 28-31. 'Then Peter got down out of the boat, walked on the water and came toward Jesus. But when he saw the wind, he was afraid and, beginning to sink, cried out, "Lord save me!" Immediately Jesus reached out his hand and caught him. "You of little faith," he said, "why did you doubt?"'

(But Peter believed enough to get out of the boat and to walk on the water, and this in a huge storm; he who didn't know how to swim. He had to have some faith to do this. Not too many would dare doing this, even on calm waters, especially without knowing how to swim.)

John 21, 8. 'The other disciples followed in the boat, towing the net full of fish, for they were not far from shore, about a hundred yards.'

(300 feet. In John 21, 6, these seven men could not haul the net because there were too many fish.

In John 21, 8, they could haul it with one man less, since Peter was in the water. How could he make it to shore? The story doesn't tell. Maybe he hung himself to the net full of fish, making it heavier and harder to hull yet.)

John 21, 9-10. 'When <u>they landed</u>, they saw a fire of burning coals there with fish on it, and some bread.

(This) Jesus said to them, "Bring some of the fish you have just caught."'

(The men then were all on the ground.)

John 21, 11. 'Simon Peter climbed aboard and dragged the net ashore. (By himself.) It was full of large fish, 153, but even with so many the net was not thorn.

(Neither was Peter's back. But why Peter had to drag the net ashore, if the other six men have done it?)

153 large fish; this would be reasonable enough to say they were at least ten pounds each, since seven men couldn't haul the net. But Peter dragged it by himself; this is kind of strange, isn't it? If these are the kind of great signs and miracles performed by Paul and his disciples; frankly, they are pitiful. See again;)

Matthew 24, 24. 'For false Christs and false prophets will appear and perform great signs and miracles to deceive even the elect—if that were possible.'

The true Jesus also said that we will recognize the tree by its fruits. Just make sure not to forget that.)

John 21, 12. '(This) Jesus said to them, "Come and have breakfast." None of the disciples dared ask him, "Who are you? They knew it was the Lord.'

(It seems to, that there was some kind of a doubt in this last verse.)

John 21, 13-14. 'Jesus <u>came</u>, took the bread and gave it to them,'

(But he was already there by the fire before them.)

'And did the same with the fish. This was now the third time, Jesus approached to his disciples after he was raised from the dead.'

(But according to this story; it is just the other way around that happened; it was the disciples who approached him. And for the very first time of the story of Jesus, and according to this lying author; Jesus ate and gave food to his disciples without praying or giving thanks for this blessing. To me this is another proof that this Jesus in the gospel of John is a false Christ and that he and this John are impostors and liars of the worse kind, because they lied about the word of God.

And when they were at it, why not put a bit more rubbishes and exaggeration to finish with.)

See John 21, 25. Jesus did many other things as well. If every one of them were written down, I suppose that even the whole world would not have room for the books that would be written.'

(And of course, everyone knows that there are a lot more weeds than vegetables in a garden, and they grow faster and higher. Like Jesus said it; the Bible is like a garden; it contains more lies than truth.

When it comes to this false Christ and this impostor, this John, author of this gospel; they have made a lot of harm, because way too many people believed and still believe in their lies.

When the true Jesus spoke about the abomination that causes desolation in the holy place; I think he already knew to what extent the desolation will be and how painful it will be for us. And when he told us to stand firm to the end; he knew this won't be easy for his disciples, but he knew too that this was necessary.

Never in my whole life I have heard anyone talked about the things I am talking about in this book of mine concerning the holy place.

I know that Louis Riel had discovered a lot of these things too, because I could read between the lines of his story. But the truth about his story was so manipulated and hidden that it is hard to figure out how much he knew. I know for example that he changed the day of the Lord from Sunday to Saturday. This is something that has upset the Catholic Church a lot, especially coming from a man that has studied to become one of their priests. I know too that he locked up a priest and some nuns, who betrayed him. I know that he repeated the Lord's Prayer instead of the Ave Maria; before being delivered from evil on the scaffold.

I also know that he is with the great God's men, like Abraham, because he stood firm up to the end, to the end of the rope and up to his death; like Jesus did it, and this to defend the truth. To him too, death was better than lies, and I hope that God will give me as much courage and as much strength at the time of physical death threats.

I counted 122 times where the word, 'father,' is written in the gospel of John, and this without his false Christ mentioning even once that he is the Father, who is in heaven. The true Messiah has done it many times in Matthew. It is not because someone puts a capital F to father that this means he is the Father in heaven. I even think that if this false Christ has never said where his father is; this is because he didn't want people to know where he is. It is kind of embarrassing to pretend to be the Christ and at the same time saying that his father is Satan or Paul. This is certainly not something that would have helped him build the biggest religious empire in the world, which are Christianity and all of those lying religions. I also think that his father is the one who said about himself being the father of many and this without touching a woman.)

See 1 Corinthians 4, 14-15. 'I (Paul) am not writing this to shame you, but to warn you, as <u>my dear children</u>. Even though you have ten thousand guardians in <u>Christ</u>, you do not have many fathers, for in Christ Jesus <u>I became your father</u> through the gospel.'

(And this is why so many Christians call their priests and pastors, 'fathers.' But as the true Messiah said to his disciples; they have One Father and he is in heaven. This is not Paul and it is not Satan either.

But this declaration from Paul is only a bad imitation about what God said in;)

Psalms 2, 7. 'I will proclaim the decree of the Lord: He said to me, "You are my Son; today I have become your Father."'

(According to this; God became the Father of is Son long after he was born.

The Jesus who is in Matthew mentioned 15 times: 'The Father who is in heaven, six times, 'the Lord of heaven,' and seven times, 'the heavenly Father.' All of the other times, we knew about whom he was talking about.

According to what I have counted, the word, 'Father,' pointing to God by the Messiah is written 43 times in the Holy gospel of Matthew.

CHAPTER 3

All of the rubbishes have continued from the gospel of John through the Acts of the Apostles. Oups! I should rather say; in the Acts of Paul at more than 95%.

Acts 1, 3. 'After his sufferings, he showed himself to these men and gave many convincing proofs that he was alive. He appeared to them over a period of forty days and spoke about the kingdom of God.'

(So, according to this one; according to Luke; Jesus would have spoken basically only about the kingdom of God before and after his death, and not at all about the kingdom of heaven. We could almost believe that he was not the same man who was resurrected. Especially after reading from the writing and the lies of his enemies that almost no one could recognize him.

What Jesus was preaching mainly all along his ministry, was the kingdom of heaven, about his kingdom, and he hardly talked about the kingdom of God, like all of the others have done, beside Matthew, of course. Luke didn't speak about the kingdom of heaven either. You will see all along his writing that Luke spoke and preached about Paul, and not much about Jesus.

Jesus' kingdom was and is near and his accessible to everyone who follows him. His teaching shows us how to enter the two kingdoms, the kingdom of heaven and the kingdom of God. The Messiah has also warned us about the ferocious wolves that attract people in the kingdom of the devil.)

Acts 1, 4-5. 'On one occasion, while he was eating with them, he gave them this command: "Do not leave Jerusalem, but wait for the gift my Father promised, which you have heard me speak about. For John baptized with water, but in a few days you will be baptized with the Holy Spirit.'

(This is absolutely false, and again the same catchy tune, preached by Paul and his disciples; because the true Jesus baptized all of his disciples with the Holy Spirit from the very beginning of his ministry, and this with each and every word from God he spoke to them, and not only after his resurrection. The Acts here are only the continuation of the lies that we have seen in the Gospel of this John, who made the false Christ speak about the lies and the contradictions.

Here this false Christ told his disciples not to leave Jerusalem, but in Matthew the true Messiah told his apostles to go wait for him in Galilee; which is a long walk away from Jerusalem. In Acts 1, 4, the apostles are told not to leave Jerusalem and in Acts 1, 12, they returned to Jerusalem they have never left.

And not only that, but before his death, the true Messiah told his apostles to go wait for him in Galilee, on the mountain he pointed out to them and not in Jerusalem, and this for a very good reason too. Jesus had already told them that Jerusalem was killing, stoning those who were sent to it.)

See Matthew 23, 37. 'O Jerusalem, Jerusalem, you who kill the prophets and stone those sent to you.')

(The Jews were stoning, the Romans were crucifying."

See Matthew 3, 11. 'He will baptize you with the Holy Spirit and with fire.'

(And believe it; this was done in all the days the Messiah spent with his disciples. And it is from that declaration from John the Baptist that Jesus' enemies added the tongues of fire. In fact, it is the Holy Spirit, who told Peter that Jesus was the Christ. See Matthew 16, 16. And this happened long, long before the Messiah was ready to go to the Father who is heaven.

Peter didn't see those tongues of fire, and none of the other apostles have seen them either. Did Matthew talk about them? The answer is no. This although would have been something to talk about, something special, I mean something unforgettable, if this was true.

And it is from the mentioning of the baptism of John the Baptist that the tongues of fire were invented by

Jesus' enemies. I know for myself that God speaks to me and that His Spirit is lighting me, but I have never seen any tongues of fire yet. I happened to see some fireflies in some summer days, but no tongues, of fire, I mean to say. It is just another witchcraft story invented by the wicked to make people believe the lies, and the Jesus' apostles had nothing to do with this.)

See again Acts 2, 3. 'They saw what <u>seemed</u> to be tongues of fire that separated and came to rest on each of them.'

(And all of this happened without burning anyone or anyone's ass. But I hope that you too are seeing him coming, this false Christ, who has prepared the coming of Paul in the picture. The one this false Christ sent in the sheep pen to seduce, and we know now what he has done this ferocious wolf.

See also that this devil was using a bit of truth to seduce, just like the serpent did it in the Garden of Eden. Without this bit of truth; he would be believed by no one. The words used to seduce are: 'The kingdom of God,' and, 'The Spirit of truth.'

Here in Acts 1, 18, not only Luke lied, but he put a lie in the mouth of Peter. Don't believe Luke, because Peter, the one who held the keys of the kingdom of heaven has been faithful and truthful to the end.

Some people will ask me how I can be so sure about that. Well, Jesus, the Messiah, told Peter that he will be sitting on a throne with him and all the other apostles to judge the twelve tribes of Israel. This is enough for me to trust Peter instead of the liars.

Acts 1, 18. 'With the reward he got for his wickedness, Judas bought a field;'

(This is completely false again, since that field was bought by the scribes, the Pharisees and the chief priest with the treason's money. Judas didn't buy anything; he went to kill himself after the treason.)

See Matthew 27, 6-7. 'The chief priest picked up the coins and said, 'It is against the Law to put this into the treasury, since it is blood money. So <u>they</u> decided to use the money to buy the potter's field as a burial place for foreigners.'

(And the lies over lies continue in Acts 1, 18.)

'There he (Judas) fell headlong, his body burst open and all his intestines spilled out.'

(This is another lie, some more manure for the weeds, for the lies, because Judas didn't die from an accident where he fell down and spilled out his intestines, but he went to hang himself. This is even why Jesus, the Messiah, said this about him; "It would be better for him if he had not been born."

I just wonder how the scholars could tolerate so many lies and contradictions in the Holy Bible, and I have a hard time believing they didn't see them; they who are the most educated about the Scriptures.)

Acts 1, 19. 'Everyone in Jerusalem heard about this, so they called that field in their language, Akeldama that is, Field of Blood.'

(I think that if that story told by Luke was true; the name of that field should have been different and have been called, 'The field of shit from the traitor's intestines.' To see the truth go read;)

Matthew 27, 5. 'So Judas threw the money into the temple and left. Then he went away and hanged himself.'

See again Acts 2, 3. 'They saw what <u>seemed</u> to be tongues of fire that separated and came to rest on each of them.'

(This would have been such an event that absolutely no one could have forgotten. And according to that story, all of the apostles were reunited in that place.)

See Acts 2, 1. 'When the day of the Pentecost came, they were all together in one place.'

(So Matthew had to be there too with them and if that story was true; Matthew too would have talked about a story of that importance. But Matthew didn't do it; which means to me that this has never happened. This is just another lie like many others from the same author.

God has put his Spirit on many as He did with Jesus and with all of his Prophets, and there were not there any tongues of fire. This was just another invented story and a lie to mislead people. Besides, Jesus had already baptized them all with the Holy Spirit, with the word of God. See again;)

See Matthew 3, 11. 'He will baptize you with the Holy Spirit and with fire.'

(And fire didn't necessarily mean tongues of fire. This baptism from the Messiah was and is in the word of God. This is the baptism that Jesus was giving to his apostles and disciples all of the days of his ministry. I won't be surprised to hear one of these days that, 'with fire,' was added to Matthew 3, 11 by the wicked, just to corroborate their wicked story, because, as far as I know; Jesus, the Messiah, who is nothing but love, didn't burn anyone and neither did the Holy Spirit.

Acts 2, 4. 'All of them (the Jesus' apostles) were filled with the Holy Spirit and began to speak in other tongues, as the Spirit enabled them.'

(That too would have been a very special and unforgettable event and that other than Luke would have talked about, but no one else did. This is another lie and another invented story. These are the kind of stupid stories that contribute to create atheists in the world, and that too is a deed of Satan. Anything and everything that pulls the human beings away from God is Satan's ultimate goal.

What is written in Acts 2, 17-21, and was put in the mouth of Peter is copied and pasted from whatever is written in Joel 2, 28-32. But these words are not for the time of Peter, but for the end of this actual world.

What is written in Acts 2, 25-28 is coming from the Psalms 16, 8-11, and this almost word for word. This demonstrates very well that Satan and his children too know the Holy Scriptures and the truth, but as always; they use the truth to mislead people. Besides, the words that were put in the mouth of Peter are not words from an unschooled person; which Peter was apparently; contrary to Paul and Luke, who were the most educated.

Here in Acts 2, 29-30, there are a mixture of truth and lies, apparently coming from Peter's mouth.)

Acts 2, 29-30. 'Brothers, I can tell you confidently that the patriarch David died and was buried, and his tomb is here to this day. But he was a prophet (this is false) and knew that God had promised him on oath that He will place one of his descendants on his throne.'

(Well yes, the King David was a king of the Jews, but he was not a prophet and he had to contact a prophet many of times. It is true though that it is one of David descendant, who will be placed on David's throne, but eternally. Here, by admitting that Jesus is one of David's direct descendants; he makes liars all of those who say that Jesus is God's only Son. By saying that Jesus is God's only Son; they say that all the other men are sons of the devil, and this, I don't take it, not at all.

Then David, far from being a prophet himself, was consulting the prophet Samuel and Nathan, the prophet. Nathan, the son of David, was a prophet, but not David, and this is one thing that Peter knew very well, because Peter was instructed by the Messiah. Don't you go believe that Peter said such a thing or that he lied!)

See 2 Samuel 12, 13. 'Then David said to Nathan, "I have sinned against the Lord." Nathan replied, "The Lord has taken away your sin. You are not going to die."'

(If I am not mistaking, the Acts of the Apostles were written by Luke, Paul's best loved friend. These Acts I would rather call the Acts of Paul, because they are about Paul for more than 90%, and maybe more than 95%. It is hard to tell, but they are mainly about Paul, that's for sure.

Acts 2, 31. 'Seeing what was ahead, He spoke of the resurrection of the <u>Christ</u>, that he was not abandoned to the grave, nor did his body see decay.'

(We saw it earlier and we'll see it again, that this was mainly Paul, who spoke about Jesus in an arrogant way, saying, 'for Christ, from Christ, by Christ,' and so on. But Peter didn't do this. When Peter talked about Jesus, the Messiah; he was saying, 'Our Lord Jesus Christ. This was respect for his name. When Peter pronounced the word, 'Christ,' he was not talking about the Messiah, but to him and this was Jesus who was asking his apostles, who they thought he was, something we can read in;)

Matthew 16, 16-17. 'Simon Peter answered, "You are the Christ, the Son of the living God." Jesus replied,

"Blessed are you, Simon son of Jonah, for this was not revealed to you by man, but by my Father in heaven."'

(Can you see that the Spirit of God has spoken to Peter as well, and this long before Jesus died.

(The same thing happened again, plus a huge lie in;)

Acts 2, 36. 'Therefore let all of Israel be assured of this: God has made this Jesus, whom you (Jews) crucified, both Lord and <u>Christ</u>.'

(This is false and a huge lie again, because the Lord Jesus was killed, crucified by the Romans, and if Peter would have accused the chief priests and spoke to them this way and at any time; they would have him crucified too. These were lies put in the mouth of Peter and Peter has nothing to do with this. Believe it!

What wouldn't Luke and Paul have done to put down the Jews and to elevate the Romans? All of this, of course, with the only goal that was to create their religion, as we know it today as being roman and this huge empire known as, Christianity.' And as you too most likely know now; it is all based on lies.

Peter was gutsy maybe, but he was not suicidal. But don't be fooled; Peter didn't make any false accusation of this sort and he didn't lie this way either. This was just a lying way to demonstrate, or at least try to demonstrate that Peter was not that good after all. This was just disparagement from Luke and Paul against the Jesus' apostles, especially against Peter, because he was the most considerate of all of them. Do you see? Peter was the one to whom the Messiah gave the keys of the kingdom of heaven.

This was dementia and jealousy from Jesus' enemies. What is better for the devil than to make people believe that the one Jesus chose to bind and to loose on earth is a liar. This is the abomination of the desolation again that Jesus, the Messiah, spoke about in Matthew 24, 15.)

See also Matthew 18, 18. 'I tell you the truth, whatever you bind on earth will be bound in heaven, and whatever you loose on earth will be loosed in heaven.'

(Jesus' enemies don't like that; so they did and do all they possibly can to tarnish the reputation of those that Jesus has chosen to continue his ministry. And this was starting with Peter, the most considerate of them all, and this according to Paul.

Acts 2, 37. 'When the people heard this, they were cut to the heart and said to Peter and to the other disciples, "Brothers, what shall we do?"'

(Sure, they were cut to the heart for being accused by this number one apostle and wrongly of killing the Messiah. Come on!

Acts 2, 38. 'Peter replied, "Repent and be baptized, every one of you, in the name of Jesus Christ for the forgiveness of your sins. And you will receive the gift of the Holy Spirit.'

(Peter, who was with Jesus from the very beginning of Jesus' ministry, since he was the first apostle to be chosen by the Messiah, knew perfectly all of the Master's messages and he knew that the forgiveness of sins came with the repentance and not from baptism.

Jesus didn't say: 'Repent and be baptized,' but he said: 'Repent for the kingdom of heaven is near.'

Besides, Jesus' baptism is the baptism of the Holy Spirit, and not the baptism of water, as John the Baptist was doing and he is the one who said it. John the Baptist was not a liar either. He lived and died for the truth. Peter and the other apostles were following faithfully whatever the Messiah has prescribed, and they didn't baptize with water either, not more than Jesus did it.)

Acts 2, 46. 'Every day they (the Jesus' apostles) continued to meet together in the temple courts.'

(What a lie and falseness this is again. And this is on top of being another manipulation of the Scriptures again! In the French Bible and in the King James Bible; they were not in the temple courts, but they were in the temple.

The temple was the house of the scribes, of the Pharisees and of the chief priests and almost all of them were almost always a threat to the Jesus' disciples, and this before and after the death of the Messiah. They didn't quit the desire to destroy that sect because the Master was killed.)

Acts 2, 47. 'Praising God,'

(This is most likely true, but for the rest; it is very questionable, especially in the temple.?????????)

'And enjoying the favour of all the people.'

(This is false again. One party of the people, who wanted to eliminate Jesus and his disciples, didn't stop to do this after the death of the Messiah, because his disciples continued to hide and to assemble behind locked doors.)

See John 20, 19. 'On the evening of that first day of the week, when the disciples were together, with the doors locked for fear of the Jews.'

(No matter what the truth is, the version of John is contradicting the version of Luke here, but I really believe that both of them are liars. All of these are lies put in the mouth of Peter. They would have told themselves; 'If God can put the truth in a mouth of one man; we can put lies in the mouth of men too.'

Here in Acts 3, 13-14, the person who is speaking is blaming the Jews for the death of the Messiah and is basically praising the Roman, the governor Pilate, for not wanting Jesus to die.)

Acts 3, 13-14. 'The God of Abraham, Isaac and Jacob, the God of our fathers, has glorified his servant Jesus. You handed him over to be killed, and you disowned him before Pilate, though he decided not to let him go. You disowned the Holy and Righteous One and asked that a murderer be released to you.'

(Neither Peter or John would have dared speaking to the chief priests and risking their life unnecessarily this way. If they did it; they would have been killed in no time at all. It took a lot less than this for them to stone someone like Stephen. And the message they have received from the Messiah was to enter a deserving house, not to enter the temple, there where their lives would have been constantly in danger.

The Jesus' apostles didn't become crazy after the Messiah' death, on the contrary; they become more aware of the danger of losing their lives. And being killed would have not helped our cause at all, because the true would have died with them. Without Matthew being able to write; we would have just about nothing true about the Messiah.

See Matthew 10, 11-13. 'Whatever town or village you enter, search for some worthy person and stay at his house until you leave.'

(Be sure of one thing, Peter and all of the other apostles had respect and obedience and they have listened to the Master.

So, don't you go believe the lie that they were spending all of their time or any time at all in the temple, because this is not true! But I repeat it because it is very important; it is not Peter or the true John, apostle of Jesus who lied, but rather the liar, this Luke who wrote the Acts of the supposedly apostles.

This author mentioned, 'Christ,' here again in;)

Acts 3, 18. 'But this is how God fulfilled what He had foretold through all the prophets, saying that his Christ would suffer.'

(I am absolutely sure that Peter has never spoken that way about the Messiah. In fact, Peter has absolutely nothing to do with what is written in the Acts. We have seen earlier that Luke has spent all of his time with Paul; which was far away from Peter.

I went to check it out and the word, 'Christ,' is not mentioned at all in the Old Testament of the Bible. The first time we can see it written in the Bible is at the beginning of the gospel Matthew.

In Acts 3, 22-23, there are some truth and some lies, as usual, just enough truth to make people believe in it.)

Acts 3, 22-23. 'For Moses said, "The Lord your God will raise up for you a prophet like me from among your own people; you must listen to everything he tells you. Anyone who does not listen to him will be completely cut off from among his people.'

(Let see now the true story in Deuteronomy 18, 17-19. Here it is not Moses speaking, but God, the Almighty speaking to Moses. Which is not quite the same, isn't it?)

Deuteronomy 18, 17-19. 'The Lord said to me: (Moses) What they say is good. I will raise up for them a prophet like you (Moses, a man pure and simple) from among their brothers; (the Jews) I will put my words in his mouth and he will tell them everything I command him. If anyone does not listen to My words that the prophet speaks in My Name, I Myself (God) will call him to account.'

(To call someone to account doesn't necessarily mean being cut off from his people for one thing. And I think that all the people will be called to account and this for better or worse. Anyway, the one who wrote the Acts has deformed the truth; just like Satan knows how to do it so well and as he did it many times.

There is more deformation here in;)

Acts 3, 25. 'And you are heirs of the prophets and of the covenant God made with your fathers.'

(This is the same lie Paul told his disciples.)

'He said to Abraham, "Through your offspring all peoples on earth will be blessed.'

(See the true story from the Almighty in Genesis 26, 4-5, but the ones who are against the Law of God didn't want to tell the whole story, the whole truth. Believe it; this was not Peter.)

See Genesis 26, 4-5. 'I will make your descendants as numerous as the stars in the sky and I will give them all these lands, and through your offspring all nations on earth will be blessed, because Abraham obeyed Me and kept my requirements, my commands, my decrees and my Laws.'

(Contrary to Luke, Peter was righteous and faithful and he would have told the whole truth about that story, as I just did.

There is a change of tone in what is following. It is not the so-called Peter who is speaking anymore, but someone else who talked about him.)

Acts 4, 1-3. 'The priests and the captain of the temple guard and the Sadducees came up to Peter and John while they were speaking to the people. They were greatly disturbed because the apostles were teaching the people and proclaiming in Jesus the resurrection of the dead. They seized Peter and John, and because it was evening, they put them in jail until the next day.'

(What was I saying earlier? See again;)

Acts 2, 47. 'Praising God,'

(This is most likely true, but for the rest, it is very questionable, especially in the temple, and enjoying the favour of all the people.'

(In any case; all the people must not include the chief priests, the captain of the temple guard and the Sadducees. We also know that the Pharisees and the scribes did everything in their power to stop Jesus' movement.

Then see the same lie that was put in the mouth of Peter again by one or more of his enemies.)

Acts 4, 5-10. 'The next day the rulers, elders and teachers of the Law met in Jerusalem. Annas the high priest was there and so were Caiaphas, John, Alexander and the other men of the high priest's family. They had Peter and John brought before them and began to question them: By what power or what name did you do this?" Then Peter filled with the Holy Spirit said to them: "Rulers and elders of the people! If we are being called to account today for an act of kindness shown to a cripple and are asked how he was healed, then know this, you and all the people of Israel: It is in the name of Jesus Christ of Nazareth, whom you crucified but whom God raised from the dead, that this man stands before you healed.'

(The author of these writings has put again here the lie in the mouth of Peter and all of this by making him accusing wrongly the Jews of killing Jesus, the Messiah, while they were not the ones who have actually killed him, but this was done by the Gentiles, by the Romans. Luke's goal as always, of course, was to exculpate the Romans and to blame the Jews, just like Paul has done it. This is a devilish machination and is the exact same lie Paul told in;)

1 Thessalonians 2, 14-15. 'You suffered from your own countrymen (the Jews) the same things those (Paul's) churches suffered from the Jews, who killed the Lord Jesus and the prophets and also drove us out. They displease God and are hostile to all men.'

(I don't mean to say that the Jews are completely innocent of the assassination of the Messiah, because they are the ones who have accused and delivered him to the Gentiles, but they didn't kill him themselves. The Jews weren't executing anyone by crucifixion; the Romans did it and this after mocking him, insulting him and flogging him. But the author of the Acts is insisting to make all the blames for the death of the Messiah carried by the Jews. He is evidently a Roman.

Not to mention that if Peter would have truly accused the chiefs priests wrongly and to their faces; he and John would have been stoned on the spot. The two of them have survived, so this means that this has never happened. This is nothing but a very big lie again.

Some people will tell me that Peter and John were under the protection of the Holy Spirit. And I will tell them that Jesus, the Messiah was too, but this didn't stop the wicked to hill him.)

Acts 4, 13. 'When they saw the courage of Peter and John and realized that they were unschooled ordinary men, they were astonished and they took note that these men had been with Jesus.'

(This is what I was saying earlier, that Peter and John had no education at all. This means then that this was not the John, Jesus' apostle, who wrote the gospel of John or the Revelation, and Peter didn't write either. I also think that neither one of the two had a single day in class. The education they both have received was coming from Jesus, from the Messiah. They have received the word of God and the Holy Spirit. They have received life, the most important of all the instructions and of all the blessings.)

Acts 4, 34-35. 'There were no needy persons among them. For from time to time those who owned lands and houses, sold them, brought the money from the sales and put it at the apostles' feet, and it was distributed to anyone as he has need.'

(So, the one who just sold is house and gave the money from it to the poor was in need of a house again too. All of this is rubbish and is only one part of the process they used to create this huge empire of the religions they built up and the Jesus' apostles had nothing to do with this. All of this was Paul's policy, as we can read again in;)

2 Corinthians 8, 13-14. 'Our desire is not that others might be relieved while you are hard pressed, but there might be equality. At the present time your plenty will supply what they need. Then there will be equality.'

(Except that a huge percentage of that money, their plenty, was for his diabolic empire that Paul and company built up.

The Messiah has never taught or told his apostles to do such a thing. The Messiah rather told them this here and I am absolutely sure that they have listened to him.)

See Matthew 10, 8. 'Freely you have received, freely give.'

(And this was not to give freely all of their goods, but to give freely the word of God.

On the other hand, all of the religions have not given freely their teaching and this on a very big scale.

There are many million dollars churches all over the world and in just about every town and village; all built with the money collected from the innocent blinds. They were blinded and brain-washed without knowing what happened to them. Do these so-called religions, apparently created by Jesus, sell their proprieties to give the money to the poor?

If the next story in these Acts was true; not only Ananias and his wife would have fell dead, but all of those who have cheated also, because God is just and so is his Messiah and his apostles.

Acts 5, 1-11. 'Now a man named Ananias, together with his wife Sapphira, also sold a piece of property. With his wife's full knowledge he kept back part of the money for himself, but brought the rest and put it at the apostles' feet. Then Peter said, "Ananias, how it is that Satan has so filled your heart that you have lied to the Holy Spirit and have kept for yourself some of the money you received for the land? Didn't it belong to you before it was sold? And after it was sold, wasn't it the money at your disposal? What made you think of doing such a thing? You have not lied to men but to God. When Ananias heard this, he fell down and died. And great fear seized all who heard what had happened. And the young men came forward, wrapped his body, and carried him out and buried him. About three hours later his wife came in, not knowing what had happened. Peter asked her, "Tell me, is this the price you and Ananias got for the land?" "Yes," she said, "this is the price." Peter said to her, "How could you agree to test the Spirit of the Lord? Look! The feet of the men who buried your husband are at the door, and they will carry you out also. At that moment she fell down at his feet and died. Then the young men came in and, finding her dead, carried her out and buried her beside her husband. Great fear seized the whole church and all who heard about these events.

(This was the real reason for all that exercise and for this pile of lies. This was to create fear among people and for the people to give to these crooks their money and their goods without lying and cheating. But these crooks were taking care of the money from the poor innocent people, just like the churches have done it for centuries. It is written that it will fall the great Babylon and I hope I have something to do with that.

But what rubbish and what an abomination this was! If all the people who lied and cheated about their money would fall dead; there would not be enough people on earth the make a world. And this was not Peter either, who participated to such an abomination, to this swindle or any of the Jesus' apostles. Such a plot to scare people was wicked and none of the Messiah's people would have done that. I won't be surprised at all to hear one day that this happened, that such a plot happened to scare people off was a reality, but neither Peter nor any of the other Jesus' apostles were part of it. The ones who did this are the same ones who managed to create the beast, the huge empire of Christian religions and this is completely diabolic. No one led by the Holy Spirit would do such a thing. I think that such abominable scam was invented by Paul and Luke with two precise goals. One was to force people to give them their money without cheating and the other was to tarnish Peter's reputation. And what was better than to involve Peter in this scam to succeed such a plot?

To see and to understand who has invented such abomination, go read what Paul has written about your goods in;)

Galatians 6, 6. 'Anyone who receives instruction in the word must share all good things with his instructor.'

(None of the Jesus' disciples will ask you or anyone to sell whatever for whomever, and the Jesus' apostles didn't do this either. It is Paul and company, who built this great empire of wicked religions who did this, and the end of their scams is also at the door.)

Acts 5, 17-20. 'Then the high priest and all his associates, who were members of the party of Sadducees, were filled with jealousy. They arrested the apostles and put them in the public jail. But during the night an angel of the Lord opened the doors of the jail and brought them out. Go, stand in the temple courts,"'

(Here too, in the French Bible and in the King James Bible, it is not in the temple courts, but in the temple. This is just a bit more manipulation. Not only have they put lies in the mouth of Peter, in the mouth of the Messiah, but also in the mouth of an angel of the Lord. What can be more diabolic than this?)

'He said, "and tell the people the full message of the new life."'

(I can believe that an angel of the Lord has the power to open jail doors and to free the Jesus' apostles, but I cannot believe that he would tell them to go throw themselves in the mouth of the wolves; mainly because of the instructions they have received from the Messiah. An angle of the Lord wouldn't have told the Jesus' apostles to do the opposite of what Jesus taught them.

Only an arrogant like Satan and like Paul did and would dare go in someone else church (temple, synagogues) to teach his own teaching. No one would do that nowadays anymore than it was done back then; unless, like I said, he is as arrogant as Satan is and has an army to help him to do so. Jesus tried this and the scribes wanted and tried to throw him down a cliff, but this is according to Luke, a liar. See again Luke 4, 28-29.

The same lie put in the mouth of Peter is repeated here in;)

Acts 5, 30. 'The God of our fathers raised Jesus from the dead—whom <u>you</u> (the Jews) had killed by hanging him on the tree.'

(This same lie is to put the shame of the killing of the Messiah on the shoulders of the Jews instead of on the Romans. I can see that this has worked out for them, considering the number of people who joined the Roman Catholic Church. We have to understand that the majority of their members became so with their eyes closed, because they were baptized before having their eyes opened. They are converts acquired cheaply, who have became members of the beast without their consent, and this too is worthy of Satan.)

Acts 5, 40. 'His speech persuaded them. They called the apostles in and had them flogged. Then they ordered them not to speak in the name of Jesus, and let them go.'

Let's go see in Matthew 10, 17-18, what Jesus told his apostles.)

Matthew 10, 17-18. 'Be on your guard against men; they will hand you over to the legal councils and flog you in their synagogues. On my account you will be brought before governors and kings as witnesses to them and to the Gentiles.'

(I don't go in a temple or in synagogues or in churches, mainly because I hate lies, especially the ones about the word of God. But I have the impression that I will be questioned soon about my declarations and about my work. We cannot be working for the will of God without being persecuted by the world and by the children of the devil.)

Acts 7, 56. '"Look," Stephen said, "I see heaven open and the Son of Man standing at the right hand of God."'

(It is here, I think, that Paul had the brilliant and malicious idea to make his entry in the sheep pen. This was just after Paul heard the words of Stephen, and this just before he died. Paul would have told himself: 'I want to discourage these peoples from their faith in Jesus, their faith in this Messiah and instead of this, we send them directly to God, and this is not our goal at all, on the contrary.'

Here in Acts 7, 58, they have tried to smooth out the implication of the participation of Paul in the murder of Stephen.)

Acts 7, 58. 'They dragged him out of the city and began to stone him. Meanwhile, the witnesses laid the clothes at the feet of a young man named Saul.'

(This means Paul. Don't be fooled though, because Paul was pursuing the Jesus' disciples as far as the foreign cities and he was throwing them in jail. Then he was forcing them to blaspheme, and if this is true; he was doing this with death threats. I am also sure that he was putting them to death after listening to their testimonies, with the goal of using them to mislead people during his so-called ministry.

Some people will ask me how I could be sure he was killing the Jesus' disciples. This is because I know he is a murderer and a liar from the beginning.)

Acts 8, 1. 'And Saul (Paul) was there, giving approval to his (Stephen's) death.'

(Here again, they tried to reduce the importance of the implication of Paul with that murder.)

'On that day a great persecution broke out against the Church of Jerusalem, (they didn't say how many were killed) and all except the apostles were scattered throughout Judea and Samaria.'

(This was the only Church that Jesus founded. And guess who the leader of this persecution was? I doubt though that Jesus' disciples went to Samaria, because Jesus, the Messiah, told them not to enter the towns of Samaria.)

See Matthew 10, 5-6. 'Do not go among the Gentiles or enter any town of the Samaritans. Go rather to the lost sheep of Israel.'

(This most likely meant there was no Jew in Samaria. So, Jesus told them to go to the Jews and according to another message, the salvation is coming from them and so is the truth.

See John 4, 22. 'You Samaritans worship what you don't know; we worship what we do know, for salvation is from the Jews.'

(This is a declaration; I am sure, that made many sons of the devil, like Hitler, jealous.

See, on the other hand, what the prophet Jonah has declared a lot earlier.

Jonas 2, 9. 'What I have vowed I will make good. Salvation comes from the Lord.'

(In the French Bible, instead of the Lord here, it is, 'the Almighty.'

On the other hand, the Jew people, the people of Israel is God's first born.

Then, it was them, the scattered Jesus' disciples, who had the knowledge of the word of God, with the knowledge of the truth, who gave Paul a lot of headaches all along his way, because they arrived in the synagogues before him. And of course, what Paul had to tell them was quite the opposite of the words of these disciples. Paul, for example, was telling the Jews that the Law of God was about to disappear and that the baby males didn't have to be circumcised anymore. The Jews didn't believe this liar; they didn't believe Paul, but millions of pagans did and I hope they will recognize themselves by reading these lines.)

See Acts 21, 21. 'They have been informed that you (Paul) teach all the Jews who live among the Gentiles to turn away from Moses,'

(This was away from the Law of God, away from God's commandments and away from the circumcision.)

'Telling them not to circumcise their children,'

(Which is an everlasting covenant between God and all of the Jews.)

'Or live according to our customs.'

(Paul didn't think he had done enough against that Church, so he continued the war against the only Church the Messiah has founded and against the Jews.)

See Acts 8, 3-4. 'But Saul (Paul) began to destroy the Church. (Jesus' disciples) Going from house to house, he dragged off men and women and put them in prison. Those who had been scattered preached the word wherever they went.'

(But as we can see in Acts 21, 21, Paul has continued to do this long after his so-called conversion to the so-called Jesus. But to be able to do all of this; Paul needed his little army, and I am persuaded also that those were the Jesus' disciples that Paul was pursuing as far as the foreign cities, trying to eliminate them. Of course, Paul's army is never mentioned in the New Testament of the Bible. And why not? This is because Paul was a Roman.

The Jesus' apostles with the idea of James, Jesus' brother, managed to stop Paul from harassing the Jesus' disciples just about everywhere in the world. And it seems to be from that time only that Paul turned to the Gentiles. It was from Rome that Paul was pulling all the strings of his empire. This was from Rome that Paul was giving all his orders to his many churches. This is what we can see in all of his letters.)

See Acts 26, 11. 'Many a time I went from one synagogue to another to have them punished, and <u>I tried</u> to force them to blaspheme. In my obsession against them, I even went to foreign cities to persecute them.'

(And this demon has always had a clear conscience and fell guilty of nothing. He couldn't have been breaking the Law, because as he was saying; the Law has disappeared with the death of the Messiah on the cross. See to start with;)

Ephesians 2, 15. 'By abolishing in his flesh the Law with its commandments and regulations. His purpose was to create in himself one new man out of the two, thus making peace.'

(And this is where among other places, that Paul said that Jesus has abolished the Law of God; Jesus who said that not even the least stroke of a pen will disappear from the Law.)

See also 1 Corinthians 4, 3. 'I care very little if I am judged by you or by any human court; indeed, I (Paul) do not even judge myself. My conscience is clear.'

(I don't exactly know how many lies and contradictions are there in Paul's writings, but it seems to me being as numerous as the grains of sand from the sea. It's been more than twenty years now that I have been looking for them and I still find some.

In Acts 8, 5, there is again the way of Paul of speaking about Jesus, the Messiah.)

Acts 8, 5. 'Phillip went down to a city in Samaria and proclaimed the Christ there.'

(There are two contradictory things to retain here. A Jesus' disciple wouldn't have talked about Jesus this way, for one thing, and if this Phillip was one of the twelve apostles; he wouldn't have been in Samaria at all either. The ones who were and are following Jesus are obeying him. So this was written by Jesus' enemies only to make Jesus' apostle looked disobedient.)

Acts 8, 9-12. 'For some time a man named Simon had practiced sorcery in the city and amazed all the people of Samaria. He boasted that he was someone great,'

(This sounds a lot like Paul for sure.)

'And all the people, both high and low, gave him their attention and exclaimed, "This man is the divine power known as the Great Power."'

(Remember I was saying in my previous book that with black magic; an agile man could make people believe in miracles. Here we are.)

'They followed him because he had amazed them for a long time with his magic. But they believed Philip as he preached the good news of the <u>kingdom of God</u> and the name of Jesus Christ, they <u>were baptized</u>, both men and women.'

(In the entire gospel of Matthew about Jesus, our Master, the Messiah, Matthew has never mentioned that Jesus was baptizing with water and neither were his disciples or apostles. And I am sure of it too; all of the Jesus' disciples were preaching the kingdom of heaven, as Jesus was doing it, and not the kingdom of God as Jesus' enemies did it. So Philip, just like the other Jesus' apostles, was not there in Samaria, for one thing, and he was doing what the Master has commanded him to do.

See again Acts 8, 1. 'On that day a great persecution broke out against the Church of Jerusalem, and all except the apostles were scattered throughout Judea and Samaria.'

So, Peter, John, neither Philip nor any of the other apostles went to Samaria, simply because the Messiah, our Master asked them not to go there. This was actually the very first instruction the Messiah gave to his apostles, and don't you go think they have forgotten about that. See again;)

Matthew 10, 5. 'Do not go among the Gentiles or enter any town of the Samaritans.'

(This was clear enough, don't you think? And the lies continue.)

Acts 8, 14. 'When the apostles in Jerusalem heard that Samaria had accepted the word of God, they sent Peter and John to them.'

(The one or those who wrote these lies knew very well that Jesus told his apostles not to enter any town of the Samaritans and if they wrote these lies; it is just to tarnish the reputation of the Jesus' apostles. But don't you go believe these lies and these liars, because they are diabolic. And be sure of one thing; this is that the Jesus' apostles have obeyed him.

This was at the same time a vicious attack against the Jews, and this was done by the Romans like Paul. This was most likely done by Paul or by Luke, or by both of them.

If I could rename the Acts of the Apostles, as they are presented to us in the book of the New Testament; I would call them, 'The Acts of Dementia,' by the demons insatiable of lies.)

Acts 8, 18-20. 'When Simon saw that the Spirit was given at the laying of the apostles' hands, he offered them money and said, "Give me also the ability so that everyone on whom I lay my hands may received the Holy Spirit. Peter answered, "May your money perish with you, because you thought you could buy the gift of God with money!"'

(This was not Peter who handed people over to Satan. This was done by Paul. Peter has learned to call the sinners, like Jesus, our Master was doing it. But anyway, Peter was not at all in Samaria. And the goal of this Simon was not that bad after all; since he wanted for other people to receive the Holy Spirit too. I know about others who pretended to be Jesus' disciples and did a lot worse.)

Acts 8, 38. 'And he gave orders to stop the chariot. Then both Phillip and the eunuch went down into the water and Philip baptized him.'

(This is a kind of a proof that this Philip was not a Jesus' disciple. Firstly, this is because he was in

Samaria, there where Jesus told his apostles not to enter, and secondly because he baptized with water and not with the Holy Spirit; which means with the word of God.

But there is another explanation; this is that this whole story was completely invented by Jesus' enemies to make people believe that the Jesus' apostle weren't obeying him, and that too is diabolic.

I strongly believe that all of those who will read this book of mine and accept the truth will receive the baptism of the Holy Spirit, the baptism of truth, no matter how shocking it is for them.

Many of those churches, not to say all of them that baptize people nowadays with water are hiding the truth to their congregation, and I think that this too is diabolic. Read again;)

Romans 1, 18. 'The wrath of God is being revealed from heaven against all the godlessness and wickedness of men (women) who suppress the truth by wickedness.'

(And basically all of the churches are doing this. I wouldn't want to be in their shoes. As I said it earlier, in the entire holy gospel of Matthew; there is no question at all of Jesus or his disciples baptizing with water. Jesus, the Messiah, and all of his disciples were baptizing with the Holy Spirit, with the word of God.

And it is here in what is following that the ferocious wolf made is entry in the sheep pen.)

Acts 9, 1-6. 'Meanwhile, Saul (Paul) was still breathing out <u>murderous threats</u> against the Lord's disciples. He went to the high priest and asked him for letters to the synagogues in Damascus, so that if he found any there who belong to the Way, (Jesus' Church) whether men or women, he might take them as prisoners in Jerusalem. As he neared Damascus on his journey, suddenly a light from heaven flashed around him. He fell to the ground and heard a voice say to him, "Saul, Saul, why do you persecute me?" Who are you, Lord?"'

(As you too will be able to tell later on, Paul was an expert in contradictory phrases. Paul asked who he was and called him Lord at the same time. And we'll find out what kind of lord his lord is a bit later.)

'Saul asked. "I am Jesus, whom you are persecuting." He replied.'

(Now here in the New International Version Bible; there is a big part missing. It is also missing in the Bible placed by the Gideons. I will then take it from the King James Bible.)

'It is hard for thee to kick against the pricks. And he (Paul) trembling and astonished said, Lord what wilt thou have me to do? And the Lord said unto him.'

(Back now to the New International Version Bible.)

'"Now get up and go into the city, and you will be told what you must do."'

(The least we can say about this demon is that he was bold to make people believe that Jesus, the

Messiah, would have chosen a murderer and liar and sent him to go contradict his apostles and preach against the circumcision and against the Law of God. Paul was not sent by the Messiah, but he was sent by Satan.

Besides, Paul's introduction was not made by one of Jesus' apostles or by Jesus. Paul introduced himself and his introduction is full of lies. Paul has even said that he was blinded by Jesus, and we all know that Jesus was blinding no one, on the contrary. Jesus was opening the eyes of the blinds and this more than one way.

By reading carefully, as we were told by the Messiah in Matthew 24, 15, the so-called conversion of Paul to Jesus in the Acts 9, 7, and comparing it to the same story written in Acts 22, 9, there is a true controversy. In one version Paul's companions heard, but were seeing no one, and in the other version; it is the total opposite.

Remember the very important message from Jesus: 'A bad tree cannot produce good fruits.' A liar doesn't tell the truth.)

See Proverbs 5, 22. 'The evil deeds of a wicked man ensnare him; the cords of his sin hold him fast.'

CHAPTER 4

Romans seen by a Jesus' disciple

As for the rest of the Acts of Paul, concerning my evaluation and if you didn't see it yet; you will find it in my precious book: The Wolf in The Sheep Pen.

Although, I still continue to evaluate his diabolic deeds from Romans 1.

What is better than a heading, supposedly coming from Paul, but that is in reality from one of the Jesus' apostles, to make people swallow the rest of his venom? I mean his lies in the rest of his epistles.)

See Romans 1, 3. 'Regarding his Son, who as to his human nature was a descendant of David.'

(This is not what the Christian's churches founded by Paul are preaching, and when you'll see some truth in the so-called letters from Paul; don't think it is from Paul, because, as Jesus, the Messiah said it:) 'A bad tree cannot produce good fruits.'

(The Paul's Christian's churches are teaching that Jesus is born from God through the operation of the Holy

Spirit, and according to the John of Paul; the Holy Spirit was not yet in the world.)

See John 14, 26. 'But the Comforter, the Holy Spirit whom the Father will send in my name, will teach you all things and will remind you of everything I have said to you.'

See also John 15, 26. 'When the Comforter comes, whom I,'

(This supposedly Jesus who is in the gospel of John.)

'Will send to you from my Father, he will testify about me.'

(My dear friends, the one who is pointed out here is Paul; the one who knows all and sees all, even without being present.)

See also John 16, 13. 'But when he, the Spirit of truth, comes, he will guide you into all truth. He will not speak on his own; he will speak only what he hears, and he will tell you what is yet to come.'

See also John 7, 39. 'By this he meant the Spirit, whom those who believed in him were later to receive. Up to that time the Spirit had not been given, since Jesus had not yet been glorified.'

(The Spirit was not yet given, because he was not yet glorified, but the Spirit would be his father.????

The truth doesn't come from the mouth of a liar. To refresh your memory, I bring you to;)

2 Thessalonians 2, 1-5. 'Not to become to easily unsettled or alarmed by some prophesy, report or <u>letter supposed to have come from us</u> (the Jesus' apostles)

saying that the day of the Lord has already come. Don't let anyone deceive you in any way, for that day will not come until the rebellion occurs and the man of lawlessness is <u>revealed</u>, the man doomed to destruction.'

(We know him now, he is revealed.)

'He will oppose and he will exalt himself over everything that is called God or is worshipped, so that he sets himself in God's temple, proclaiming himself to be God. Don't you remember that when I was with you I (Jesus' apostle) used to tell you these things?'

(My dear friends, know that Paul is well set in the heart of more than three billions of Christian people, and this is what explains the fact that more and more people are ignoring the word of God, ignoring the truth, because these churches are preaching Paul and not the Messiah. They are not preaching Jesus and his kingdom of heaven. To Jesus the word of God was not for sell like Paul's churches have done it and are still doing it.

Paul's disciples were not his brothers, but they were his children, as we are going to see soon; even if he didn't want to touch women and he was teaching his disciples not to touch them either.

Paul could not say easily: 'Our Lord Jesus Christ,' while talking about the Messiah, but we can read in his writings the following terms; 'In Christ, by Christ, for Christ, of Christ,' and his name backward, 'Christ Jesus.' Paul was not able to be in adoration for God either.

And finally, we can see that some letters from the Jesus' apostles were stolen and used by Paul and company to make his disciples believe he was a true apostle and of course; many were caught and seduced by this liar; who is many times more of a traitor than Judas was. It is just the craft of Satan.

Here is another proof that Paul could not declare his love for God. See first what Jesus, the Messiah, said about the greatest God's commandment in the Law in;)

Matthew 22, 37-40. 'Jesus replied; 'Love the Lord your God with all your heart and with all your soul and with all your mind. This is the greatest commandment. And the second one is like it; love your neighbour as yourself. All the Law and the Prophets hang on these two commandments."

(See now what all the Law of God is for Paul, and also see a bad imitation of the first and greatest God's commandment in;)

Galatians 5, 14. '"The entire Law is summed up in a single command: "Love your neighbour as yourself."'

(This is false for one thing, and this is the whole Law of God for Paul. And there is no question for him to love God with all of his heart. And we all know that the homosexuals also love their neighbours as themselves, and even more than themselves. This won't open for them the doors of the kingdom of heaven.)

Romans 1, 4. 'And who through the Spirit of holiness was declared with power to be the Son of God by his resurrection from the dead: Jesus Christ our Lord.'

(In the French Bible on line as well as in my French Bible of Louis the Second, after, 'the resurrection from the dead,' there is a parenthesis, as if the writer wanted to separate the words of the Jesus' apostles from the words of Paul. This is what I do too to separate my words from the words of the Bible.

Jesus was not declared to be the Son of God and the King of the Jews only after his resurrection. In fact; Jesus was declared the Son of God and King of the Jews while he was still in the belly of his mother.

This was Paul, who was preaching grace and faith instead of the Law of God and the obedience to the God's commandments. The God's commandments that say we have to love God with all of our heart were not for Paul, they are not for Satan and they are not for his disciples either.)

Romans 1, 7. 'To all in Rome, who are loved by God and called to be saints.'

(To be called saint like Paul and Luke, no thanks. But if his enemies have called Jesus, the Messiah, Beelzebub, and said he has a demon, why not then say that Satan is a saint? Jesus said that only One is good and he wasn't even talking about himself. So then, who are all of those saints who are not saints and who were called saints by Rome? Aren't they all some saint demons?)

See Matthew 10, 25. 'If the head of the house has been called Beelzebub; how much more the members of his household!'

Romans 1, 9. 'God, whom I serve with my whole heart in preaching the gospel of his Son, is my witness how constantly I remember you.'

(The god of Paul is not the true God and the Jesus of Paul is not the true Messiah, and Paul is not a Jesus' disciples either, because the true Messiah said not to swear, and to swear is to take God as a witness. The Messiah said not to do this. The Messiah said even more about this; he said that to do it is coming from the evil one. See and this is very important, Matthew 5, 34-37, to see a confirmation of what I am talking about.)

Matthew 5, 34-37. 'But I (Jesus) tell you. Do not swear at all; either by heaven, for it is God's throne; or by the earth, for it is his footstool; or by Jerusalem, for it is the city of the Great King. And do not swear by your head, for you cannot make even one hair white or black. Simply let your 'Yes' be 'Yes,' and your 'No' be 'No;' anything beyond this comes from the evil one.'

The Jesus' disciples are obeying him, but Paul didn't do that, and just like about all the liars are doing it; they take God as witness in trying to make people believe in their lies. This is what Paul did in Romans 1, 9, and in many other occasions.)

Romans 1, 12. 'That is, that you and I may be mutually encouraged by each other's faith.'

(Well, we know now that Paul was teaching faith and grace to the detriment of the Law of God and we also know too now that the demons too believe and shudder. See to better understand;)

James 2, 19-20. 'You believe that there is one God. Good! Even the demons (like Paul) believe that—and shudder. You foolish man, (Paul) do you want evidence that faith without deeds is worthless?'

(It is though what Paul has preached. See him in;)

Romans 3, 28. 'For we (Paul and company) maintain that a man is justified by faith apart from observing the Law.'

See also James 2, 24. 'You see that a person is justified by what he does and not by faith alone.'

See also James 2, 26. 'As the body without the spirit is dead, so faith without deeds is dead.'

(So, your faith and the faith of your disciples without deeds, Paul and you, all of Paul's disciples, is dead and useless, just like James, Jesus' brother said it. And this is what Jesus, the Messiah, said too.)

See Matthew 11, 18-19. 'For John (the Baptist) came neither eating nor drinking, and they say, "He has a demon." The Son of Man (which means, God's Prophet) came eating and drinking, and they say, 'Here is a glutton and a drunkard, a friend of tax collectors and sinners, but wisdom is proved right by her <u>actions</u>.'

(There is another message about Jesus' deeds that is even more evident for him to be justified by his deeds.)

Matthew 16, 27. 'For the Son of Man is going to come in his Father's glory with his angels, and then he will reward each person according to what he has done.'

(This is not according to everyone's faith, no matter whom Jesus was talking about. Do you believe Jesus, the Master of truth, or Paul and his lies? And don't you think that Jesus didn't have faith. He has faith and the Law, in the deeds that justified him.

Paul is still promoting the faith here in;)

Romans 1, 16-17. 'I am not ashamed of the gospel, because it is the power of God for the salvation of <u>everyone who believes</u>; first for the Jew, then for the Gentile. For in the gospel a righteousness from God is revealed, a righteousness that is by faith from first to last, just as it is written, "The righteous will live by faith."'

(The more I read in Paul and company's writings, the more I understand that Paul was trying to justify himself and he was also trying to justify Satan and his demons, because they too believe in God and in the Messiah.

I rather believe in the Messiah, who said that men will live by the word of God. See Jesus in;)

Matthew 4, 4. 'Jesus answered, "It is written: 'Man does not live on bread alone, but on every word that comes from the mouth of God.'

(Faith in God and in the Messiah is only good if it leads people to observe the God's commandments. Paul, this demon, gave himself a lot of troubles to make his disciples swallow his lies. It is very clear to me that he had in mind the will of Satan and not at all the will of God. The will of God is that everyone obeys his Law, his commandments, just like Jesus said it.

See again Matthew 19, 16-17. 'Now a man came up to Jesus and asked, "Teacher, what good thing I must do to get eternal life?" "Why do you ask me about what is good?" Jesus replied. "There is only One who is good. If you want to enter life, obey the commandments."'

See also Deuteronomy 7, 1. 'Therefore, take care to follow the commandments, decrees and Laws I gave you today.'

(Jesus has preached God, his commandments, his Laws and his will, but Paul has preached the faith without deeds, which is useless. Paul is the worthless shepherd who kept his disciples in darkness as he is mentioned in;)

Zechariah 11, 17. '"Woe to the worthless shepherd, who deserts the flock! May the sword strike his arm and his right eye! May his arm be completely withered, his right eye totally blinded!"'

(And this is why Paul had this thorn in his flesh. He was missing his right eye and he had an arm completely withered. This is why that at the beginning and before some of his disciples knew him well; they were almost ready to pull out their own eyes to give them to him. This is why also that the viper couldn't hurt or kill him. See Galatians 4, 15 and Acts 28, 3-5.)

Galatians 4, 15. 'What has happened to all you joy? I can testify that, if you could have done so, you would have torn out your eyes and given them to me.'

Acts 28, 3-5. 'Paul gathered a pile of brushwood and, as he put it on the fire, a <u>viper</u>, driven out by the heat, fastened itself on his hand. When the islanders saw the snake hanging from his hand, they said to each other, "This man must be a <u>murderer</u>; for though he escaped from the sea, justice has not allowed him to live. But Paul shook the snake off into the fire and suffered <u>no ill effects</u>.'

(Here is a message that is surely coming from a Jesus' disciple, because they had the truth in mind and in their mouth, contrary to Paul and his pagan's churches.)

Romans 1, 18. 'The wrath of God is being revealed from heaven against all the godlessness and wickedness of men (women) who suppress the truth by wickedness.'

Romans 1, 24. 'Therefore God gave them over in the sinful desire of their hearts to sexual impurity for the degrading of their bodies with one another.'

(What an abomination this is! This is not God, who hand over people to sins and to Satan; this is the desire and the deed of Satan, who is most likely the god and father of Paul.

The same infamy and worse are repeated here again in;)

Romans 1, 26-32. 'Because of this, God gave them over to shameful lusts. Even <u>their women</u> exchanged natural relations for unnatural ones.'

(Paul just said that it was God, who made them this way.)

'In the same way the men also abandoned natural relations with women and were inflamed with lust for one another.'

(This is what happens when men are told and believed the one who said; 'It is better for men not to touch women and to love one another among themselves.')

'Men committed indecent acts with other men, and received in themselves the due penalty for their perversion. Furthermore, since they did not think it worthwhile to retain the knowledge of God, He gave them over to a <u>depraved mind</u>,'

(Here in the French Bible, it is rather written they have a lack of intelligence. Which means they are poor in spirit, and according to the Messiah; the kingdom of heaven belongs to them.

But those people are just as intelligent as Paul is; they were just indoctrinated by him not to touch the opposite sex. They are inspired by Satan.)

'To do what ought not to be done. They have become filled with every kind of wickedness, evil, greed and depravity. They are full of envy, murder, strife, deceit and malice. They are gossips, slanderers, God-haters, insolent, arrogant and boastful; they invent ways of doing evil; they disobey their parents; they are senseless, faithless, heartless, ruthless. Although they know Gods' righteous decree that those who do such things deserve death, they not only continue to do these very things but also approve of those who practice them.'

(In that last litany from Paul; I was under the impression he was describing himself.

Who in the New Testament of the Bible was more of a slanderer than Paul? None! Who in the New Testament of the Bible was more of a gossiper than Paul? None! Who in the New Testament of the Bible was more of an arrogant, insolent and boastful than Paul? None! Who in the New Testament of the Bible was more senseless, faithless, heartless, ruthless than Paul? None! Who in the New Testament of the Bible was more against the Law of God, against his commandments and against circumcision than Paul? None! Who in the New Testament of the Bible contradicts more Jesus and God than Paul? None! Who in the New Testament of the Bible was less repentant than Paul? None! So, who is God's and Jesus' worse enemy?

Paul here has said no less than God would have created homosexuality with men and women. What an abomination to say such a thing about God! But the more I think about it; the more I think that Paul's god is Satan. The ones who live an evil life do it by the power of Satan and because of him, not because of the goodness of God.

Isn't he, Paul, who approved the murder of Stephen? There is no one in the New Testament of the Bible who is more arrogant, more bold, more crafty and more of a gossiper than Paul.

See the craftiest one in;)

2 Corinthians 12, 16. 'Be that as it may, I have not been a burden to you. Yet, crafty fellow that I am, I (Paul) caught you by trickery!'

(He is the same crafty one that we can read about in;)

Genesis 3, 1. 'Now the serpent was more crafty than any of the wild animals the Lord God had made.'

(Paul was not only the craftiest, but he was also the worse murderer of the New Testament and I also believe he is also the worse liar.

Romans 2, 1. 'You, therefore, have no excuse, you who pass judgement on someone else, at whatever point you judge the other, you are condemning yourself, because you who pass judgement do the same thing.'

(Would this be the same one who said this here written in;)

1 Corinthians 5, 3. 'Even though I am not physically present, I (Paul) am with you in spirit. And I have already <u>passed judgement</u> on the one who did this, just as if I was present.'

(Not only this Paul, this spirit sees all, but he also allows himself to judge others, and this contrary to the teaching of the Messiah, that we can read in;)

Matthew 7, 1. 'Do not judge, or you will be judged.'

(We have to believe that Paul didn't care to be judged by anyone. See also;)

1 Corinthians 4, 3. "I care very little if I am judged by you or by any human court; indeed, I (Paul) do not even judge myself. My conscience is clear.'

(Paul is the one who was a murderer, a blasphemer, and a liar from the beginning and the one who had a clear conscience, because he felt guilty of nothing. This is how he became a saint in the heart of many people in this world. But we have seen at his trial that he didn't like to be judged be others after all. See Paul in;)

Acts 23, 3. 'Then Paul said to him, (to the judge) 'God is going to strike you whitewashed wall! You sit there to judge me according to the law, yet you yourself violate the law (roman law) by commanding that I be struck!'

(That has to be the roman's law, since Rome was ruling over Israel in those days. But the fact remains that Paul was not happy about it even if he cared very little to be judged. What it would have been if he cared a lot? Paul, who said he was not judging himself would have also said this here in;)

1 Corinthians 11, 31. 'But if we judge ourselves rightly, we would not be judged.'

(I guess he didn't judge himself rightly after all, and maybe if he did; he wouldn't have got a slap on the mouth.

But all of this seems to demonstrate that Paul seemed to say one thing and the opposite, but I don't think this is really what had happened. What had happened, in my opinion, is that sometime in Paul's writings, we can read the say of the Jesus' apostles and disciples, letters that Paul and company would have stolen, and other times; these would be Paul's proper words. Even if this is not really proper for a man who said he was a Jesus' apostle. But I am sure that all of this is causing a lot of confusions to the ones who don't understand yet the stratagem of Paul, the craft of the devil.

What is following demonstrates this even clearer. Be careful as you read, as Jesus asked us to do;)

Romans 2, 1-8. 'You, therefore, <u>have no excuse</u>, you who pass judgement on someone else, (like Paul has done) at whatever point you judge the other, you are condemning yourself, because you who pass judgement do the same thing. Now we know that God's judgement is based on truth. So when you, a mere man, pass judgement and yet do the same things, do you think you will escape God's judgement?'

(God's judgement, this is not the judgement of Paul.)

'Or do you show contempt for the riches of his kindness, tolerance and patience; not realizing that God's kindness leads you toward repentance?'

(Paul, whose conscience was clear, was not preaching repentance at all either, as Jesus and his disciples were doing. Paul and his disciples didn't need repentance, simply because, as Paul was telling them; 'For sin shall not be your master, because your are not under Law, (like Paul is not) but under grace.')

'But because of your stubbornness and your unrepentant heart, you are storing up wrath against yourself for the day of God's wrath, when his righteous judgement will be revealed. God "will give to each person according to what he has done."'

(This is the total opposite of what Paul was preaching. Paul was not preaching that we will be judged according to our deeds, but according to our faith in Jesus Christ.)

'To those who by persistence in doing good seek glory, honour and immortality, He will give eternal life. But for those who are self-seeking and who reject the truth and follow evil, there will be wrath and anger.'

(All of what I just wrote from Romans 2, 1-8, is not from Paul at all, and yet, it is placed among Paul's writing to the Romans.

I won't be surprised at all to find out one day that this letter came from the Jesus' apostles and sent to Paul. Paul in turn would have used it and pretended it was from him. He is crafty the enemy.

(Do you see? In that letter, there is blame to who was judging others, which Paul has clearly done. Paul, who's master is the master of false pride, and who's conscience was clear; was way to proud to blame himself or to repent.

Not only Paul was judging others, but he was also teaching his disciples to do the same thing. This is, in my opinion, a very serious sin. See Paul in;)

1 Corinthians 6, 2-3. 'Or do you not know that the saints will judge the world? If the world is judge by you, are you not competent to constitute the smallest law courts? Do you not know that we will judge the angels? How much more matters of this life?'

(These wouldn't have been the Jesus' apostles or the Jesus' disciples who would have taught against Jesus' teaching this way.

Paul didn't waste any time to judge the angels of heaven either.)

See Galatians 1, 8-9. 'But even if we or <u>an angel from heaven</u> should preach a gospel other than the one we (Paul and company) preached to you, (full of lies, contradictions and abominations) let him be eternally condemned!'

(This again is for Paul to sit himself above God's angels and to condemn them is to take God's place.)

'As we have already said, so now I (Paul) say again, if anybody is preaching to you a gospel other than what you accepted, let him be eternally condemned.'

(These were not Jesus' apostles or Jesus' disciples, who have judged either men or angels from heaven, at least not yet, and it was not them either, who have condemned or damned anyone. Paul has done it and he has also handed people over to Satan; which is not at all the teaching of the Messiah, on the contrary.)

See Timothy 1, 20. 'Among them, (then out of many) are Hymenaeus and Alexander, whom I (Paul) handed over to Satan to be taught not to blaspheme.'

(Jesus came to call the sinners and this was not to hand them over to Satan, quite the contrary. It was rather to deliver them from the claws of the devil, but Paul has condemned them.

Then from Romans 2, 12, to Romans, I don't know yet; this devil broke loose against those who blamed him. And if the Jesus' apostles blamed him; this was because he was speaking against the Law of God, against the circumcision, against the Jews who were under the Law and against Israel, against God's people.

But did you see Paul's craftiness? Paul started by introducing a nice letter that came from one of the Jesus' apostles; pretending it was from him and hoping to be believed next about the rest of his satanic letters. It was artful, wily, crafty, cunning and tricky, but also diabolic, lying and abominable.

If I consider all the people he got caught in his trap; I have to admit that this was also very efficient.

Paul did the same thing to start his second chapter, just in case the first one wasn't quite enough.

It is very long, depressing and disgusting, but I still have to denounce this demon, because this is the Job of a Jesus' disciple to do it, just like the Jesus' apostles have done it in Romans 2, 1-8, and in Acts 21, 21.)

Romans 2, 12-?. 'All who sin apart from the Law will also perish apart from the Law,'

(And according to Paul, all have sin. Then, according to him, all will perish. Paul seemed to think that all will be with him and with Satan in hell. We all know also that perished in the Bible means condemned.)

'And all who sin under the Law will be judged by the Law.'

(We will all be judged according to the Law of God anyway; this is a sure thing, no matter if we are under the Law, or if we think we are above it, or outlaw like Paul, but not all will be judged by Paul. At least his judgement is completely and absolutely worthless; just like the judgement of those who sit in a confessional to judge others, pretending to be their fathers.)

'For it is not those who hear,'

(Here in the French Bible, it is not those who hear, but those who listen to the Law, and listening is obeying.)

'The Law who are righteous in God's sight, but it is those who obey the Law who will be declared righteous.'

(But Paul said that no one will be justified by observing the Law? Paul didn't want to have anything to do with it.)

See Romans 3, 28. 'For we (Paul and company) maintain that a man is justified by faith apart from observing the Law.'

(Well, as far as I know; those who listen to the Law of God are those who obey it. But this is not the first time that Paul wrote a contradictory phrase. In the King

James Bible, it is not those who obey the Law, but the doers of the Law are justified. Now, what is a doer of the Law? As far as I know, a doer is a maker, and as far as I know too; only One has made the Law of God and this is God Himself, no one else.

Many of times Paul seemed to contradict himself in his letters, but this is not necessarily always the case. When you see the truth in the New Testament of the Bible; this is because it is coming from the true Jesus and from some of his disciples. But when you see the lies, the abominations and the contradictions to the word of God and to Jesus' teaching; this is coming from Paul, from Satan and his disciples. This makes sense, isn't it? But this is the reason why there are things that are hard to understand in Paul's letters. See 2 Peter 3, 15-16.)

'Indeed, when Gentiles, who do not have the Law.'

(The Law of God is for the whole world, for the Jews and for the others. But this is most likely why Paul was against the Law, against the circumcision and against the Jews so much; he was a Roman, so a Gentile, who was jealous and envious of the Jews and of the Jesus' apostles, just as Satan is.)

'Do by nature things required by the Law, they are a Law by themselves,'

(No one is a law by himself, certainly not a Law of God; this is completely stupid.)

'Even though they do not have the Law, (like Paul) they show that the requirements of the Law are written in their hearts,'

(Here, Paul tried to make his disciples believe that God would have made his last covenant with him and his disciples; a covenant that is still to come nowadays. See Jeremiah 31,33.

But it is with the <u>house of Israel</u> that this last covenant that is still to come will be made, as God said, and not with the house of <u>Rome</u>. But again, this declaration from God has surely made Paul and Satan jealous.)

'Their consciences also bearing witness, and their thoughts now accusing, now defending them.'

(As always, or at least very often; Paul spoke a lot to say nothing or to put his auditors to sleep, and this is why one of those fell down the third floor sleeping during one of his endless speech. See Acts 20, 9.)

'This will take place on the day when God will judge men's secrets (actions) through Jesus Christ, as my gospel declares.'

(These are our actions that according to Paul don't count for men to be justified before God.

I don't think this last phrase is from Paul. Many will ask me why I say that. This is because there is no truth coming out of the mouth of a liar; certainly not out of the mouth of Satan.)

'Now you, if you call yourself a Jew,'

(To my knowledge, no one except Paul called himself a Jew. We are a Jew or we are not a Jew. And if Paul was truly a Jew; then he has badly betrayed his people. They have assassinated Louis Riel for a lot less than what Paul has done. And if Paul was raised with King Herod; then I doubt very much that he was a Jew. I doubt a lot also that, if Paul was a Jew, he could have preached Jesus of Nazareth and preached God freely in Rome.)

'If you rely on the Law and brag about your relationship with God; and know his will and approve of what is superior because you are instructed by the Law; if you are convinced that you are the guide of the blind, a light for those who are in the dark, an instructor of the foolish, a teacher of the infants, because you have in the Law the embodiment of knowledge and truth—you then, who teach others, do you not teach yourself? You who preach against stealing, do you steal? You who say that people should not commit adultery, do you commit adultery? You who abhor idols, do you rob temples? You who brag about the Law, do you dishonour God by breaking the Law?'

(In my French Bible, instead of the five last questions asked here by Paul; these are five accusations of doing them and as far as I understand; this is judging. And doing so is to pretend to be God.)

'As it is written: "God's Name is blasphemed (mainly by Paul) among the Gentiles because of you."'

(This last litany from Paul was directly pointed against Jesus, against the Jesus' apostles and against the Jews.)

'Circumcision has value if you observe the Law, but if you break the Law, you have become as though you had not been circumcised.'

(The circumcision, this covenant that God has established it with Abraham and his descendants always remains as is, because according to God Himself; it is an everlasting covenant. Then there is no such a thing as incircumcision. Once a male has been circumcised, there was no going back for him, especially at the time of Paul. It is different nowadays. Today a man who really wants it can even change sex. But I think that this was from Paul's part a slap in God's face. Then I also searched for the words, 'uncircumcision,' and, 'incircumcision,' in the dictionary and on the Internet, and I couldn't find them.)

'If those who are not circumcised (the gentiles) keep the Law's requirements, will they not be regarded as though they were circumcised?'

(Can you imagine those poor people of Paul's time, who were forced to listen to Paul's foolish speeches, because Paul and his army had the power to kill them all? Paul has probably thought he was observing the Law because he loved his Luke, his Timothy and his Titus as himself, because to him, this is the summed up of the whole Law of God; even though he hated the Jews.

Without lying, no one can say keeping the Law's requirements and also say he is not under the Law, like

Paul said about himself and about his disciples. And it is also for God to judge, not for Paul or for Satan.

'The one who is not circumcised physically and yet obeys the Law <u>will condemn you</u> who, even though you have the written code (the Law of God) and circumcision, are a Law-breaker.'

(The ones who are not circumcised physically are not all like Paul, who was always ready to judge, to condemn everyone and to hand them over to Satan. And if some of them are ready to condemn the Jesus' disciples and the Jews; this is just because they have learned it from Paul and they are listening to Paul, because this is evil.)

'A man is not a Jew if he is only one outwardly, nor is circumcision merely outward and physical.'

(This is completely false. The circumcision as God has established it between Himself and men is, in fact, visible in the flesh. And why then did Paul circumcise Timothy in that case? And if circumcision on men was so obvious to Paul, maybe this was because Paul was seeing to many penises, or yet he was frustrated with his.

See for your own information the covenant God has made with Abraham in;)

Genesis 17, 9-14. 'Then God said to Abraham, "As for you, you must keep my covenant, you and your descendants after you for the generations to come. This is my covenant with you and your descendants after you, the covenant you are to keep: Every male among you shall be circumcised. You are to undergo circumcision, and it will be the sign of the covenant between Me and you. For the generations to come every male among you who is eight days old must be circumcised, including those born in your household or bought with money from a foreigner—<u>those who are not your offspring</u>. Whether born in your household or bought with your money, they must be circumcised. My covenant <u>in your flesh</u> is to be an <u>everlasting</u> covenant. Any uncircumcised male who has not been circumcised in his flesh, will be cut off from his people; he has broken my covenant.'"

(And as far as I know; the Jew people has always respected this covenant to this very day. Paul, either he was a Jew or not, has violated this covenant by speaking against it to others. And it is mostly why he was cut off from Israel. It is also most likely why he hated the Jews so much. And I continue with Romans 2, 29.)

'No, a man is a Jew if he is one inwardly; and circumcision is circumcision of the heart, by the Spirit, not by the written code.'

(Here the written code means the Law of God, the One Paul put aside to replace it by the grace and faith in, 'Christ.' In any case, I wouldn't want my heart to be circumcised the way I was circumcised somewhere else.)

'What advantage, then, is there in being a Jew, or what value is there in circumcision?

(The circumcision is a covenant God has made with men and in their flesh and it is visible and everlasting, but Paul knew it. Paul was just trying to cause confusion. But

Paul didn't want this covenant with God. He didn't want it for himself or for his disciples. These are Paul, Satan and his demons, who don't want this covenant with God and Paul proved it plenty of times.)

'Much in every way! First of all, they (the Jews, Jesus' disciples) have been entrusted with the very words of God. What if some did not have faith? Will their lack of faith nullify God's faithfulness? Not at all! Let God be true, and every man a liar. (Talk for yourself Paul) As it is written: "So that you may be proved right when you speak and prevail when you Judge."'

(A man cannot be found to be a liar and proved to be right at the same time. This is another stupidity from Paul. Here in the French Bible, it is not, 'when you judge,' but, 'when you are judged.' It is actually the exact opposite. But again James, Jesus' brother, had a very clear message for Paul in:)

James 4, 11-12. 'Brothers, do not slander one another. Anyone who speaks against his brother or judges him (Paul has done it a lot) speaks against the Law and judges it.'

(That too Paul has done it a lot, especially when he said it was an old code, has aged and was ready to disappear.)

'When you judge the Law, you are not keeping it, (we know too now that Paul was not keeping it) but sitting in judgement on it. There is only One Lawgiver and Judge, the One who is able to save and destroy. But you—who are you to judge your neighbour?'

(To me the answer to this is very clear. This was done by Paul, who wanted to take God's place. No wonder that his successors and imitators are sitting in confessionals to judge others and pretending to be their fathers. No one can be found right before God when he speaks the lies; especially not when he lies about the word of God. Not all men are liars like Paul was and still is, because his lies are still going on in his writings and this, in the most sold book in the world. Not all men wanted and do want to judge others, especially the Jesus' apostles and the Jews, like Paul did it either, as we can see this from the beginning of Romans. But what a liar! He is a liar mainly about the word of God, about the truth. How Paul, or who ever, could be found right before God after lying about the word of God? It is absolutely impossible. And I continue with Romans 3, 5.)

'But if our unrighteousness (lie) brings out God's righteousness more clearly, what shall we say?'

(This is still a very foolish language, because none of the unrighteousness can bring God's justice.)

'That God is unjust in bringing his wrath on us? I am using a human argument.'

(It is a fact that Paul spoke as a fool, just like he did it and as he admitted himself in;)

2 Corinthians 11, 16. 'I (Paul) repeat: Let no one take me for a fool. But if you do, then receive me just as you would a fool, so I may do a little boasting.'

(You can boast all you want Paul; I too receive you as if you are a fool, but a fool as crafty as the devil. See also;)

2 Corinthians 11, 21. What anyone else dares to boast about—I (Paul) am speaking as a fool, I also dare to boast about.'

(So then, here in Romans; it is not the only time when Paul has spoken as a fool and he knew it. And Romans continues.)

'Certainly not! If that were so, how could God judge the world? (Don't you worry how, because God will know how to judge the world and how to judge you also.)

'If my falsehood (lies) enhances God's truthfulness and so increases his glory, why am I still <u>condemned</u> as a sinner?'

(Because your lies, Paul, make you to be a liar; something you are from the beginning and you will be judged consequently. But you won't be judged by yourself this time and if you lied about the truth, about the word of God; this makes you an abominable sinner, and according to your own say; you didn't repent either, because you fell guilty of nothing. Here in the French Bible and in the King James Bible; it is not written, 'condemned,' but, 'judged.' And if Paul has been judged or condemned; this must have been done by his own disciples, and according to his own teaching, because Jesus' disciples had no right to judge others. Besides, no one but a devilish person could say that his lies could enhance God's truthfulness and increases his glory.)

'Why not say—as we are being slanderous reported as saying and as some claim that we say—"Let us do evil that good may result?"'

(Sure, I will make love to my neighbour's wife, so she could feel good and this thinking I could receive blessing from God for doing so and for his glory. If this is not a foolish and diabolic language, then tell me what else it is. Can you imagine some children reading these foolish things? No wonder a priest told my grand-father not to let his children read the Bible, that this might drive them crazy.

But on the other hand, if one of them would have found the contradictions that I have myself found; the world might have had opened its eyes much sooner. Although, this diabolic empire was still too powerful in those days and the massacre of the God's children would have been a real disaster. I might even have not been here to do it.

This was still the same at the time of Louis Riel. As it is written; 'the rebellion has to occurs first,' (the French translation of this in the dictionary says; "the giving up public and voluntary of a religion, religious empire,") 'and the man of lawlessness is revealed, the man doomed to destruction.'

(This is what is happening with my books, and by the will of God.)

'Their (Jesus' disciples) condemnation is deserved.'

(This is still foolishness. Paul was the one who judged, condemned and handed people over to Satan, and this is something the Jesus' disciples didn't do. And Paul has pretended being slandered by the Jesus' disciples, what else? What wouldn't the devil have done to make the Jesus' disciples look worse than he is?)

'What should we conclude then? Are we any better? Not at all! We (Paul and company) have already made the charge that Jews and Gentiles alike are all under sin. As it is written: "There is no one righteous, not even one;'

(Paul could speak for himself and for his companions. The devil was please to say that all have sins and that there was no one righteous on earth, but he was fooling himself. His fan club is huge, I can admit that, but he doesn't have all the people. Paul here was talking about Israel at the time it was all caught in corruption, but they all have paid for their sins as usual and God is fair. Paul was telling his disciples that there was not even one righteous person on earth. See on the contrary what Jesus said about this in;)

Matthew 9, 13. 'For I have not come to call the <u>righteous</u>, but sinners.'

(This means then that there were righteous back then too. Even though Luke lied a lot; there is a message in his gospel that demonstrates it very well and contradicts Paul clearly.)

See Luke 1, 5-6. 'In the time of Herod king of Judea there was a priest named Zachariah, who belonged to the priestly division of Abijah; his wife Elizabeth was also a descendant of Aaron. Both of them were upright in the sight of God, observing all of the Lord's commandments and regulations blamelessly.'

(So, who is, or who are the liars? Who said that there was not even one righteous person in the world and that no one could be justified by observing the Law of God? The truth is the exact opposite. Everyone will be justified before God by the way that he or she has observed the Law. Of course, the fact remains that to be righteous in this corrupted world; each of us needs to have God in his life, and this was not the case with Paul and his disciples. This is why he could say that all (Paul and his companions) have sins. And I continue with Paul and his Romans.)

'"There is no one who understands, (this is false,) no one who seeks God. (This is also false.) All have turned away, they have together become worthless; (this is also false) There is no one who does good, not even one."'

(This devil would want that everybody believes that this is the way in the whole world and with everyone. Maybe so, but this is the way in Paul's camp. And I continue again with Paul and his Romans.)

'"Their throats are open graves; their tongues practice deceit. The poison of vipers is on their lips.'

(This was rather Paul, who practiced deceit, who had the poison of vipers on his lips, and what he did here in Romans; isn't this the worse kind of gossiping?)

'Their mouths are full of cursing and bitterness.'

(Listen to the mouth of the one who is talking here.)

'Their feet are swift to shed blood; ruin and misery mark their ways, and the way of peace they do not know. There is no fear of God before their eyes.'

(Paul had quite a way to speak against the Jesus' apostles and against the Jews. But when I think about it seriously, Paul was talking to the Romans against the Jews, but I think he was describing himself and the Romans. And what can we say about the Romans, who have killed more than one and a half million Jews from the year 67 to 73? What to say about the Romans who killed the Messiah? Paul has never said a word against them. He rather blamed God and the Jews for his death.

Line after line we can see that here in Romans; what we can read is the language of Satan against the God's people. What else could we expect from him? And that continues.)

'Now we know that whatever the Law says, it says to those who are under the Law, so that every mouth may be silenced,'

(Paul proved by his own dirty words here and among many other times that he is the lawless one, because he could not keep his mouth silenced and he spoke abundantly against the Law of God.)

'And the whole world held accountable (guilty) to God.'

(This is still the devil's desire, that everybody is found guilty before God, but we know that he is the lawless one and so is Paul, as he said it himself. Then comes one of the biggest lie ever mentioned by the devil, and yet, billions of peoples have believe it.)

'Therefore no one will be declared righteous in His (God's) sight by observing the Law; rather, through the Law we become conscious of sin.'

(Adam and Eve and all of those who came after them through Moses, including Cain, Noah and all of the others were conscious of sin, and this was long before the Law was giving to Moses.)

'But now a righteousness from God, apart from the Law,'

(The righteousness that Paul is talking about here is the Messiah, but Jesus, the Messiah, was never apart from the Law, on the contrary, and the proof is written in Matthew 5, 17-18, among others.)

'Has been made known, to which the Law and the prophets testify.'

(You have proved many of times, Paul that you are the lawless one, the man doomed to destruction, but the God's prophets and the Jesus' disciples were observing the Law of God, contrary to you.)

'This righteousness from God comes through faith in Jesus Christ <u>to all who believe</u>.'

(Sure, like Satan and all of his angels, all of his demons and all of his children believe too. And because Paul became the father of so many; there are many who believe they can be saved only by believing in Jesus

Christ and this, without observing the Law, since they are following Paul, the worthless shepherd, the worthless master. See again Zachariah 11, 17.

The gospel of the Romans is so rotten up till now that it took me two weeks to go through it so far and I am not done yet. And I continue with Paul and his Romans.)

'There is no difference, for <u>all</u> have sinned and fall short of the glory of God, and are justified freely by his grace through the redemption that came <u>by Christ Jesus</u>.'

(The death of the Messiah; you dared called that freely, Paul? All have sinned, maybe so, but it is not all who don't repent; contrary to you, Paul, who is just too proud to do so. And we all know that Satan is the king of the false pride. The Messiah said that it is those who obey the commandments who are entering life; they are those who are justified before God, not necessarily those who believe in him.)

'God (who doesn't like sacrifices) presented him (his Son) as a sacrifice of atonement, through faith in his blood. He did this to demonstrate his justice,'

(To condemn his Son to death to save sinners would be, according to me, one of the worse injustices ever, and if any man would do that today; he would be condemned to life in prison. God, who is perfectly fair and just, didn't do that either. This is one of the worse lie from Paul, from Satan, and a huge part of the people of the world has swallowed that lie, this venom. The Messiah, the Son of Man was condemned by men and he was assassinated by men, by some Gentiles. This is the truth. And those Gentiles, those Romans, instead than accepting their responsibility for that crime, turned around and accused God for their crime. What else can we expect from Satan? And I continue with Paul and his Romans.)

'Because in his forbearance He had left the sins committed beforehand unpunished—'

(This is absolutely false, because Adam, Eve and Cain, and almost all the peoples of the time of Noah and of Sodom and Gomorrah were punished for their sins.)

'He (God) did it to demonstrate his justice at the present time, so as to be just and the One who justifies those who have faith in Jesus.'

(This is a huge lie from Paul's part again, and is also preaching faith to the detriment of the obedience in the Law of God.)

'Where, then, is <u>boasting</u>? It is excluded. On what principal? On that of observing the Law? No, but on that of <u>faith</u>. For we (Paul and company) maintain that a man is <u>justified</u> by faith apart from observing the Law.'

(Faith without deeds is as dead as you are, Paul, and as useless as you are for the will of God. Besides, it is not all who has the tendency to boast like Paul did. See again James, Jesus' brother in;)

James 2, 26. 'As the body without the spirit is dead, so faith without deeds is dead.'

(And I continue with this interminable Paul's litany of lies and his Romans.)

'Is God the God of the Jews only? Is He not the God of the Gentiles too? Yes, of Gentiles too, since there is only one God, who will justify the circumcised by faith and the uncircumcised through that same faith.'

(The thing is that the Jews and the Gentiles don't have the same faith. All of the God's good prophets said it, including Jesus.)

See Matthew 22, 31-32. 'But about the resurrection of the dead—have you not read what God said to you? 'I am the God of Abraham, the God of Isaac, and the God of Jacob.' God is not the God of the dead but of the living.'

(So, God is not the God of those who all have sins. God is not the God of those that are not under his Laws. The livings are those that are not under the power of Satan. The livings are with God and God is supporting them as He is supporting and helping me to go through all the lies, all the contradictions and all the abominations that Paul has made here in Romans and everywhere else.

None of the demons, none of Satan's angels and none of the not repented sinners will be justified by their faith in Jesus; even though Jesus would die another thousand times. See again what Jesus, the Messiah, said he will tell those who all have sins in;)

Matthew 7, 23. 'Then I will tell them plainly, 'I never knew you. Away from me, you evildoers.'

(And this either they believe in him or not; like Satan and all the demons do. It is a sure thing that all of those who are with Satan have sins, but it is different with all of those who are with God. It seems though that Paul, or whoever wrote in Romans, is in the camp of the sinners and that he doesn't need to repent to be justified, but only needs to have faith in the one who said to repent to enter life. And I continue this torture with the abominations from this Paul and his Romans. Do you see now the poisonous venom that came after the few good words from a Jesus' disciple at the beginning of Romans?)

'Do we, then, nullify the Law by this faith?'

(Paul and Satan would like to, but they can't. They though, didn't miss their shot to cause disparagement against it, in favour of the faith.)

'Not at all! Rather, we uphold the Law.'

(Maybe they uphold it, but they don't want any of it, and Paul said it many times.)

'What then shall we say that Abraham, <u>our forefather</u>, discovered in this matter?'

(Abraham is not the father of such a demon.)

'If, in fact, Abraham was justified by works, he had something to boats about—'

(The fact is that Abraham was not like Paul, and he was not a boaster and looking for glory in lies.)

'But not before God.'

(Abraham was not a boaster before God or anywhere else.)

'What does the Scripture say? "Abraham believed God, and it was credited to him as righteousness."'

(I will show you why and what for Abraham was justified before God, and this is not because of his faith in God alone, like Paul, the liar, said it was, but by his actions also. Just like James, Jesus' brother said it;)

'Faith without deeds is dead and useless.')

See Genesis 26, 4-5. 'I (God) will make your descendants as numerous as the stars in the sky and I will give them all these lands, and through your offspring all nations on earth will be blessed,

(Only because Abraham believed in God, like Paul said? No!) 'Because Abraham obeyed Me and kept my requirements, my commands, my decrees and my Laws.'

(And this is the truth coming directly from God's mouth.)

'Now when a man works, his wages are not credited to him as a gift, but as an obligation. However, to the man who does not work but trust God who justifies the wicked; his faith is credited as righteousness.'

(The words of this Paul are lies after lies and succeeding one another like a diabolic and endless litany. What Paul has just said here is no less than saying that God is unjust, unfair. See what's next.)

'David says the same thing when he speaks of the blessedness of the man to whom God credits righteousness apart from works.

(What a lie this is again! See James in;)

James 2, 14. 'What good is it, my brothers, if a man claims to have faith but has no deeds? Can such a faith save him?'

(See the follow up of this litany.)

'"Blessed are they whose transgressions are forgiven, whose sins are covered. Blessed is the man whose sin the Lord will never count against him."'

(The only sin the Lord will never count against he or she is only the one that was repented, but Paul is not one of them. See also the word of God in;)

Exodus 20, 7. 'You shall not misuse the Name of the Lord your God, for the Lord will not hold anyone guiltless who misuse his Name.'

(Woe to you, J's Witnesses.......who do just that every day. Not only you do, but you make people who talk about you do the same thing. See also;)

Proverbs 11, 21. 'Be sure of this: The wicked will not go unpunished, but those who are righteous will go free.'

(Isn't this the exact opposite of what Paul said?)

Proverbs 16, 5. 'The Lord detests all the proud of heart. (Like Paul) Be sure of this: They will not go unpunished.'

(And this, either they are under the Law of God or not, and either they believe to be saved by the death of Jesus or by faith or not.

See what's next of this litany of lies.)

'Is this blessedness only for the circumcised, or also for the uncircumcised? We (Paul and company) have been saying that Abraham's faith was credited to him as righteousness.'

(See what James, Jesus' brother, had to say about Abraham's justification in;)

James 2, 21-24. 'Was not our ancestor Abraham considered righteous <u>for what he did</u> when he offered his son Isaac on the altar? You see that his faith and his actions were working together, and his faith was made complete by what he did. And the Scripture was fulfilled that says, "Abraham believed God, and it was credited to him as righteousness," and he was called God's friend. You see that a person is justified by what he does and not by faith alone.'

(The teaching of James is also totally the opposite of the teaching of Paul and company. Thanks to James. See what is next.)

'Under what circumstances was it credited?'

(I say this was done through Abraham's obedience to the will of God. This is evidently not for Paul.)

'Was it after he was circumcised, or before? It was not after, but before! And he received the sign of circumcision, a seal of righteousness that he had by faith while he was still uncircumcised. So then, <u>he is the father of all who believe</u> but have not been circumcised, in order that righteousness might be credited to them.'

(But even when Abraham was not circumcised yet; he was listening and obeying God and following his commands. This is something Paul didn't want to do at all, even if he was circumcised, according to him, of course.

How could Paul say, without lying, that Abraham was to become the father of all the uncircumcised, when God by making this new covenant with him, said that all males of his posterity should be circumcised? And Abraham is not the father of Satan or of his uncircumcised demons who believe and tremble. This is a sure thing. But even before Abraham was circumcised; he was faithful to God, he loved God; he listen to God and he obeyed God's Laws and commands, which is not the case with Paul or with Satan. God said that the uncircumcised like Paul and his disciples are cut off from his people. That seems to me clear enough.)

See Genesis 17, 9-14. 'Then God said to Abraham, "As for you, you must keep my covenant, you and your descendants after you for the generations to come. This is my covenant with you (Abraham) and your descendants after you, the covenant you are to keep. Every male among you shall be circumcised. You are to undergo circumcision, and it will be the sign of the covenant between Me and you. For the generations to come every male among you who is eight days old must be circumcised, including those born in your household or bought with money from a foreigner—those who are not your offspring. (Either he is a Jew or a Gentile.) Whether born in your household or bought with your money, they must be circumcised. 'My covenant <u>in your flesh</u> is to be an <u>everlasting</u> covenant.'

(But Paul didn't want any of it, not for him or for any of the Gentiles. So, he was against the will of God and also against all the people of Israel.)

'Any uncircumcised male who has not been circumcised in his flesh, will be cut off from his people; he has broken my covenant.'"

(Is that clear enough for you?

See what is next for more lies in;)

Romans 4, 12. 'And he is also the father of the circumcised who not only are circumcised, but who also walk in the footsteps of the faith that our father Abraham had before he was circumcised.'

(In any cases, this devil of Paul gave himself a lot of troubles to make his disciples and the world believe that circumcision is nothing, that faith alone justify people, and that observing the Law has no value at all. All of these can only come from the devil, from the lawless one, then from God's enemies.

See again what God had to say about Abraham's footsteps, and this had nothing to do with his faith, but had everything to do with his deeds. This is why Abraham was justified before God, and this is the very same thing with Abraham's posterity, with his descendants.)

Genesis 26, 4-5. 'I (God) will make your (Abraham's) descendants as numerous as the stars in the sky and I will give them all these lands, and through your offspring all nations on earth will be blessed, because Abraham obeyed Me and kept my requirements, my commands, my decrees and my Laws.'

(To follow Abraham's footsteps is first of all to obey God's Laws and this is what proves our faith in Him. This is not quite what Paul has said and done. And what did a certain, 'christ,' say in;)

John 8, 39? '"If you were Abraham's children," said (this) Jesus, "then you would do the things Abraham did."'

(This was obeying God, following God's Laws, get his descendants circumcised, among other things. Then this means also that God had Laws to follow even before He gave his Laws to Moses and Abraham was obeying them long before he was circumcised.

Then the BS continues with Paul, more lies to his Romans. And did the Gentiles swallow them, as if this was honey!)

'It was not through Law that Abraham and his offspring received the promise that he will be heir of the world,'

(What a lie! Not only Paul has contradicted the Messiah, his brother James, Jesus' disciples and Jesus' teaching, but he cold bloodily contradicted the Almighty too.)

'But through righteousness that comes by faith. For if those who live by Law are heirs, faith has no value,'

(Faith has no value at all if you don't live by the Law. This is what James, Jesus' brother said: 'In the same way, faith by itself, if it is not accompanied by action, is dead.'

(And of course, what is dead is useless and has no value,)

'And the promise is worthless,'

(The promise hasn't been worthless, because Abraham's posterity is almost incalculable.)

'Because Law brings wrath.'

(Yes, the Law makes Satan and his angels quite upset and bring wrath to those who disobey it.)

'And where there is no Law there is no transgression.'

(And this is why the lawless one said that his conscience was clear, because he is not under the Law. So he is without transgression, without sin, but the truth is much different than this. Only God's enemies don't want any of his Laws. For God's children, his Laws are the perfect guideline to please God.)

'Therefore, the promise comes by faith, so that it may be by grace and may be guaranteed to all Abraham's offspring—not only to those who are of the Law but also to those who are of the faith of Abraham. He is the father of us all.

(What a lie this is again! Abraham is the father of God's children, but he is not the father of Satan's children. Satan and his children will discover at the last judgement what the promise and the guaranteed there will be for the lawless ones, but Jesus, the Messiah, already told us about it, and it is written in Matthew 13, 42.

See again the follow up of this litany of lies.)

'As it is written: "I have made you the father of many nations." He is our father in the sight of God, in whom he believed—the God who gives life to the dead and calls things that are not as though they were.'

(Who would believe that Paul didn't know that God is the God of the living? God is not the God of the dead, but of the living. This is the truth from God and from the Messiah. Abraham is not the father of the murderers, or of the liars, or of the blasphemers either. Satan is the god of the dead and Paul worked for him.)

'Against all hope, Abraham in hope believed and so became the father of many nations, just as it had been said to him, "So shall your offspring be." And without weakening in his faith, (false) he faced the fact that his body was as good as dead—since he was about a hundred years old—(it is the exact opposite that happened) and that Sarah's womb was also dead. Yet he (Abraham) did not waver through <u>unbelief</u>'

(This is also false according to the truth that is written in;)

Genesis 17, 17. 'Abraham fell facedown; <u>he laughed</u> and said to himself, "Will a son be born to a man a hundred years old?"'

(The one in Romans, this Paul here, who said that Abraham didn't waver through unbelief, lied big time, and this is not the first time.)

'Regarding the promise of God, but was strengthened in his faith and gave glory to God,'

(But what kind of strengthened faith of Abraham Paul was talking about here? Abraham was face down to the ground and he was laughing about what he just heard.)

'Being fully persuaded that God had power to do what He had promised. This is why, "it was credited to him as righteousness."'

(What a pile of rubbishes this is again. Paul talked through his hat, because neither Abraham nor Sarah believed in it, and as always, Paul used the word of God in the Scriptures to mislead and to lie. In this case here; Paul said that Abraham was justified by his faith and not by his deed. But you too will see, as I did, that Abraham and Sarah didn't believe this at all.)

See Genesis 17, 16-17. God said to Abraham about Sarah, 'I will bless her and I will surely give you a son by her. I will bless her so that she will be the mother of nations; kings of peoples will come from her. Abraham fell facedown; he laughed and said to himself, "Will a son be born to a man a hundred years old? Will Sarah bear a child at the age of ninety?'

(Which was the faith of Abraham and of Sarah that Paul was talking about for him to be justified by his faith, at least concerning for them to have a child at their old age? Of course, Paul was looking for all means and for anything he could find in the Scriptures to help him making people believe in his lies, especially his disciples and the Jews he wanted to mislead. But the Jews and Jesus' apostles knew the truth even better than I do, and at least as good as Paul did. This is mainly why he could never succeed to convince the Jews. It is the gentiles who got caught in his trap, because they were ignoring the truth, for most of them, and they didn't bother to check out if what Paul was telling them was the truth or not. But you too now, as you read in this book of mine, can see the result when someone knows the truth. Jesus said: 'Seek and you will find.'

(And if we have to seek to find the truth; this is because the truth is hidden, mainly by the liars and their churches.

Paul has also mentioned the faith of Sarah somewhere in Hebrews, about for her to have a child in her old age. See what she herself said about that in;)

Genesis 18, 11-13. 'Abraham and Sarah were already old and well advanced in years, and Sarah was past the age of childbearing. So Sarah laughed to herself as she thought, "After I am worn out and my master is old, will I now have this pleasure? Then the Lord said to Abraham, "Why did Sarah laugh and say, "Will I really have a child, now that I am old?'

(Did she believe that? Did she have faith in this?

And the lies continue from Romans 4, 23.)

'The words, "It was credited to him," were written not for him alone, but also for us, to whom God will credit righteousness—'

(God will credit righteousness to the righteous, not to Satan and his demons,)

'For us (the demons) who believe in Him who raised Jesus our Lord from the dead.'

(Don't think that Satan and his demons didn't believe in it, with all of the lies they spoke about Jesus' resurrection, like the third day and much more.)

'He was delivered over to death for our sins.'

(This is false. Jesus was sent to us to instruct us, because of our offences and our ignorance.)

'And was raised to life for our justification.'

(And this is false again. Jesus was led to death by the Pharisees, because he was telling the truth and that all of those who were following him everywhere were making the temple and the synagogues losing money. It was for their religion and for their income that the Jews feared. Jesus was assassinated by the Romans, because they feared he becomes a very powerful king. A king of the Jews, who could resurrect his soldiers as soon as they fall in combat, could not be defeated according to the Romans. The Pharisees offered the Romans on a silver plate, the one the Romans wanted dead since he was born.

Back now to this litany of lies.)

'Therefore, since we have been justified by faith, we have peace with God through our Lord Jesus Christ,'

(Yet Satan and his angels, who also believe in God and in Jesus Christ, since they have done everything in their power to eliminate Jesus, even while he was still in his cradle, still don't have peace with God to this day. So what kind of grace is he talking about?)

'Through whom we have gained access by faith into the grace in which we now stand. And we rejoice in the hope of the glory of God.'

(All of these Christians, Paul's children, are saying having faith and that they are not under the Law but under grace, and at the same time, they all say they all have sins. What kind of grace this really is?)

'Not only so, but we also rejoice in our sufferings, because we know that suffering produces perseverance; perseverance, character; and character, hope. And hope does not disappoint us, because God has poured out love into our hearts by the Holy Spirit, whom He has given us. You see, at just the right time, when we were still powerless, Christ died for the ungodly.'

(This is false. Jesus lived for the ungodly, for the sinners, by calling them to repentance and this for the remittance of their sins, and the grace that comes out of it is to live clean, delivered from evil and delivered from Satan. This is what the Messiah has preached and this is quite a grace, contrary to what Paul has preached.)

'Very rarely will anyone die for a righteous man, though for a good man someone might possibly dare to die.'

(How many men and women have died serving their country?)

'But God demonstrates his own love for us in this: While we were still sinners, Christ died for us. Since we have now been justified by his blood,

(Was that by his blood or by faith? One has to make up his mind.)

'How much more shall we be saved from God's wrath through him! For if, when we were God's enemies, we were reconciled to Him through the death of his Son,'

(With faith or not, without repentance; there is no possible reconciliation with God, word of the Messiah, which is the word of God. And how could Paul and the Romans say being reconciled with God after killing his Son and without repentance, but just by faith? This is just none sense.)

'How much more, having been reconciled, shall we be saved through his life?'

(God has let us know through his prophet Isaiah, among others, how we will be justified by the Messiah, and this was not by his blood, or by his death on the cross, or by anyone's faith.)

See Isaiah 53, 11. 'By his knowledge my righteous servant will justify many.'

(This happened when Jesus started his ministry.)

See Matthew 4, 17. 'From that time on Jesus began to preach; "Repent, for the kingdom of heaven is near."'

(It is with sincere repentance that we are washed out of our sins, and only then we are reconciled with God. Besides, we don't need a confessional and neither a false father to do it. But to be sincerely repented allows us to enter the kingdom of heaven, the marvellous kingdom of the Messiah. The repentance can be accomplished by faith, but faith without repentance is totally worthless.

To be able to repent for all of our sins; one has first to love God with all of his heart. This is something that Paul could not say or do, and this is why he was against the Law of God, and said the Law is about to disappear. This, of course, was a huge lie. To tell someone how to get rid of his sins doesn't mean; 'give them to me, I will carry them for you.'

Follow up from Romans 5, 11.)

'Not only is this so, but <u>we</u> also <u>rejoice</u> in God through our Lord Jesus Christ, through whom we have now received <u>reconciliation</u>.'

(The assassination of the Messiah was and is to me one of, if not, the worse crime ever committed by mankind and the demons rejoiced in God for that. What a shame! Besides, there is no possible reconciliation between God and the demons, between God and the sinners without repentance, even if they have enough faith to move mountains.)

'Therefore, just as sin entered the world through one man, and death through sin, and in this way death came to all men, because all have sinned—'

(If this was the case, then what kind of grace Paul and company have received? God to be the God of the living has to be the God of those who don't have sin. Then, it is not true that all have sinned. Read again the story of Job. God, who is infinitely fair and just and He didn't condemn the whole world for the sin of one man either. Of course Paul and Satan would love to believe that all are lost and will end up in hell with him. This is in what they have put their faith in and it is up to you to believe this lie or not.

Also, sin entered the world through Satan, and not through one man like this liar said. It is not true either that sin or death came on all men. Think of Abel, Seth, Noah, Abraham, Isaac, Jacob and many others. They were walking with God and they were greatly blessed by God.)

'For before the Law was given, sin was in the world.'

(What a lie this is again! What rubbish this is! God had given his rules to Adam and Eve before they have committed their sin. This is only common sense, because, if there were there no rules, there wouldn't have been any disobedience. So then, the Law was given before the sin. Paul, as usual, said the exact opposite of what really happened. As Jesus said about him, 'he is a liar from the beginning.' So the rules and the regulations were given to mankind before anything else. What is following is a proof of that.)

See Genesis 26, 4-5. 'I will make your descendants as numerous as the stars in the sky and I will give them all these lands, and through your offspring all nations on earth will be blessed, because Abraham obeyed Me and kept my requirements, my commands, my decrees and my Laws.'

(This was said long before the tables of the Law were given to Moses.)

'But sin is not taken into account when there is no Law.'

(Paul here said that there was no Law before Moses and that sin is not taken into account when there is no Law, but at the same time he is saying that the sin of Adam and death came to all men. Isn't it the goal of Satan to confuse everyone?)

'Nevertheless, death reigned from the time of Adam to the time of Moses, even over those who did not sin by breaking a command, as did Adam, who was a pattern of the one to come.'

(What a lie this is again. There were many Patriarchs who were God's friends and stayed away from sin, like Noah, Abraham, Isaac, Jacob, Joseph, just to name a few. And if God is their God, as the Messiah said, He is the God of the living; then death didn't reign over them. This was God who reigned over them, contrary to what this liar of Paul said. But Paul has used everything he could to make God looked unfair. What else can we expect from the devil?)

'But the gift is not like the trespass. For if the many died for the trespass of one man, how much more did God's grace and the gift that came by the grace of the one man, Jesus Christ, overflow to the many?'

(And this is the same lie again. It is false to say that many died spiritually because of Adam's sin as we can read in one of God's great prophet. See what God said to the prophets Ezekiel about who is held into account for his own sin in Ezekiel 18, 1-20, and among these, read;)

Ezekiel 18, 14-20. 'But suppose that a man has a son who sees all the sins his father commits, and though he sees them, he does not do such things: He does not eat at the mountain shrines, or look to the idols of the house of Israel. He does not defile his neighbour's wife. He does not oppress anyone or require a pledge for a loan. He does not commit robbery, but gives his food to the hungry and provides clothing for the naked. He withholds his hand from sin and takes no usury or excessive interest. He keeps my Laws and follows my decrees. He will not die for his father's sin; he will surely live.'

(Did you get that, you Paul and his followers?)

'But his father will die for his own sin, because he practiced extortion, robbed his brother and did what was wrong among his people. Yet you ask, 'Why does the son not share the guilt of his father?' Since the son has done what is just and right and has been careful to keep all my decrees, he will surely live. The soul who sins is the one who will die. The son will not share the guilt of the father, nor will the father share the guilt of the son. The righteousness of the righteous man will be credited to him, and the wickedness of the wicked will be charged against him.'

(This means my friends that all of the BS, from Paul about death reigning over all mankind from Adam to Moses; you can put it in the toilet and pull out the chain. The sin of Adam and Eve were charged against Adam and Eve, not to the rest of the world. But the rest of the world had to learn from that lesson.

But who lied about such important matter? The answer to this question is Satan and a son of Satan. Just like the craftiest of all used the word of God to mislead Adam and Eve; he continued to do so with the rest of the world, and again by using the word of God, and this didn't stop to this very day. And if the devil tried to make God look like he is an unfair Being, how much more the rest of the humanity? And I continue with Romans.)

'Again, the gift of God is not like the result of the one man's sin. The judgement followed one sin and brought condemnation, but the gift followed many trespasses and brought justification.'

(What a pile of rubbishes this is again. Only one trespass makes a man a sinner, just like only one murder makes a man a murderer like Paul, and as his conscience was always clear and that he felt guilty of nothing; he didn't repent either. As far as I can tell from what I read; Paul didn't enter the kingdom of heaven either. Also, the death of the Messiah is not what I would call a free gift either.

One has to understand here, that the gift of God that Paul is talking about is the condemnation of the Messiah to death by his Father, by God. But what Paul is not telling you here, is that God, Himself, called such an action an abomination. And of course, whoever knows God, at least a little, knows that God could not condemn an action, saying it is an abomination and commit such an action Himself.

See again what God, Himself, said to his first born, to his people about someone who condemns his son or daughter to death in;)

Deuteronomy 18, 10-12. 'Let no one be found among you (Israelites) who <u>sacrifices</u> (give) his son or daughter in the fire, (kill in fire or any other ways) who practices divination or sorcery, interprets omens, engages in witchcraft, or casts spells, or is a medium or spiritist or who consults the dead.'

(Whoever prays somebody else than God.)

'Anyone who does these things is detestable (abomination) to the Lord, and because of these detestable practices (abominations) the Lord your God will drive out those nations before you.' (Israel!

And I continue in Romans 5, 17 with this litany of lies from Paul that seems endless.)

'For if, (but this is not the case) by the trespass of one man, death reigned through that one man, how much more will those who received God's abundant provision of grace and the gift of righteousness reign in life through the one man, Jesus Christ.'

(The fact is that the Messiah was not alone in his time and he is not alone today. Jesus has the Father, he has his apostles and a multitude of disciples to continue his work.)

See Acts 2, 41. 'Those who accepted his message were baptized, and about three thousand were added to their number that day.'

See also Acts 4, 4. 'But many who heard the message believed, and the number of men grew to about five thousand.'

Jesus, the Messiah, is not alone at all and he has with him the most powerful Father in heaven. Jesus and the Almighty are against their enemies. Jesus has a team that he will be proud of to the end of the war for victory. And I continue in Romans.)

'Consequently, just as the result of one trespass was condemnation for all men, so also the result of one act of righteousness was justification that brings life for all men.'

(This is a huge repeated lie from Paul again. The Messiah said that what brings life to people is the obedience to the God's commandments. It is not from one act of righteousness by the Messiah that justifies all men. The three years of the ministry of Jesus, what he left to his apostles and to his disciples to perpetuate his messages of the word of God; this is what has and will justify many men. His death is nothing, since all men die, but the word of God stays. See again the truth in;)

Isaiah 53, 11. 'By his knowledge my righteous servant will justify many and he will bear their iniquities.'

(And the Messiah did this by telling us to repent for all of our sins and by making God known to us, the Father and his will. But as always, the devil is using this image of the condemnation to condemn everybody; which is to his advantage, of course. And just like one of his speech that last forever to the point that one of his listeners fell asleep and down to the ground from the third floor. Paul continued to put people to sleep. Remember what Jesus said in his parable of the weeds,) 'While everyone was sleeping.'

(As it is his habit, Paul has continued to put people to sleep with this story of Adam and Eve and their sin, and with all kind of lies. God is just and He could not have punished the whole world for the sin of only one man. Adam and Eve were punished and all of the other men will be punished also for their own sins, just like God has made it known to his prophet Ezekiel. See what's next.)

'For just as through the disobedience of the one man the many were made sinners,'

(This is no less than saying that by punishing Adam; He contributed in making many more sinners. This is another abomination told by Paul, and how many believed him?)

'So also through the obedience of the one man the many will be made righteous.'

(And this is also a pile of rubbishes. It is the sin of everyone that makes everyone guilty of his sin; just like it is the obedience of everyone to the Law of God that makes everyone righteous before God. It is just as this happened with Abraham. And this is only common sense.)

'The <u>Law was added</u> so that the trespass might increase. But where sin increased, grace increased all the more.'

(What an infamy this is again! This is another blasphemy from Paul or from whoever wrote this. To say that God made the sins increased by giving his rules and Laws to the humanity, this is no less than a blasphemy. But this is not the only time Paul has done it.)

'So that, just as sin reigned in death, (it is rather death that reigned in sins) so also grace might reign through righteousness to bring eternal life through Jesus Christ our Lord.'

(Jesus, the Messiah, told us what brings eternal life to people, and this is not through grace and neither through faith, but through the obedience in God's commandments, through the obedience in the Laws of God, the Laws that Paul wanted disappeared as he mentioned many of times. See again Jesus in;)

Matthew 19, 16-17. 'Now a man came up to Jesus (the true one) and asked, "Teacher, what good thing I must do to get eternal life?" "Why do you ask me about what is good?" Jesus replied. "There is only One who is good. If you want to enter life, obey the commandments."'

(Which one do you believe, Jesus the true Messiah, or Paul the liar, who said the exact opposite? Let's get back to Paul's abominations.)

'What shall we say, then? Shall we go on sinning so that peace may increase? By no means! We died to sin; how can we live in it any longer? Or don't you know that all of us were baptized into Jesus Christ were baptized into his death.'

(This is rubbish again. It was and it still is with every word of God that Jesus is baptizing and at his death he could not baptize anyone, because he could hardly open his mouth to say anything.)

'We were therefore buried with him through baptism into death in order that,'

(I wish this demon was buried too; he wouldn't have had the time then to lie this much.)

'Just as Christ was raised from the dead through the glory of the Father, we too may live a new life. If we have been reunited with him like this in his death,'

'(No lawless one will be reunited with the Messiah at his death, or anywhere else, or by any other way; Jesus who said that not the least stoke of a pen will disappear from the Law.)

'We will certainly also be united with him in his resurrection. For we know that our old self was crucified with him,'

(The ones who were crucified with him were also on a cross, and they are not necessarily saved.)

'So that the body of sin might be done away with, that we should no longer be slave to sin—because anyone who has died has been freed from sin.'

(The one who is dead doesn't sin anymore, but it is false to say that he is freed from sin, because the none repented sins will follow him all the way to the judgement and to hell, no matter what the liar said.)

'Now <u>if</u> we died with <u>Christ</u>, we believe that we will also live with him.'

(And if this demon said such a thing, such abomination; this is most likely because, as he also said before, Jesus took all of the sins of the world on him; that he became a curse; thus making him the biggest sinners of all. For your information read Galatians 3, 13.)

'For we know that since <u>Christ</u> was raised from the dead, he cannot die again; death no longer has mastery over him. The death he died, he died to sin once for all,'

(This is another stupidity. Jesus didn't die to sin or for sin, since no fault was found in him. Jesus sacrificed his life to save the sinners. The one who sacrificed his life for sins is Satan and he loves sins to the point of scarifying his whole existence for them.)

'But the life he lives, he lives to God. In the same way, count yourselves dead to sin but alive to God in Christ Jesus.'

(All of this sounds good, isn't it? Watch out for what is coming and how the lawless one introduced his policy of perdition to you.)

'Therefore do not let sin reign in your mortal body so that you obey its evil desires. Do not offer the parts of your body to sin, as instruments of wickedness, but rather offer yourselves to God, as those who have been brought from death to life; and offer the parts of your body to Him as instruments of righteousness. For sin shall not be your master, because you are not under Law, but under grace.'

(He is subtle and crafty the evil one and this is how he has created thousands of saints that are not, by eliminating the Law. He has eliminated the sin in the mind and in the heart of his disciples with his fake grace. But we already saw it; the Law of God will never disappear. He is the same who said this in?;)

Romans 3, 23. 'For all have sinned and fall short of the glory of God.'

(I don't see the advantage to be a lawless one and to be under grace, if all have sinned, because God loves his children to be faithful and righteous. And I continue with

Paul and the Romans, because unfortunately, he is not done yet.)

'What then? Shall we sin because we are not under the Law but under grace?'

(Not to be under the Law of God is to be like the lawless one. This is exactly what it is said and written about Satan.

Jesus, the Messiah, said it, and him, you can and you must believe; that to have eternal life you must obey the God's commandments, then to be under the Law of God.)

'By no means! Don't you now that when you offer yourselves to someone to obey him as a slave, you are slaves to the one whom you obey—whether you are slaves to sin, which leads to death, or to obedience, which leads to righteousness? But thanks be to God that, though you used to be slaves to sin, you wholeheartedly obeyed the form of teaching to which you were entrusted.'

(This meant, to obey the lies of Paul, to the craft of Satan.)

'You have been set free from sin,'

(The only thing that set people free from sin is the sincere repentance, but did Paul mention it? Not at all! Paul said repeatedly; that it is the death of the Messiah that frees them from sin, and it is a huge lie that he wanted them to believe in. Many believed him, because they have listened and believed Satan rather than listening to the Messiah.)

'And have become slaves to righteousness.'

(No one is slave to God; because He let us free will to do what ever we want, but God also told us the consequences. If this was not the case; the whole world would belong to Him.)

'I put this in human terms because you are weak in your natural selves.'

(Was not Paul pretending to be God here again?)

'Just as you used to offer the parts of your body in slavery to impurity and to ever-increasing wickedness, so now offer them in slavery to righteousness leading to holiness.'

(No one can reach holiness by being a lawless one.)

'When you were slaves to sin, you were free from the control of righteousness.'

(No one who is slave to sin is free from the control of God's judgement, on the contrary.)

'What benefit did you reap at that time from the things you are now ashamed of? Those things result in death. But now that you have been <u>set free from sin</u> and have become <u>slaves to God</u>, the benefit you reap leads to holiness and the result is eternal life.'

(Paul here has continued his same lie; that they obtain eternal life by the death of the Messiah, but we saw it before, the holiness and eternal life can be earned only by obeying the God's commandments. This cannot be achieved by not being under the Law of God like Paul told them, and this, no matter the greatness of grace and the greatness of their faith. See what's next in Romans 6, 23.)

'For the wages of sin is death,'

(This is before sincere repentance, but did Paul mention it? Not at all!)

'But the gift of God is eternal life in Christ Jesus our Lord.'

(There is nothing free in the death of a man like the Messiah. The gift that came from God is for Him to send us a prophet not to die, but to inform, to instruct us about his will, and this is what the Messiah did. We can also read in Isaiah that the Messiah surrendered himself to death. It is then false to say that God sacrificed him.)

See Isaiah 53, 12. 'Because he poured out his life unto death.'

(See what's next in Romans.)

'Do you not know brothers—for I am speaking to men who know the law—that the law has authority over a man only as long as he lives?'

(The Romans surely knew the laws of Caesar, the laws of Rome, but not necessarily the Laws of God. This was not against the laws of Caesar that Paul was against and talked against, but this was against the Laws of God that he called slavery. See Paul in;)

Romans 13, 1. 'Everyone must submit himself to the governing authorities, for there is no authority except that which God has established. The authorities that exist have been established by God.'

(So, according to Paul here, God would have put in place in Rome, some authorities to kill all the baby boys under two years of age, to make sure that Jesus, the new born King of Israel couldn't escape.??????? According to Paul, this would be God who put Hitler in authority to kill six millions Jews of his own people. Besides, we all know that all the kingdoms of this world belong to Satan. I would say Israel apart and the kingdom of heaven.)

See Matthew 4, 8-9. 'Again, the devil took him (Jesus) to a very high mountain and showed him all the kingdoms of the world and their splendour. "All this I will give you," he said, "if you will bow down and worship me."'

(The authorities that God put in place, in my opinion, are more men like Abraham, Noah, Joseph, David and Jesus. The diabolic authorities like Hitler and Caesar are rather coming from Satan. Return to Romans.)

'For example, by law a married woman is bound to her husband as long as he is alive, but if her husband dies, she is released from the law of marriage. So then, if she marries another man while her husband is still alive, she is called an adulteress. But if her husband dies, she is released from the law and is not an adulteress, even though she marries another man. So, my brothers, you also died to the Law through the body of <u>Christ</u>, that you might belong to another, to him who was raised from the dead, in order that we might bear fruits for God.'

(The least we can say is that Paul knew how to put people to sleep; which brings us back again to the parable of the weeds. To say we are separated from the Law of God, by the death of the Messiah on the cross;

he, Jesus, who said that not the least stroke of a pen will disappear from it. This is no less than an abomination.)

'For when we were controlled by the sinful nature, the sinful passions aroused by the Law (this is abomination again) were at work in our bodies, so that we bore fruit for death. But now, by dying to what once bound us, (held us as prisoners) we have been released from the Law so that we serve in a new way of the Spirit, and not in the old way of the written code.'

(The Law of God, which is to Paul too old to be followed. Are you still looking for the lawless one? The abominable is always continuing his lying speech. As if Jesus, the Messiah, the one who said that not the least stroke of a pen will disappear from the Law of God, not the smallest letter for as long as the earth exist, would have released anyone from the Law by dying on the cross. When Jesus said this here:)

'Therefore, when you see the abomination that causes desolation—standing in the holy place.'

(This is in the Scriptures, this is in the Bible. This is about this abominable, the devil well established in the heart of people that Jesus the Messiah, was talking about. Jesus also mentioned something else in the same verse;)

'Which was spoken of through Daniel the prophet—let the reader understand.'

(And if the reader should understand and be careful as he reads; this is because the abomination that causes desolation is among the Holy Scriptures.

(Well, let's see what the prophet Daniel had to say about the abomination that causes desolation in;)

Daniel 11, 36-37. 'The king will do as he pleases. He will exalt and magnify himself above every god and will say unheard-of things against the <u>God</u> of gods. (This is what Paul has done.) He will be successful until the time of wrath is completed, for what has been determined must take place. He will show no regard for the gods of his fathers or for the one desired by women, nor will he regard any god, but will exalt himself above them all.'

(He is also described very well by one of Jesus' apostles, and this is not by Paul, in 2 Thessalonians 2, 1-10. My friends, this man is the true description of Paul, the lawless one, who is above the Law of God, and I think the true Revelation is in Daniel; the one Jesus, the true Messiah, mentioned quite a few times. Here is another example among many of them in;)

Daniel 12, 2. 'Multitudes who sleep in the dust of the earth will awake; some to everlasting life, others to shame and everlasting contempt.'

(See and compare this now with Jesus declaration in;)

Matthew 13, 41-43. 'The Son of Man (Jesus, the Messiah) will send out his angels, and they will weeds out of his kingdom (of heaven) everything that causes sin and all who do evil.'

(These include the forceful men who laid hold on his kingdom, and shut it down in people's faces and all who say they all have sins.)

'They will throw them in the fiery furnace, where there will be weeping and gnashing of teeth. Then the righteous will shine like the sun in the kingdom of their Father.'

(This will be then and only then in the kingdom of God. These two are in accordance with one another. See what's next in Romans 7, 7.)

'What shall we say, then? Is the Law sin?'

(According to Paul in Galatians 3, 13, the Law of God is a curse.)

'Certainly not! Indeed, I would not have known what sin was except through the Law.'

(What is better for Satan than to blame the Law of God for his own sins?)

'For I would not have known what coveting really was if the Law had not said, "Do not covet." But sin, seizing the opportunity afforded by the commandment, produced in me (Paul) every kind of covetous desire.'

(This is what the Messiah said about Satan also.)

'For apart from the Law, sin is dead.'

(And this is why Paul said he is not under the Law of God, so guilty of nothing and also why he said his conscience was always clear. For Paul his sin is dead, it doesn't exist anymore. But the truth is totally something else, because the Law of God is for everybody, either they want it or not and either they accept this fact or not. This is something that all will find out when comes the judgement.)

'Once I was alive apart from the Law;'

(This is false, the lawless one is dead as death can be dead.)

'But when the commandment came, sin sprang to life and I died. I found that the very <u>commandment</u> that was intended to bring life actually brought death.

(The Law of God, his commandments brought death to Satan and to his disciples, because they don't want to have anything to do with what is from God.)

'For sin, seizing the opportunity afforded by the commandment, deceived me, (Paul) and through the <u>commandment</u> put me to death.

(Sin leads to death, but the repentance leads to the resurrection, so it leads to life. This is what Jesus, the Messiah, has preached, but Paul has never mentioned this, and yet, this was the most important message from the Messiah to save the world. Men can hardly live without committing sins, but everything is possible to God, as the Messiah said it. So with God in our life; it is possible to stay away from sin, no matter what the devil says.)

'So then, the Law is holy, and the commandment is holy, righteous and good.

(And this is why the devil doesn't want any of it.)

'Did that which is good, then, become death to me? By no means! But in order that sin might be recognized as sin, it produced death in me through what is good,'

(What causes death is sin, so it is nothing good, contrary to what Paul has just said, and he contradicts himself from one verse to another.)

'So that through the commandment sin might become utterly sinful.

(It is not through the God's commandment that sin becomes sinful, or condemnable, but through the devilish spirit of the devil. But Paul said earlier that if he has sin, it is because of the Law. Can you imagine Jesus, the Messiah, speaking this way to his uneducated disciples and apostles? All of them would have sent him away before falling asleep, or becoming crazy and they would all have continued to fish; which was a lot less complicated.)

'We know that the Law is spiritual, but I am unspiritual, sold as a slave to sin.'

(And you were bought by Satan, I know it. Besides, the Law of God is also tangible.)

'I do not understand what I do. For what I want to do I do not do, but what I hate I do.'

(Isn't it what they say about someone scatterbrained?)

'And if I do what I do not want to do, I agree that the Law is good. As it is, it is no longer I myself who do it, but it is sin living in me.'

(This is one way to exculpate oneself. And this is why Paul said his conscience was clear and he felt guilty of doing nothing wrong. To Paul everything he has done wrong is the fault of God's Law. This is a speech to put the whole world to sleep and this is why most of it is sleeping and is in need of a wake up call and in need of light.)

'I know that nothing good lives in me,'

(It is very clear to me that God, who is infinitely good, is not living in someone that bad, or in the devil.)

'That is, in my sinful nature. For I have the desire to do what is good, but I cannot carry it out. For what I do is not the good I want to do; no, the evil I do not want to do—this I keep on doing.'

(This is what is happening to the people who don't want God and his Laws in their lives.)

'Now if I do what I do not want to do, it is no longer I who do it, but it is sin living in me that does it.

(This is the way Paul chose to exculpate himself, some excuses, instead of following Jesus and to repent for his sins.)

'So I find this Law at work: When I want to do good, evil is right there with me. For in my inner being I delight in God's Law; but I see another law at work in the members of my body, waging war against the law of my mind and making me a prisoner of the law of sin at work within my members.'

(Paul's condition here; isn't it what it is said about a soul, or a person possessed by many demons? This makes me think about the rich man in hell in Luke's story.)

See Luke 16, 22-23. 'The rich man also died and was buried. In hell, where he was in torment.'

(I can't help thinking that for Paul to talk like he did; he had to be badly in torment too. This Paul has a speech to make anyone sick; contrary to Jesus' speech that seems to heal people. It is not surprising that one of

Paul's disciples fell asleep and fell down from the third floor, because Paul's speech is not only bad enough to fall asleep on a windowsill, but boring enough for anyone to fall asleep standing on both legs.)

'What a <u>wretched</u> man I am!'

(Here is what the dictionary says about such a man: 'A poor devil, a villain.')

'Who will rescue me from this body of death? Thanks be to God—through Jesus Christ our Lord! So then, in my mind I am a slave to God's Law, but in my sinful nature a slave of the law of sin. Therefore, there is now no condemnation for those who are in Christ Jesus,'

(Those who are in Jesus don't denigrate the Law of God, on the contrary.)

'Because through Jesus Christ the Law of the Spirit of life set me free from the <u>law of sin</u> and death.'

(For one thing, sin is not a law, but is against the Law of God, just like the devil is.)

'For what the Law <u>was</u> powerless to do in that it <u>was</u> weakened by the sinful nature,'

(The Law of God, as Jesus, the Messiah said it, will never disappear, not even the least letter from it, so it is still the same. This is from Paul denigrating the Law of God again, but the Law is still in force, no matter what the devil says.)

'God did by sending his own Son in the likeness of sinful man to be a sin offering.'

(This is no less than blasphemy, impure and simple and is not surprising coming from Satan.)

'And so He condemned sin in sinful man,'

(Didn't rather God condemned man because of his sins?)

'In order that the righteous requirements of the Law might be fully met in us, who do not live according to the sinful nature, but according to the Spirit.'

(But Paul also says that all have sins.)

'Those who live according to the sinful nature have their minds set on what that nature desires; but those who live in accordance with the Spirit have their minds set on what the Spirit desires.'

(The sinful nature that Paul is talking about and against here is the love of the flesh, love between men and women; which was created by God to accomplish his first goal that is for men to be fruitful and to fill up the earth. But the speech of the lawless one has succeeded to do the exact opposite; meaning creating priests, false fathers, friars and nuns, false mothers, homosexuals and lesbians and pedophiles, who have listened and are listening to Satan instead of listening to God. This whole speech from Paul is directly related to what he said in 1 Corinthians 7, 33-34. Paul's speeches are the speeches of the ferocious wolves.)

'For to be carnally minded is death,'

(On the contrary; it is life. The love of the flesh, the love between men and women was created by God to perpetuate his creation, so to perpetuate life itself. This natural nature is perpetuating life from the beginning and this despite all the attempts from the devil to stop it with wars, with murders and with his message that it is good for a man not to touch a woman. Satan knows very well that when the earth will be filled; this will be his end and he is not in a hurry for this to happen.

The whole creation was created to perpetuate itself through sex, through flesh, and thanks to God, what He has done is good. What is hostile to God is for Satan to contradict God, and to me this is blasphemy. The whole creation and the way it is done are far from being hostile to God. But by reading what Paul says about it; I think it is rather hostile to Satan.)

'But the mind controlled by the Spirit is life and peace; the carnally minded is hostile to God. (This is false again.) It does not summit to God's Law, nor can it do so. Those controlled by the sinful nature cannot please God.'

(And Paul said we all have sin. Can you see him coming? Paul tried to make people believe we all belong to Satan,)

'You, however, are controlled not by the sinful nature but by the Spirit, if the Spirit of God lives in you.'

(This is an attractive message from the seducer to invite people to do the exact opposite of the will of God. He is inciting his disciples to remain single, for men not to touch women, to live in communities and to love each other among themselves. This is no less than dementia and the opposite of the will of God. We have the result of this policy just about every day with the scandals of pedophilia and homosexuality. We hear about them, the friars, the nuns and about the priests quite often.)

'And if anyone does not have the Spirit of Christ, he does not belong to Christ.'

(Now, when Jesus, the Messiah, was talking about the Spirit; he was not talking about his spirit, but he was talking about the Holy Spirit, the Spirit of his Father, the Spirit of God. And as we continue to read in Romans; we can see another lie right away.)

'But if Christ is in you, your body is dead because of sin.'

(This is a lie again, because it is not the body that dies because of sin, but the soul. If the body would die because of sin; there would not be too many people alive on earth. Read again;)

Ezekiel 18, 20. 'The soul who sins is the one who will die. The son will not share the guilt of the father, nor will the father share the guilt of the son. The righteousness of the righteous man will be credited to him, and the wickedness of the wicked will be charged against him.'

(But as you can see for yourselves; Paul has spoken only to mislead people.

And I continue in Romans for more lies. It is depressing, I know, to see so many lies and contradictions in the Holy Bible and I felt it too, but take courage, the light is at the end of this dark tunnel. The more you'll know the truth; the better you'll see the devil coming. So when you'll hear someone lying to you, either he is a priest or a pastor, either he is a friar or a nun; you'll know on which side he or she is.)

'Therefore, brothers, we have an obligation—but it is not to the sinful nature, to live according to it. For if you live according to the sinful nature, you will die, but if by the Spirit you put to death the misdeeds of the body, you will live,'

(The resurrection of the mortal bodies will not happen before the end of the ages, just as it is written in;)

Daniel 12, 2. 'Multitudes who sleep in the dust of the earth will awake; some to everlasting life, others to shame and everlasting contempt.'

(But as you can see for yourselves, Paul has only spoken to mislead people.

'Because those who are led by the Spirit of God are sons of God.'

(We all are led by the Spirit of God through the commandments, by God's Laws, but only the ones who do the will of the Father in heaven are Jesus' brothers, sisters, and mothers, so sons and daughters of God.)

'For you did not receive a spirit that makes you a slave again to fear,'

(What Paul said here is that you are not slave of the Law; which means that you are not obligated to serve God.

The fear of God is still necessary to bring the people to respect Him and to call Him Lord, instead of just, 'Christ,' while speaking about Him. You can be sure that none of the Jesus' disciples and none of the Jesus' apostles have called Jesus, 'Christ,' while speaking about Him.

They all have way too much respect for Him to do that, to do what Paul, the arrogant has done.)

'But you received the Spirit of sonship. And by him we cry, Abba, Father." The Spirit Himself testifies with our spirit that we are God's children.'

(God's children are not without his Laws and neither against the circumcision in the flesh, because this is an everlasting covenant between Him and his children. God is like Jesus, the Messiah, said it: 'He is the Father of the living.' This means He is the Father of those without sin, the Father of those who obey his Laws, just like Abraham did it.)

'Now if we are children, (if) then we are heirs—heirs of God and co-heirs with Christ, if indeed we share in his sufferings in order that we may also share in his glory. (Paul said it, 'if,') I consider that our present sufferings are not worth comparing with the glory that will be revealed to us. The creation waits in eager expectation for the sons of God to be revealed.'

(So now, Jesus is not the only Son anymore.)

'For the creation was subjected to frustration, not only by its own choice, but by the will of the One who subjected it, in hope that the creation itself will be liberated from its bondage,'

(Paul here meant the slavery to the Laws of God. This looks enormously like a blame against the Creator.)

'To decay and brought into the glorious freedom of the children of God.'

(This litany of blasphemies from Paul seems endless, and I can't wait to see the end of it.)

'We know that the whole creation has been groaning as in the pains of childbirth right to the present time.'

(The pains of the childbirth are for the pregnant women and not for the creation. Although, Paul mentioned one time suffering the pains of childbirth. I hope for him he could get the caesarean surgery, since he was quite friendly with Caesar.)

See Galatians 4, 19. 'My dear children, for whom I am again in the pains of childbirth until Christ is formed in you.'

(Jesus, who is the Messiah, and is the one who said not to call anyone on earth, 'father,' didn't certainly not educate this Paul, who has pretended to be the father of all his disciples, and this without even touching a woman. But now after reading this last verse; I have to wonder if Paul didn't think he was their mother.

See what the Jesus' apostles had to say about the lawless one that Paul is in;)

2 Thessalonians 2, 4. 'He will oppose and he will exalt himself over everything that is called God or is worshipped, so that he sets himself in God's temple, proclaiming himself to be God.'

(This is it; Paul proclaimed to be the father of many. But here is what Jesus, the Messiah, said to his apostles in;)

Matthew 23, 9. 'And do not call anyone on earth, 'father,' for you have one Father, and He is in heaven.'

(The Father who is in heaven; this is not Paul, even if he was telling his disciples he is. Paul said it many times, but see, among others times, what he said in;)

1 Corinthians 4, 14-15. 'I am not writing this to shame you, but to warn you, <u>as my dear children</u>. Even though you have <u>ten thousand guardians in Christ</u>, you do not have many fathers, for in <u>Christ Jesus</u> <u>I became your father</u> through the gospel.'

(In another word, Paul is saying that, 'Christ,' is nothing to them in comparison to what Paul is. A blasphemer one day, a blasphemer always!

For the rest of Romans; I will only mention what is the most evident, because this is just too much.)

CHAPTER 5

Romans 8, 24. 'For in this hope we are saved.'

(To me it is not hope; it is a certainty, and all can be certain too, if they do the will of the Father who is in heaven, by observing the God's commandments, by observing the Laws of God. And the will of God is to listen to the Messiah, God's Son and what he had to say, and also to be fruitful and to fill up the earth with the tool He gave us, the flesh.

To hope for the eternal life, it is not truly to believe in it. Might as well just fall on your face and laugh, because that is doubting. On the other hand, to truly believe in what Jesus, the Messiah, told us; this is to have the conviction that what he told us is the truth.

Then, follow the Law of God, obey his commandments and the eternal life will be yours and don't count on your faith only, as the liar has suggested, by telling you that the deeds are worthless.)

Romans 8, 26. 'We do not know what we ought to pray for.'

(If Paul knew God and Jesus and mainly God's will; he would have known, because here what Jesus, the Messiah, said in;)

Matthew 6, 9-13. 'This, then, is how you should pray: "'Our Father in heaven, hallowed be your Name, your kingdom come, your will be done on earth as it is in heaven. Give us today our daily bread. Forgive us our debts, as we also have forgiven (this here is very important) our debtors. And lead us not into temptation, but deliver us from the evil one.'

(I have personally asked Him what I could do for Him, and this is what made a huge difference in my life. Can you imagine the father of twelve children, who all have their hand out to ask him for money, and not one of them is offering him any help?

Jesus didn't leave us in the gloom, in darkness and in ignorance like Paul, the worthless shepherd has done with his disciples. Jesus is the light and this is why his disciples can see and light up others. This is if they want to see, of course.

And if Paul was a Jesus' disciple; he would have known how to pray and what to ask for and what to say to his disciples. He would also have known where to pray instead of telling them to pray everywhere, contrary to Jesus, who said to go in our room to do it. But we already know that Paul could not say loving God with all of his heart. So for him to pray God.???? Don't think he could. For Paul to say, 'Our Father who is in heaven,' when his father is Satan; he could not afford to do that and he didn't want to do that either.)

Romans 8, 32. 'He (God) who didn't spare his own Son, but gave him up for us all.'

(What a lie this is again, and not only a lie, but a blasphemy, an abomination and it is a multitude that is misled by that devil. See again;)

Isaiah 53, 12. "Because <u>he</u> (Jesus) poured out his life unto death.'

(Now at least we know who propagated this awful lie about God scarifying his own Son. I knew it, but it is a good thing that the rest of the world knows it too. This lie came out of the mouth of God's enemy, out of the mouth of the Messiah's enemy. This lie came out of the mouth of Satan, out of the mouth of Paul.)

Romans 8, 33. 'Who will bring any charge against those whom God has chosen?'

(Who doesn't know that it is Satan who will give himself this pleasure?)

'It is God who justifies.'

(But Paul already said that only faith in, 'Christ,' justifies, and this without observing the Law of God. Let's look again at;)

Romans 3, 28. 'For we (Paul and company) maintain that a man is justified by faith apart from observing the Law.'

Romans 8, 34. 'Who is he that condemns?'

(We all know now that it was Paul who gave himself this pleasure. See Paul in;)

1 Timothy 1, 20. 'Among them, (then out of many) are Hymenaeus and Alexander, whom I (Paul) handed over to Satan to be taught not to blaspheme.'

(To blaspheme for Paul was most likely for them to contradict him. It is most likely what happened to Paul too; to be handed over to Satan for blaspheming and for having forced other to do it too. Paul must have learned this from Satan also, because Jesus, the Messiah, didn't do it. I mean handing people over to Satan. On the contrary, Jesus, the Messiah, has done everything in his power to pull the sinners away from the claws of Satan. This is in fact what he gave his life for.

Here is another abomination, full of lies and contradictions from Paul's part here in;)

1 Corinthians 5, 3-5. 'Even though I (Paul) am not physically present, I am with you in <u>spirit</u>. (That sees all) And I (Paul) have already passed judgement on the one who did this, just as if I was present. When you are assembled in the name of our Lord Jesus and I (Paul) am with you in <u>spirit</u>, and the power of our Lord Jesus is present, hand this man over to Satan, so that the sinful nature may be destroyed and his spirit saved the day of the Lord.'

(This is the abomination of desolation the prophet Daniel spoke about and that Jesus mentioned in Matthew 24, 15, and is also mentioned in Daniel 11, 36-37.

God has to come to my help here, because I have a hard time to tolerate this desolation, all of these abominations that I discover as I read in this false gospel full of abominations.

You have seen as well as I did that Satan, just as he did in the Garden of Eden with Adam and Eve, doesn't hesitate at all to use the name of Jesus and the Holy Name of God to pass his sordid messages.

Here are more hypocritical and lying litanies from Paul in;)

Romans 8, 34-39. 'Christ Jesus who died—more than that, who was raised to life—is at the right hand of God (everybody knows that) and is also interceding for us.'

(Who are the 'us,' that Paul is talking about? Are these Satan and his angels?)

'Who shall separate us from the love of <u>Christ</u>? Shall trouble or hardship or persecution or famine or nakedness or danger or sword? As it is written: "For your sake we face death all day long; we are considered as sheep to be slaughtered." No, in all of these things we are more than conquerors, through him who loved us.'

(The love for the sinners and the will to save them doesn't necessarily mean love for Satan.)

'For I am convinced that neither death nor life, neither angels nor demons, neither the present nor the future, nor any powers, neither height nor depth, nor anything else in all creation, will be able to separate us from the love of God that is in Christ Jesus our Lord.'

(What has always separated us and will always separate us from the love of God is sin, wickedness. Paul and his gang are saying they all have sin, so they are separated from the love of God; besides, they don't know who to pray, how and why to pray or where to pray.)

See Psalm 45, 7. 'You (God) love righteousness and hate wickedness.'

(The lie, especially about the word of God, is an unequal wickedness and is only worthy of Satan.

See now Romans 9 and the follow up with Paul's abominations.)

Romans 9, 1-2. 'I speak the truth in Christ—I am not lying, my conscience confirms it in the Holy Spirit.'

(This is swearing by God again and his words must have been burning in his mouth, but Jesus, the Messiah, said not to do it. More yet; he said that whoever does it, this is coming from the evil one. See Matthew 5, 33-37.)

'I have great sorrow and unceasing anguish in my heart.'

(Would this be the same man who said this here in;)

Romans 12, 8. 'If it is encouraging; let him encourage; if it is contributing to the needs of others, let him give generously; if it is leadership, let him govern diligently; if it is showing mercy, let him do it cheerfully.'

(See also;)

Galatians 5, 22. 'But the fruit of the Spirit is love, joy, peace, patience, kindness, goodness, faithfulness.'

(None of these qualities can be attributed to Paul. I prefer, and by far, the people who practice what they preach.)

Romans 9, 3-5. 'For I could wish that I myself (Paul) were cursed and cut off from Christ'

(These are two wishes that most likely came through for him, because no one can lie constantly and abundantly about the word of God and remain unpunished.)

'For the sake of my brothers, those of my own race,' (Are these Romans or Jews?) 'The people of Israel. Theirs is the adoption as sons; theirs the divine glory, the covenants, the receiving of the Law, the temple worship and the promises.' Theirs are the patriarchs, and from them is traced the human ancestry of Christ, who is God over all, forever praised! Amen.'

(No one can tell that this man didn't like litanies. But it is most likely for all of these reasons that the devil is jealous and envious of the Jews.

This is the lie that even all the Jews to this very day cannot take, and neither do I.)

There is a part in Romans 9, 5 that is not translated correctly, as it is in the French Bible and in the King James Bible.)

Romans 9, 5. 'Whose are the fathers and of whom as concerning <u>the flesh Christ came</u>, <u>who is over all</u>, God blessed for ever.'

(The meaning here is totally different than it is in the International Bible version. Why, would you ask me? This is because the liar has already said that the true father of Jesus is the Holy Spirit. And if the true human father of Jesus is not Joseph, a true descendant of David; he can not be the Messiah. And I am conscientious that this declaration will disturb many of those who still believe in the lies of the devil.

Romans 9, 6-8 contain a lot of rubbishes too.)

Romans 9, 6-8. 'It is not as though God's word had failed. For not all who are descended from Israel are Israel. Nor because they are his descendants are they all Abraham's children. On the contrary, "It is through Isaac that your offspring will be reckoned." It is not the natural children who are God's children, but it is the children of the promise who are regarded as Abraham's offspring.'

(Of course there are sons of the devil just about everywhere, and Paul is a good example of that, but the children of God are those who do his will, as Abraham did it. And all the human beings are natural children.

Only Adam came directly from God. The world had to have a beginning at some time.

There are a lot of rubbishes again in;)

Romans 9, 9-13. 'For this is how the promise was stated: "At the appointed time I will return, and Sarah will have a son." Not only that, but Rebekah's children had one and the same father, our father Isaac. Yet before the twins were born or had done anything good or bad—in order that God's purpose in election might stand: Not by works but by Him who calls—she was told, "The older will serve the younger." Just as it is written: "Jacob I loved, but Esau I hated."

(What God hates is what is wrong, wickedness, sin, but where there is also the lie in this whole story, there where Paul lied; this is when he said the promise was made to Isaac because of Abraham's faith, not by his works; when the fact is, the truth is that the promise was made to Isaac because of Abraham's works or deeds.)

See Genesis 26, 3-5. 'Stay in this land for a while, and I (God) will be with you (Isaac and his descendants) and will bless you. For to you and your descendants I will give all these lands and will confirm the oath I swore to your father Abraham. I will make your descendants as numerous as the stars in the sky and I will give them all these lands, and through your offspring all nations on earth will be blessed,'

(Then we are all blessed today because of the Jews; by the promise God made to Isaac.)

'Because Abraham obeyed Me and kept my requirements, my commands, my decrees and my Laws.'

(And this is by Abraham's deeds and this is the truth, but Paul didn't mention this, because he always lie by saying this here that is written in;)

Romans 3, 28. 'For we (Paul and company) maintain that a man is justified by faith apart from observing the Law.'

(Well then, the promise and the oath that God swore to Abraham was made because of Abraham deeds, his obedience of the Laws of God, and this long before the Ten Commandments were given to Moses and it is for this same reason that Abraham was justified before God.

Do you see the craft of Satan? Exactly like he did it in the Garden of Eden with Adam and Eve; he uses the word of God to mislead you. To the opposite; I use the word of God to open your eyes, and I hope this is working for you and that you appreciate it.

To ask the question is practically blasphemy, but it is not the first time that Paul has done it.)

Romans 9, 14-16. 'What then shall we say? Is God unjust? Not at all! For He says to Moses; "I will have mercy on whom I have mercy, and I will have compassion on whom I have compassion." It does not, therefore, depend on man's desire or effort, but on God's mercy.'

(According to Jesus, the Messiah, this statement would also be a lie from Paul, because this depends mainly on the repentance of everyone. And knowing that God is fair and just; without even questioning this; He will have mercy and compassion on everyone who deserves it. But as always, Paul again has used the word of God to mislead and he even tried here to make people believe that God was doing favouritism.)

Romans 9, 17. 'For the Scripture says to Pharaoh: "I raised you up for this very purpose, that I might display my power in you and that my Name might be proclaimed in all the earth."

(Is it really the Scripture that would have said this, or the Almighty Himself? The rest of Romans 9 is nothing else than rubbishes.'

Romans 9, 30-33. 'What then shall we say? That the Gentiles, who did not pursue righteousness, have obtained it, a righteousness that is by <u>faith</u>; but Israel, who pursued a Law of righteousness, has not attained it. Why not? Because they pursued it not by <u>faith</u> but as if it were by <u>works</u>. They stumbled over the "stumble stone." As it is written: "See, I lay in Zion a stone that causes men to stumble and a rock that makes them fall, and the one who trusts in him will never be put to shame."'

(The ones who stumble over the stumble stone, are mainly those who, like Paul, are refusing to obey the Laws of God that are in place for the Gentiles as well as for the Jews. This is what Jesus, the Messiah said. The ones who are confused are those who are listening to Paul, instead of listening to Jesus, who said that not the least stroke of a pen will disappear from the Law. But Paul took pleasure in saying the opposite. What else can we expect from the devil?

And the lie continues in;)

Romans 10, 1-4. 'Brothers, my heart's desire and prayer to God for the Israelites is that they may be saved. (BS, he hated them.) For I can testify about them that they are zealous for God, but their zeal is not based on <u>knowledge</u>.'

(The people of Israel, the Jews are the God's first born, and right from the beginning they received from God the knowledge of his will. So what Paul is talking about here, other than to denigrate them? God spoke directly with Adam, with Noah, with Abraham, Isaac and Jacob, and with Moses. God has always sent to the Jews some prophets to instruct them, including Jesus, the Messiah. Then, to say the Jews don't have the knowledge of God's justice is a huge lie from the part of the devil again and again some disparagement against them. If the Jews have the knowledge of the will of God, this is because they have listened to Him, and they were punished enough to find out. And again, this son of the devil didn't hesitate to use the word of God to lie and to mislead.

In the French Bible it is rather written that Israel is a people without intelligence, while in fact, it is the most intelligent people on earth.

Then to say that someone is not intelligent is basically saying he is a fool. Paul called the Jews brothers many times. See what Jesus, the Messiah, said about such person in;

Matthew 5, 22. 'But I (Jesus) tell you that anyone who is angry with his brother will be subject to judgement. Again, anyone who says to his brother, 'Raca,' is answerable to the Sanhedrin. But anyone who says, 'You fool.' will be in danger of the fire of hell.'

(So, according to the Messiah, Paul deserved all of this at the same time.)

'Since they did not know the righteousness that comes from God and sought to establish their own, they did not summit to God's righteousness. Christ is the end of the Law, so that there may be righteousness for everyone who believes.'

(This must be the biggest lie from the devil since the one he made to Adam and Eve in the Garden of Eden. Jesus, the Messiah, said that not the least stroke of a pen will disappear from the Law for as long as the earth exists, that if the Law disappears the earth and heavens will disappear too. Which means never.

Again, who do you believe, Jesus, the Messiah, or Paul, this liar of the devil?)

'Righteousness for everyone who believes.'

(Paul said. Do I have to remind you that Satan too believes and so do his demons and his angels and maybe more than anyone else? This would even be the reason why they did so much to hide the truth and incited you to believe in their lies.)

Romans 10, 5. 'Moses described in this way the righteousness that is by the Law: "The man who does (practices) these things (the commandments) will live by them."'

(Jesus, the prophet like Moses, has said the very same thing than Moses in;)

Matthew 4, 4. 'Jesus answered, "It is written: 'Man does not live on bread alone, but on every word that comes from the mouth of God.'

(And this includes the Law of God and all of his commandments. And this is what Paul refused to do and this is also what he preached; the lies and the disobedience to the Law of God, by preaching faith that is dead, worthless without observing the Law. Satan is not there to tell you the truth and neither to save you, but he is there to lie, to mislead and to bring you in hell, and if you give him a chance to do it, he will.

And the abomination continues in;)

Romans 10, 6-9. 'But the righteousness that is by faith says; "Do not say in your heart, 'who will ascend into heaven?'" That is to bring <u>Christ</u> down, or, 'Who will descend into the deep?' That is to bring Christ up from the dead.'

(God only could bring Jesus up from the dead, and Jesus is not with the dead. Jesus is alive and he is with the living; he is with God. The Christ that is with the dead is the false Christ, the Antichrist.)

'But what does it say? "The word is near you; it is in your mouth and in your heart," that is, the word of faith we (Paul and company) are proclaiming:'

(That we know it too, Paul, and we also know that you preached faith to the detriment of the Law of God and that this is the work of Satan. All will know it before the end of times and I'll do my very best for that to happen.)

'That if you confess with your mouth, Jesus is Lord," and believe in your heart that God raised him from the dead, you will be saved.'

(All of this is a lie. You can say anything you want; it is only the one who does the will of God, the will of the Father who is in heaven who will be saved, no matter what he believes or believed in. And the will of God is that all human beings obey his Laws, obey his commandments. Not to forget that Satan too believes that God has resurrected Jesus from the dead and it is most likely for that reason that he deployed so many efforts for people to believe in his lies.

See what Jesus, the Messiah said. Read this for your information in;)

Matthew 7, 23. 'Then I (the Messiah) will tell them plainly, 'I never knew you. Away from me, you evildoers."

(Those are some who believed in Jesus Christ, but didn't sincerely repent and didn't do the will of God who is in heaven.)

Romans 10, 10-11. 'For it is with your heart that you believe and are justified, and it is with your mouth that you confess and are saved. As the Scripture says, "Anyone who <u>trusts</u> in him will never be put to <u>shame</u>."'

(Here in the French Bible; it is not trusts and shame, but, 'believes,' and, 'confused.' Well, it is the one who believes in Paul who is confused, and not just a little. I already know many Christians who are confused. Let me tell you that the devil too believes in Jesus and he will be put to shame and so will be his demons. But let me tell you that Satan and his demons are not confused, because they know exactly what they are doing and this is evil.)

Romans 10. 12-13. 'For there is <u>no difference</u> between Jews and Gentiles—'

(This is anything. The Jews are circumcised, they are the people of God and all the others are Gentiles. To me this is quite a difference, and it was one for the Messiah also. We can realize this as we read in;)

Matthew 15, 26. 'Jesus replied, "It is not right to take the children's bread and toss it to their dogs."'

(Is the difference big enough for you? And I follow up.)

'The same Lord is Lord of all and richly blesses all who call on him, for, "Everyone who calls on the name of the Lord will be saved.'

(This is an enormous lie again, and it is exactly the opposite of what the Messiah said. See Jesus in;)

Matthew 7, 21. 'Not everyone who says to me, 'Lord, Lord,' will enter the kingdom of heaven, but only he who does the will of my Father in heaven.'

(Isn't it what I was saying earlier? Not only according to me, but also according to Jesus, according to the Messiah, Paul lied. This is because I preach Jesus, I preach the Messiah, I preach the word that came from the mouth of the Father, and the Father who is in heaven; He is God.

Paul's father, according to me, is the father of lies.)

See John 8, 44. 'He was a murderer from the beginning, not holding to the truth, for there is no truth in him. When he lies, he speaks his native language, for he is a murderer, a liar and the father of lies.'

(This is Paul at one hundred per cent.)

Romans 10, 15. 'As it is written, "How beautiful are the feet of those who bring good news!"'

(See now how it is written in the King James Bible.)

Romans 10, 15. 'As it is written, how beautiful are the feet of them that preach the <u>gospel of peace</u>, and bring glad tidings of good things!

(Why do you think, 'gospel of peace,' is missing in the New International Version Bible? This is simply because it was a point thrown directly against the Messiah who said this in;)

Matthew 10, 34. 'Do not suppose that I have come to bring <u>peace</u> on the earth. I did not come to bring peace but a sword.'

(This sword is the word of God, and it is very sharp, and it slices the lies from the truth, from good and wrong. The Messiah has put that sword in the hands of his disciples and I use it to open the eyes of those who want to see; just as he liked to do it.

Look what I found and is very interesting in;)

Isaiah 9, 15-16. 'The elders and prominent men are the head, the prophets who teach lies are the tail. Those who guide this people mislead them, and those who are guided are led astray.'

(I think this is what happened to most of the Christians in the whole world and to all who trust in a religion, instead of trusting in God. See what is written in;)

Jeremiah 17, 4-5. 'Through your own fault you will lose the inheritance I gave you. I will enslave you to your enemies in a land you do not know, for you have kindled my anger, and it will burn forever." This is what the Lord says: "Cursed is the man who trusts in man,'

(This is the one who confesses his sins to another man, to a father who is not a father.)

'Who depends on flesh for his strength and whose heart turns away from the Lord.'

(See what Paul has done trying to get some credibility here again in;)

Romans 10, 16, 'But not all the Israelites accepted the good news. For Isaiah says, "Lord, who has believed our message?"'

(Paul brought in all kind of references from the ancient prophets and from the patriarchs, and this was to bring ignorant people to believe him and according to what I can see; he has succeeded.)

Romans 10, 17. 'Consequently faith comes from hearing the message, and the message is heard through the word of <u>Christ</u>.'

(There are many people who don't hear anything and believe, and Jesus was not preaching the word of, 'Christ,' but the word of God.)

Romans 10, 18-19. 'But I ask: Did they not hear? Of course they did: "Their voice (the voice of the apostles and of the Jesus' disciples,) had gone out into all the earth, their works to the end of the world." Again I ask: Did Israel not understand? First Moses says, "I will make you envious by those who are not a nation; I will make you angry by a nation that has no understanding."'

(This was not coming from Moses, but from God's mouth to whom God spoke to, as He did with Jesus, and as He does with me.)

Romans 10, 20. 'And Isaiah boldly says, "I was found by those who did not seek Me; I revealed Myself to those who did not ask for Me.'

(Again, this was not coming from Isaiah, but from God.)

Romans 10, 21. 'But concerning Israel he (Isaiah) says. "All they long I have held my hands to a disobedient and obstinate people.'

(This is the same thing again, this was not said by Isaiah, but this is coming from God through the mouth of Isaiah, his prophet.

We can also see that Paul was not shy at all to denigrate the people of God; he who said was also his people. We can remember that Paul became all to all to win a few. Look again with me in;)

1 Corinthians 9, 19-22. 'Though I am free and belong to no man, (free like a Roman of the time) I make myself a slave to everyone, to win as many as possible. (By craftiness) To the Jews I became like a Jew, (Paul said before that he is a Jew) to win the Jews.'

(To mislead them, but isn't it what we call hypocrisy?)

'To those under the Law I became like one under the Law, though <u>I myself (Paul) am not under the Law,</u>'

(Of course not, now we all know that Satan and Paul are above the Law, especially the Law of God.)

'So as to win those under the Law. To those not having the Law I became like one not having the Law,'

(This should have been easy enough for him.)

'Though I am not free from God's Law, but I am under Christ's Law,'

(I think this has been added to Paul's statements and this got to be the Antichrist's law, because Jesus was, just like all the Jews, following the Law of God. And as far as I know, Jesus has made no new law.)

'So as to win those not having the Law. To the weak I became weak, to win the weak. I have become all things to all men so that by all possible means I might save some.'

(What the weak mostly needs in the first place, is someone strong by their side, for they do have enough weakness. But it is true that Paul became all to all. We can also notice that in these few last verses, Paul has preached Paul and not Jesus or God. No man could or can become all to all, because this requires a very large amount of hypocrisy, but the devil could and he did.

Let's see now a great part of these personalities that Paul became. He was a Jew when that was necessary to him. We just saw that and we can see that also in Acts 21, 39. See also Paul in;)

Romans 11, 1. 'I ask then: Did God reject his people? By no means! I am an Israelite myself, a descendant of Abraham, from the tribe of Benjamin.'

(I don't have much education myself, but I just wonder how someone could be a Roman and an Israelite at the same time, because the two are from two very different nations.

Paul was also a Pharisees when this was necessary to him.)

See Acts 23, 6. 'Then Paul knowing that some of them (Jews) were Sadducees and the others Pharisees, called out in the Sanhedrin, "<u>My brothers</u>, (again) I am a Pharisee, the son of a Pharisee.'

(Paul was also a Roman when that was necessary to him.)

See Acts 22, 27. 'The commander went to Paul and asked; "Tell me, are you a Roman citizen?" "Yes, I am," he answered.'

(Curiously and hypocritically, Paul was also a disciple when this was necessary to him.)

See Acts 21, 18-19. 'The next day Paul and the rest of us went to see James, and all the elders (the scribes and the Pharisees) were present. Paul greeted them and reported in detail what God had done among the Gentiles through his ministry.'

(This was inside the synagogues; there where the Gentiles have no right to enter.

Paul was also a persecutor for the needs of his cause, but this was mainly to be accepted and forgiven by those who were questioning him. Was there anyone better in the whole world for Rome than a man who was persecuting those who were threatening their religion and their country?)

See Acts 22, 4. 'I persecuted the followers of the Way to their death (the Messiah and his disciples) arresting men and women and throwing them into prison.'

(See also on the same subject.)

Acts 26, 9-11. 'I too (Paul) was convinced that I ought to do all that was possible to oppose the name of Jesus of Nazareth. And that is just what I did in Jerusalem. On the authority of the chief priest I put many of the saints in prison, and when they were put to death, I cast my vote against them. Many a time I went from one synagogue to another to have them punished, and I tried to force them to blaspheme.'

(Someone tried to make Paul look a little better than he really was here, by saying he tried to force the disciples to blaspheme. But Paul didn't just try to force them; he forced them to do it and this according to my French Bible and many other Bibles.)

'In my obsession (fury, fureur in French, führer, name that is associated with Hitler.)

'Against them, I even went to foreign cities to persecute them.'

(Paul could not do this without a little army that was following him, but that, Paul has never mentioned it.

We know now why Paul mainly was going into the Jewish synagogues just about everywhere. I even think that the name, 'Führer,' came to Hitler from Paul. Paul always knew what to say before all the commanders, before all the Pharisees and the chief priests, who are sitting in Moses' seat, before all the kings and even before Caesar, to please them and because of that fact; he always have his life speared. This is what allowed him to act as he pleased at the end in Rome; even though all the Jews except Paul were expelled from there.)

See acts 18, 2. 'Because Claudius had ordered all the Jews to leave Rome.'

(Paul was mainly a hypocrite when this was necessary to him.)

See Acts 23, 4-5. 'Those who were standing near Paul said, "You dare to insult God's high priest?" Paul replied, "Brothers, (again) I did not realized that he was the high priest; for it is written: 'Do not speak evil about the ruler of your people.'"'

(How hypocrite this was. Paul was working for them. Besides, Paul was on trial in the Sanhedrin, and he knew very well that the one who normally presides over it is a chief priest, a ruler of his people. See again;)

Acts 22, 4-5. 'I persecuted the followers of the Way to their death arresting men and women and throwing them into prison, as also the high priest and all the Council can testify. I even obtained letters from them to their brothers in Damascus, and went there to bring these people as prisoners to Jerusalem to be punished.'

(Paul, who was one of the most instructed men in Israel was not without knowing who the chief priests were and also not without knowing what was their function in the Sanhedrin. See Paul in;)

Acts 26, 10. 'And this is just what I (Paul) did in Jerusalem. On the authority of the chief priest I put many of the saints in prison, and when they were put to death, I cast my vote against <u>them</u>.'

See also Acts 26, 12. 'On one of these journeys I (Paul) was going to Damascus with the authority and commission of the <u>chief priests</u>.'

(But Paul hypocritically said he didn't know that the Judge who was sitting in the Sanhedrin to judge him was the ruler of the people. Poor him! Paul has even insulted him. As the proofs are very well established in the Scriptures, Paul was very well known from the chief priests and he knew also very well who the ruler of the people was.

It is true though that Satan can show himself under many different faces. We already know that he showed himself as a snake in the Garden of Eden.)

Romans 11, 5. 'So too, at the present time there is a remnant chosen by grace. And <u>if</u> by grace, then it is no longer by works; if it were, grace would no longer be grace.'

(This is rubbish from Paul to mix up people. A work or a deed is always a deed; unless it is destroyed. But God will certainly not destroy a good work as Good as his Law. On the contrary; He will expend it to his kingdom to come, just as He said.

But Paul has put billions of people to sleep with his so called, 'grace and faith.' But all of you would do well, as I do, to listen to the Messiah instead. To listen to the one who said this here in;)

Matthew, 16, 27. 'For the Son of Man is going to come in his Father's glory with his angels, and then he will reward each person according to what he has done.'

(This is not with the grace of Paul with all of his lies, contradictions and abominations, and neither with his faith or the faith of his disciples; he said saves and justifies.

See also;)

Isaiah 59, 17-18. 'He (God) put on righteousness as his breastplate, and the helmet of salvation on his head; He put on the garments of vengeance and wrapped Himself in zeal as in a cloak. According to what they have done so will He repay wrath to his enemies.'

(Woe to the one who is listening to Paul instead of listening to the Messiah.

From Romans 11, 7 to Romans 11, 32, this is only rubbish from Paul <u>to put people to sleep</u> and to fall, not only from the third floor, but also into the nonsense and in the lies.

Paul has denigrated the people of Israel in the eyes of the Gentiles, and this to make them believe they are much better; which is in some ways some flattering. This was to win them to his cause. I know this for a fact; I almost fell asleep by reading his lines.)

Romans 11, 33-36. 'OH, the depth of the riches of the wisdom and knowledge of God! How unsearchable his judgements, and his paths beyond tracing out! "Who has known the mind of the Lord? Or who has been his counsellor?" "Who has ever given to God, that God should repay him?" For from Him and through Him and to Him are all things. To Him be the glory forever! Amen.'

(What a hypocrite Paul is! What Paul didn't tell them, to these Romans, to these Gentiles; is that God has always and from the very beginning with Adam and Eve; God has always made his will known to them. God has made known to them his will, his thoughts, his desire, and this for us to be agreeable to Him in everything. God, contrary to Paul or to Satan, didn't leave people in the dark. God, contrary to Satan, didn't use the ignorance of people to mislead them.

With a great number of prophets and patriarchs; God has let the people know what He wanted from us and also made known to people the consequences in either way. God is just and fair and He is not at all like his enemies, who misled and still are misleading the world.)

Romans 12, 1-5. 'Therefore, I urge you, brothers, in view of God's mercy, to offer your bodies as <u>living sacrifices</u>, (wouldn't that be a deed that Paul said doesn't justify anyone?,) holy and pleasant to God—this is your spiritual act of worship. Do not conform any longer to the pattern of this world, but be transformed by the renewing of your mind. Then you will be able to test and approve what God's will is—his good, pleasing and perfect will. For the <u>grace given me</u> (Paul) I say to everyone of you:

Do not think of yourself more highly than you ought, but rather think of yourself with sober judgement, (isn't this trying to control someone's mind?,) in accordance with the measure of faith God has given you. Just as each one of us has one body with many members, and these members do not all have the same function, so in Christ we who are many form one body, and each member belongs to all the others.'

(I just wonder who the ass hole is. God doesn't like sacrifices and He said so. Here what He likes from us and this is written by many prophets.)

See Deuteronomy 9, 4. 'No, it is on the account of the wickedness of these nations that the Lord is going to drive them out before you.' (Israel!

These nations had cults and sacrifices. They were scarifying their first born sons to death, by fire. See also;)

Deuteronomy 18, 10-12. 'Let no one be found among you who sacrifices his son or daughter in fire, who practices divination or sorcery, interprets omens, engages in witchcraft, or casts spells, or who is a medium or spiritist, or who consults the dead. (Mary and all the false saints) Anyone who does these things is detestable (abomination) to the Lord, and because of these detestable practices, the Lord your God will drive out those nations before you.'

(God drove out complete nations before the people of Israel, because they were scarifying their sons to death. God said that these practices are abominations before Him, but the Christians, and maybe others, who have learned this from the devil, are saying that God has sacrificed his own Son to death to save the sinners. To say such a thing about God is to say an abomination. See also;)

Isaiah 58, 6. 'Is not this the kind of fasting (sacrifice) I (God) have chosen; to loose the chains of injustice and untie the cords of the yoke, to set the oppressed free and break every yoke?'

(Here is another very significant one in;)

1 Samuel 15, 22. 'Does the Lord delight in burnt offerings and sacrifices as much as in obeying the voice of the Lord? To obey is better than sacrifice, and to heed is better than the fat of rams.'

(But Paul preached to his disciples to offer their bodies to God in sacrifice, and he also, many of times, preached not to obey the commandments and he called them slavery. Our body is a substance that will turn to dust; this is shit. A present that would be pleasant to God is a pure soul, a soul that desires to obey God's Laws, to obey God's commandments, contrary to Paul's teachings. See also what Paul would have said in;)

Galatians 6, 3. 'If anyone thinks he is something when he is nothing, he deceives himself.'

(And this is surely what Paul wanted his disciples to offer to God, their bodies, which means, absolutely nothing.

(Here is another one that means the same thing in;)

Hosea 6, 6. 'For I (God) desire mercy, not sacrifice, and acknowledgement of God rather than burnt offerings.'

(And we can get acknowledgement of God by listening to the Messiah, not by listening to Paul.

And to finish with, see two more smooth messages from Jesus, from the Messiah in;)

See Matthew 9, 13 first. 'But go and learn what this means: 'I desire mercy, not sacrifice.'

Then Matthew 12, 7. 'If you had known what these words mean, 'I desire mercy, not sacrifice,' you would not have condemned the innocent.'

(And believe it, Jesus, the Messiah, knows God very well, and he knows also what God thinks about the sacrifices and this a lot better than Paul.

I don't think that Romans 12, 6 to Romans 12, 21 is a letter from Paul, but it is from one of the Jesus' apostles. I am sure that many will ask me why I say that and I will tell them this. Because it is written this that contradicts the teaching of Paul;)

See Romans 12, 8. 'If it is contributing to the needs of others, let him give generously.'

(Here in the French Bible, it is written, 'with liberality.' Well, this is not at all what Paul has preached and this letter is way too good for coming from Paul. Read this now in;)

1 Corinthians 16, 1-2. 'Now about the collection for God's people: Do what I told (ordered, as it is written in the King James Bible,) the Galatians churches to do. On

the first day of every week, each one of you should set aside a sum of money in keeping with his income, saving it up, so when I come no collection will have to be made.'

(This is not Jesus' teaching, who said; 'You have received freely, freely give.'

(There is more yet. It is written there: 'If it is showing mercy, let him do it cheerfully.'

(Well, this is not done by handing people over to Satan, like Paul has done.)

See 1 Timothy 1, 20. 'Among them, (then out of many) are Hymenaeus and Alexander, whom I (Paul) handed over to Satan to be taught not to blaspheme.'

(It is true that he, Paul, a blasphemer, who has forced others to blaspheme, was preaching for his own and for his kingdom.

It is also written there; 'Serving the Lord.' Knowing the way of Paul to write; he would have wrote, 'Serving Christ.'

It is also written there: 'Bless those who persecute you, bless and do not curse.'

(This is much different than cursing men and way much different than cursing an angel of heaven, if he was preaching a different gospel than the lying one that Paul was preaching.)

See Galatians 1, 8-9. 'But even if we or an angel from heaven should preach a gospel other than the one we (Paul and company) preached to you, (full of lies, contradictions and abominations,) let him be eternally condemned! (This again is for Paul to sit himself above

God's angels and to condemn them is to take God's place.) As we have already said, so now I (Paul) say again, if anybody is preaching to you a gospel other than what you accepted, let him be eternally condemned.'

(This is not what I would call, 'bless and do not curse those who persecute you.'

See also;)

1 Corinthians 12, 3. 'Therefore I tell you that no one who is speaking by the Spirit of God says, "Jesus is cursed," (but Paul did it,) and no one can say, "Jesus is Lord." except by the Holy Spirit.'

(Paul said it that Jesus is cursed. Are you surprised? Read carefully Paul in;)

Galatians 3, 13. 'Christ redeemed us from the curse of the Law, (as if the Law of God was a curse) by becoming a curse for us, (as if Jesus became a curse. Talking about the abomination in the holy place, in the Holy Bible, do you see it?) For it is written: 'Cursed is everyone who is hung on a tree.'

(This is something that can be done only by Satan and by one of his angels. To say that Jesus is God and then to say that he is cursed and so is the Law of God. Such abomination can only come from Satan. But really, this is not surprising coming from Paul, because he wished to be cursed himself.)

See Romans 9, 3. 'For I could wish that I myself (Paul) were cursed and cut off from Christ for the sake of my brothers, those of my own race, the people of Israel.'

(No one has to worry about that one, because Paul has lied and contradicted Jesus teaching enough to be separated from him; he is simply not of the same family.

It is also written there;)

Romans 12, 17. 'Do not repay anyone evil for evil.'

(This too, can not be done by handing over people to Satan.

It is also written there;)

See Romans 12, 18. 'If it is possible, as far as it depends on you, live at peace with everyone.'

(No one has disputed and fought with others as much as Paul did, and this depended mostly on him and his temperament. See an example of that in;)

Acts 15, 37-39. 'Barnabas wanted to take <u>John</u>, also called <u>Mark</u>, with them, but Paul did not think it wise to take him, because he had deserted them in Pamphylia and had not continued with them in the work. (There was no forgiveness from Paul.) They had such sharp disagreement that they parted company. Barnabas took Mark and sailed for Cyprus.'

(And we hardly heard about him since. This was rather risky to contradict this Paul. See also Paul in;)

Acts 13, 45. 'When the Jews saw the crowds, they were filled with jealousy and talked abusively against what Paul was saying.'

The Jews knew the Law and they were for the Law of God and for God's commandments, contrary to Paul. I am not jealous of Paul at all, but I have to contradict him, because he lied and a lot.

It is also written there: 'Do not take vengeance, my friends, but leave room for God's wrath, for it is written: "It is mine to avenge; I will repay," says the Lord.'

(Paul has rarely called his disciples, 'friends.' Because according to him; they were his dear children and he was their father.)

See 1 Corinthians 4, 14-15. 'I am not writing you to shame you, but to warn you, as my dear children. (And the warning was left out) Even though you have ten thousand guardians in Christ, you do not have many fathers, for in Christ Jesus I became your father through the gospel.

(Paul has many children, for a man who didn't want to touch a woman. It is true also that the devil too has many children and to Paul; to hell the Jesus' message, the Messiah's message, that says this here in;)

Matthew 23, 8-9. 'But you (my disciples) are not to be called 'Rabbi,' for you have only one Master and you are all brothers. And do not call anyone on earth 'father,' for you have one Father, and He is in heaven.'

(You understand, don't you, that this message was only for Jesus' disciples, for God's children, and that Paul has no part of it at all, and that Paul has proved this himself many of times?

There is also written this here, which is contrary to Paul' teaching: 'If <u>your enemy</u> is hungry, feed him, if he is thirsty, give him something to drink.'

(Nevermind Paul enemies; he didn't even want to feed his children. See Paul in;)

1 Corinthians 11, 34. 'If anyone is hungry, he should eat at home, so that when you meet together it may not result in judgement.'

(Don't forget that Paul's judgement is hell.

And to finish with, look at this; 'Do not be overcome by evil, but overcome evil with good.'

(And because flesh is weak, as Jesus, the Messiah said it; this is only possible with the presence of God in our life.

Some people will ask me how it is possible that some letters from a Jesus' apostle could by found in Paul's writings. We have to remember first the Jesus' messages and particularly this one in;)

Matthew 7, 17-20. 'Likewise every good tree bears good fruit, but a bad tree bears bad fruit. A good tree cannot bear bad fruit, and a bad tree cannot bear good fruit. Every tree that does not bear good fruit is cut down and thrown into the fire. Thus, by their fruit you will recognize them.'

(It is by their lies that we recognize the liars, and by whose telling the truth that we recognize the righteous. When the Jesus' disciples talk about the Master, they do it with much respect for his name; by saying; 'Our Lord Jesus Christ,' instead of just, 'Christ,' like Paul has done it. With Paul, it was just; 'in Christ, of Christ, by Christ, and so on. I counted 257 times in the New Testament where Paul referred to Jesus, to the Messiah this way. And if you think this was impossible for Paul to steal the Jesus' disciples' letters; think again and read this in;)

2 Thessalonians 2, 1-4. 'Concerning the coming of <u>our Lord Jesus Christ</u> (this is not at all the way of Paul to write) and our being gathered to him, we ask you <u>brothers</u>, not to become to easily unsettled or alarmed by some prophesy, report or <u>letter supposed to have come from us</u> (the Jesus' apostles) saying that the day of the Lord has already come. Don't let anyone deceive you in any way, for that day will not come until the rebellion occurs and the man of lawlessness is revealed, the man doomed to destruction. (We know him now, he is revealed.) He will oppose and he will exalt himself over everything that is called God or is worshipped, so that he sets himself in God's temple, proclaiming himself to be God.'

(Did you recognize him? I did. And you can be sure that it was very easy for Paul to steal letters form the Jesus' disciples he was persecuting, even through the foreign cities and throwing them in prison. If he could force them to blaspheme and kill them, we can imagine what else he could do.

Unfortunately and despite all the warnings from the Messiah and from the Jesus' disciples, many have let themselves be seduced by the man doomed to destruction, by the lawless one. He has chosen the easiest and most efficient way to do it too and this was through religions; something the Messiah was completely against.

The rest of Romans is a very big mixture of words that sometime are coming from a Jesus' disciple and some other times they are coming from Paul; which is quite confusing. Which is even more confusing is the fact that, it is a letter that is apparently started by the hand of Paul and terminated by someone else, named Tertius. This is hard to understand. Maybe Paul had different names, since he had different nationalities, who knows?

Romans 13, 1-4. 'Everyone must submit himself to the governing authorities, for there is no authority, except that which God has established. The authorities that exist have been established by God. Consequently, he who rebels against the authority is rebelling against what God has instituted, and those who do so will bring judgement on themselves. For rulers hold no terror on those who do right, but on those who do wrong. Do you want to be free from fear of the one of authority? Then do what is right and he will commend you. For he is God' servant, an agent of wrath to bring punishment on the wrong doer.'

(Here again, Paul was speaking for his own benefit and for Caesar and his country, for Rome. Because the authority of Caesar and of King Herod was certainly not the will of God to kill all the baby boys under the age of two, when Jesus was just born. This was not the will of God either to have Jesus' disciples killed by Paul ministry.

What Jesus has done wrong to deserve his condemnation and to be punished by the authorities? What was Paul doing to the authority at his trial, calling his judge of whitewashed wall? This was one of the worse insults of the time.

Jesus, his apostles and his disciples had to flee the authorities constantly; what have they done wrong? And if we can believe some of the things that are written in the Acts; see what John and Peter had to say about the authorities in;)

Acts 4, 19. 'But Peter and John replied, "Judge for yourselves whether it is right in God's sight to obey you rather than God.'

(I say like Brigitte Lafleur, a French actress I like, in one of her commercials; "Ask yourselves the right questions."

Romans 13, 5. 'Therefore it is necessary to submit to the authorities, not only because of possible punishment but also because of conscience.'

(See about the One Jesus said we should be afraid of, and this is written in the Messiah's instructions to his apostles and this, again, is completely the opposite of Paul's teaching.)

Matthew 10, 28. 'Do not be afraid of those who kill the body, but can't kill the soul. Rather, be afraid of the One who can destroy both soul and body in hell.'

Romans 13, 7. 'Give everyone what you owe him: If you owe taxes, pay taxes; if revenue, then revenue; if <u>respect</u>, then respect; if honour, then honour.'

(In the French Bible and in the King James Bible, instead of, 'respect,' it is written, 'fear.'

And we just saw it; we owe fear to God, like the Messiah said it, not to those who can kill the body, like Paul said it.

Romans 13, 8-10 is again from Paul a contradiction to the Jesus' message, and this can only come from the Messiah's enemy, this can only come from Satan.

Remember the Messiah's message written in the parable of the weeds in;)

Matthew 13, 39. 'And the enemy who sows them is the devil.'

Romans 13, 8-10. 'Let no debt remain outstanding, except the continuing debt to love one another, for he who loves his fellowman has fulfilled the Law. (This is false again; the murderers also love their wives, their children and their friends. Don't tell me they are accomplishing the Law, because they don't.) The commandments, "Do not commit adultery, do not murder, do not steal, do not covet," and whatever other commandment there may be, are summed up in this one rule: "Love your neighbour as yourself. Love does no harm to its neighbour. Therefore love is the fulfilment of the Law.'

(And this is false and a huge lie again, according to Jesus, the Messiah. What Paul is saying here is a very small part of the truth, just like the devil did it in the Garden of Eden. Remember; God told them, "You will surely die." And the devil told them, "You will not surely die." (Who do you think is telling the truth?

Let's see again what the Messiah told us about the commandments in;)

Matthew 22, 37-40. 'One of them, an expert in the Law, tested Jesus with this question: 'Teacher, which is the greatest commandment in the Law?' Jesus replied; 'Love the Lord your God with all your heart and with all your soul and with all your mind. This is the greatest commandment. And the second one is like it; love your neighbour as yourself. All the Law and the Prophets hang on these two commandments."

(All the Law and the prophets will be accomplished when the judgement of the whole world will be pronounced; otherwise Jesus wouldn't have had to ask his disciples to go make disciples of all the nations and to teach them everything he has prescribed. It is simple as that. See Matthew 28, 19-20.

As Jesus, the Messiah said it: 'All the Law and the prophets hang on these two commandments.'

Jesus didn't say that everything is accomplished, even though he has done everything he had to do. We, the Jesus' disciples, still have a lot to accomplish for the Law to be completely accomplished, and we need way more disciples to do it. I hope anyway that this book of mine, with the help of the Almighty, with the will of the Father who is in heaven, will go around the world and contribute in making Jesus' disciples everywhere. There are out there way too many who are telling lies and not enough who are telling the truth.

Here again from Romans 13, 11 through the end of Romans; I strongly believe there is a mixture of Paul's writings, and the writing of a Jesus' disciple and the writing of Tertius; who must be a friend or a disciple of Paul. This is enough for anyone to be confused. I will make my very best to clear this up and do it in a way that you can see the difference between these three. The fact to be a writer myself surely helps me to demystify the Scriptures; knowing that everyone has his own way to think and to write. Just as Paul said it himself, see;)

2 Thessalonians 3, 17. 'I Paul, write this greeting in my own hand, which is the distinguishing mark in all my letters. This is how I write.'

(And of course, this is how I recognize him just about everywhere. I will write everything and continue to write my commentaries between parentheses as I have done.)

Romans 13, 11. 'And do this, understanding the present time. The hour has come for you to wake up from your slumber, because our salvation is nearer now than when we first believed. The night is nearly over; the day is almost here. So let us put aside the deeds of darkness and put on the armour of light. (Do you see here, Paul didn't believe in the deeds of the Law and the armour of light is the Jesus' messages? Jesus, who is indeed the light, but Paul has hardly preached anything true about him.) Let us behave decently, as in the daytime, not in orgies and drunkenness, not in sexual immorality and debauchery, not in <u>dissension</u> and jealousy. (None was caught in dissension with others as much as Paul did; at least according to what we can read in the New Testament.) Rather clothe yourselves with the <u>Lord Jesus Christ</u> and do not think about how to gratify the desires of the sinful nature. (To clothe oneself with the Lord Jesus Christ is to clothe oneself with the Jesus' messages, but Paul was not even able to pronounce his name with respect; no more than he could say: 'Loving God with all of our heart, with all of our soul and with all of our thoughts.) Accept him whose faith is weak, without passing judgement on disputable matters. (Try to find someone in the whole New Testament, who disputed less than Paul with others over disputable matters. Paul was handing over to Satan anyone who dared contradict him. He even called Peter a hypocrite after being contradicted by him.) One man's faith allows him to eat everything, but another man, whose faith is weak, eats only vegetables. The man who eats everything must not look down on him who does not, and the man who does not eat everything must not condemn the man who does. For God has accepted him. Who are you to judge someone else's servant? (Yes, who are you Paul to allow yourself to judge another man, and this even without being present and without being sat on a throne? See Paul in;)

1 Corinthians 5, 3. 'Even though I (Paul) am not physically present, I am with you in spirit. And I have already passed judgement on the one who did this, just as if I was present.'

'To his own master he stands or falls. And he will stand, for the Lord (here Paul would have said, 'Christ,' instead of the Lord,) is able to make him stand. One man considers one day more sacred than another, another man considers every day alike. Each one should be fully convinced in his own mind. (The author here, no matter who he is, has missed the opportunity to speak about the day of the Lord, the Sabbath day, the last day of the week; which is a very important commandment in the Law of God.) He who regards one day as special, does so to the Lord. He who eats meat, eats to the Lord, for he gives thanks to God; and he who abstains; does so to the Lord and gives thanks to God. For none of us lives to himself alone and none of us dies to himself alone. If we live, we live for the Lord; and if we die, we die for the Lord. So, whether we live or die, we belong to the Lord. (Here again, Paul would have said, 'Christ,' instead of the Lord, as it is in what is following. He might have thought that saying, 'Christ,' three times in the same phrase was a bit too much. But in the next phrase, we are back to the way of Paul to write about Jesus, the Lord.) For this very reason, Christ died and returned to life so that he might be the Lord of both the dead and the living. (This is not only taking the name of the Lord without respect, but it is also blasphemy. If Jesus was the Lord of the dead; there would be no more sinners. Don't forget that the Christians and many others are saying that Jesus is God, but see what Jesus, the Messiah, said about God, about the Father who is in heaven in;)

Matthew 22, 31-32. 'But about the resurrection of the dead—have you not read what God said to you? 'I am the God of Abraham, the God of Isaac, and the God of Jacob.' God is not the God of the dead but of the living.'

(This is again the exact opposite of what we have just read from Paul's part. What I understand here, is that, either it is from Paul, or from one of his disciples, he put this blasphemy in the middle of one of the Jesus' disciples writings. This is what we can realize when we read what is next.)

'You, then, why do you judge your brother? Or why do you look down on your brother? For we will all stand before God's judgement seat. (It is yours to answer, Paul) It is written: "'As surely as I live,' says the Lord, 'every knee will bow before Me; every tongue will confess to God.'" (One thing is very sure; this is not done yet.) So then, each of us will give an account of himself to God. Therefore let us stop passing judgement on one another. Instead, make up your mind not to put any stumbling block or obstacle in your brother's way. (Unless he is completely crazy; this was not written by Paul, because he later on himself judged others and even taught his disciples to do it too. It is true though that Paul could allow himself to do it, because he claimed to be God himself. See Paul in;)

1 Corinthians 6, 2-3. 'Or do you not know that the saints will judge the world? If the world is judge by you, are you not competent to constitute the smallest law courts? Do you not know that we will judge the angels? How much more matters of this life?'

(It is true too that Paul mentioned once speaking as a fool and to receive him as a fool. It is a bit farther in 2 Corinthians, 11, 16-30. You will see at the same time if Paul has preached Jesus, the Messiah and his sufferings, or if Paul has preached Paul and his own problems.)

'As one is in the Lord Jesus, I am fully convinced that no food is unclean in itself. (Shit remains unclean, either you believe it is unclean or not.) But if anyone regards something as unclean, then for him it is unclean. (How false this is! One has to remember what God said through the prophets and that the Messiah declared that not the least stroke of a pen will disappear from the Law. He has also said he didn't come to abolish the prophets. Read now this here in Isaiah 65, 4, Isaiah 66, 17 and;)

Leviticus 11, 6-8. 'The (wild) rabbit, though it chews the cud, does not have a split hoof; it is unclean for you. And the <u>pig</u>, though it has a split hoof completely divided, does not chew the cud, it is unclean for you. You must not eat their meat or touch their carcasses; they are unclean for you.'

(There is absolutely nothing incomprehensible or mysterious in these few lines. And we wonder why there are so many cases of cancer in the world. What are the consequences for not listening to God? What did God say will happen to those who are not listening? "Their blood will be on their own heads." This is death. How many dies from cancer every year? And why? This is because people are listening to Paul; people are listening to Satan instead of listening to God. This is why! God is our Creator, then, He knows better than anyone what is good or not for us.)

'Do not by your eating destroy your brother for whom <u>Christ</u> died. (Jesus died while teaching us the truth and love for our neighbour or for our brother is indeed to show him the truth, either it hurts him or not. To deprive our neighbour or our brother from the truth for fear to hurt him is completely contrary to the will of God and contrary to the teaching of the Messiah. And again, this can only come from Jesus' enemy, from the one who says, 'Christ,' instead of, 'the Lord; while talking about the Messiah.')

'Do not allow what you consider good to be spoken of as evil. For the <u>kingdom of God</u> is not a matter of eating and drinking, but of righteousness, peace and joy in the Holy Spirit, (all along his ministry, Jesus, the Messiah, has preached mainly the <u>kingdom of heaven</u> and not so much the kingdom of God. And for those who are not aware of it; these two kingdoms are different and distinct from one another. But Mark, Luke, the John of Paul and Paul have spoken about the kingdom of God and this without ever mentioning Jesus' kingdom, the kingdom of heaven. The kingdom of God will only exist after the end of this world, after the last judgement for the human beings, while the kingdom of heaven, Jesus' kingdom, exists since the beginning of the Messiah's ministry. 'Repent, for the kingdom of heaven <u>is</u> near.' The kingdom of heaven is present, now. As for the kingdom of God; the Messiah talked about it too, and here is what he said about it in;)

Matthew 13, 43. 'Then the righteous <u>will</u> (future) shine like the sun in the kingdom of their Father.'

(The kingdom of God is to come for us. Those who follow Jesus know this. Those who follow Paul ignore it, because Paul has preached Paul. But the Jesus' disciples are preaching Jesus, the Messiah, and his messages, then the truth, the word of God.)

'Because anyone who serves <u>Christ</u> (this is Paul's way) in this way is pleasing to God and approved by men. Let us therefore make every effort to do what leads to peace and to mutual edification. Do not destroy the work of God for the sake of food. (Pork) All food is clean, (we all know that this is false, this is a lie again,) but it is wrong for a man to eat anything that causes someone else to stumble. It is better not to eat meat or drink wine (then why one of his disciples said that Jesus has made up to 180 gallons of it?,) or to do anything else that will cause your brother to fall. So whatever you believe about these things keep between yourself and God. (This is not quite the teaching of Jesus. To go and to preach everything that Jesus has prescribed; this is not to keep for ourselves the truth. Besides, see what is written in Romans 1, 18, and this apparently by the same author.)

Romans 1, 18. 'The wrath of God is being revealed from heaven against all the godlessness and wickedness of men (women) who suppress the truth by wickedness.'

(Apparently also, this didn't seem to scare Paul and Satan. At least, up until now anyway.)

'Blessed is the man who does not condemn himself by what he approves. But the man who has doubts is condemned if he eats, because his eating is not from faith; and everything that does not come from faith is sin. (What a pile of rubbishes these are again. Besides, Paul's condemnation, he can put it where I think. It is God's condemnation someone has to fear; just like Jesus said it. Then, according to this author, no matter who he is, I am sinning and I will be condemned because I am not convinced that Paul is telling the truth.????? And if I kill someone, and I am not convinced it is a crime or a sin; I don't sin. As I just said it; this is completely rubbish. This is most likely why Paul had a clear conscience after killing many Jesus' disciples. This devil didn't commit a sin by killing his neighbour, because he was convinced it was not a sin to kill. He, who knew the Law of God more than anyone else in the country.)

'We who are strong ought to bear with the fallings of the weak and not to please ourselves. Each of us should please his neighbour for his good, to build him up. For even Christ (Paul's way again) did not please himself but, as it is written: "The insults of those who insult you have fallen on me." For everything that was written in the past was written to teach us, so that through endurance and the encouragement of the Scriptures we might have hope.'

(Then the tone changes completely from here and so does the appellation of the name of the Messiah.)

'May the God who gives endurance and encouragement give you the spirit of unity among yourselves as your fellow Christ Jesus, so that with one heart and mouth you may glorify the God and Father of our Lord Jesus Christ.'

(And then, we are back again to the way of Paul.)

'Accept one another, then, just as Christ accepted you, in order to bring praise to God. For I tell you that Christ has become a servant of the Jews on behalf of God's truth, to confirm the promise made to the patriarchs so that the Gentiles may glorify God for his mercy, as it is written: "Therefore I will praise You among the Gentiles; I will sing hymns to your Name." Again, it says, "Rejoice, O Gentiles, with his people." (This is also to come.) And again, "Praise the Lord, all you Gentiles and sing praises to Him, all you people." (This too is still to come.) And again, Isaiah says, "The root of Jesse (if Jesus is the root of Jesse; he is not someone I would call, 'God,' but I say he is the word of God. This is to be a God's prophet; just as God said Jesus is. This is not quite the same, isn't it???? And if Jesus is the root of Jesse, he is not the root of the Holy Spirit; like the liars said he is,) will spring up, one who will arise to rule over the nations; the Gentiles will hope in him."

(And this is to accomplish the word of God, brought to us through the prophets. God who said He will put a descendent of David on the throne of Israel to reign forever. This is not to be God, but a servant of God. God didn't say that He will put Himself on the throne of Israel, but He said He will put a descendant of David. But why so many people are making God a liar? Again, this is because they are listening to the liars, they are listening to Paul and to Satan.

Paul, to tell the truth, for someone who said he was sent by Jesus didn't preach much about Jesus, but he mentioned many times the ancient prophets, and this was mainly to try to give himself some credits. This proves that he was instructed about the Scriptures, but doesn't prove at all he was a Jesus' disciples. And again, when Paul said, 'Isaiah says,' he lied, because this was not coming from Isaiah, but from God, through the mouth of Isaiah.

And as I said it before; none of Jesus' apostles or Jesus' disciples would have spoke about our Master by just saying, 'Christ.')

'May the God of hope fill you with all joy and peace as you trust in Him, so you may overflow with hope by the power of the Holy Spirit. I myself am convinced, (well, if he was not convinced; he would have sin, according to himself,) my brothers, that you yourselves are full of goodness, complete in knowledge and competent to instruct one another. I have written you quite boldly on some points, as if to remind you of them again, because of the grace God gave to me to be a minister of Christ Jesus to the Gentiles (what was Paul doing then, on his way, in all the synagogues, there where were no gentile at all?)

'With the priestly duty of proclaiming the gospel of God, so that the Gentiles might become an offering acceptable to God,'

(The Gentiles, who according to Paul are nothing. This is quite an offering acceptable to God, isn't it? Jesus had a much better opinion of us, when he said this in;)

Matthew 10, 29-31. 'Are not two sparrows sold for a penny? Yet not one of them will fall on the ground apart from the will of your Father. And even the very hairs of your head are all numbered. So don't be afraid; you are worth more than many sparrows.'

(I don't know exactly how much we worth, but I am sure it is more than nothing, according to the Messiah anyway. And if you are worth nothing; this is because you are following Paul. Someone has to laugh once in a while, at least I do.)

'Sanctified by the Holy Spirit. Therefore I glorify (in French, he also said, 'myself,' in Christ Jesus in my service to God.'

(We all know now that the devil always wants to glorify himself and this even about his weaknesses and this to the point of taking God's place. This is what he has done in the heart of many, many people.)

'I will not venture to speak of anything except what Christ has accomplished through me in leading the Gentiles to obey (to obey who? What? Because Paul didn't think that a person could be justified by observing the Law of God. This is what he said in this same false gospel, in Romans 3, 28.)

'God by what I have said and done—by the signs and miracles, through the power of the Spirit. So from Jerusalem all the way around to Illyricum, I have fully proclaimed the gospel of Christ.'

(For what I read in this gospel; I would rather call it the gospel of Paul.

Let's see one of the main warnings from the Messiah in;)

Matthew 24, 24. 'For false Christs and false prophets will appear and perform great signs and miracles to deceive even the elect—if that were possible.'

(This is what Paul is and also what he has done. I have read many times the holy gospel of Jesus that is mainly written in the book of Matthew and the only thing I could find where Paul is saying the same thing than Jesus is this, 'love one another.' And this is also something that all the wicked people on earth can do just as well as the righteous. But Paul couldn't say what the first and the main God's commandment is; which is this; 'Love the Lord your God with all your heart, with all your soul and with all your mind.'

(To ask why he could not do it is kind of answering the question; it is because Satan hates God.)

'It has always been my ambition to preach the gospel where Christ was not known,'

(Sure, this way it was much easier to make anyone swallow the lies. But this must have been difficult, because there was and there are Jews just about everywhere in the world. We have seen this in;)

Acts 21, 27. 'The Jews from the province of Asia.'

(It was also probably why Paul was entering all the synagogues, but the thing was that the Jews knew the word of God as much as Paul did and they wouldn't swallow his lies, his venom.)

'So that I would not be building on someone else's foundation.'

(This is clear enough. Paul didn't want to continue Jesus' plan and neither continue Jesus' ministry. Paul wanted to make one of his own and this is what he has done with his empire of diabolic religions.)

'Rather, as it is written: "Those who were not told about him will see, and those who have not heard will understand."'

(I made a search about this in the whole Bible to find these same words and I couldn't find them. So I don't really know if they were really written or invented by Paul. What I found about, 'those who will see and those who will understand,' is from Jesus and is written in;)

Matthew 13, 15. 'For this people's (Israel) heart has become calloused; they hardly hear with their ears, and they have closed their eyes. Otherwise they might see with their eyes, hear with their ears, understand with their hearts and turn, and I (Jesus) would heal them.'

(Jesus said they were sick, because they have not believed nor received the Messiah, the one God sent to us.

Paul's lying gospel was preached just about everywhere in the world, then by the church of Rome. But Jesus' messages were preached by his disciples who were scattered, dispersed by Paul and company. Let's see again;)

Acts 8, 1-4. 'And Saul (Paul) was there, giving approval to his (Stephen's) death. On that day a great persecution broke out against the Church of Jerusalem, (they didn't say how many were killed) and all except the apostles were scattered throughout Judea and Samaria. Godly men buried Stephen and mourned deeply for him. But Saul (Paul) began to destroy the Church. (Jesus' disciples) Going from house to house, he dragged off men and women and put them in prison. <u>Those</u> who had been <u>scattered</u> <u>preached</u> the word (the truth) wherever they went.'

(Jesus' disciples were preaching Jesus' gospel, just as Matthew did it.)

'This is why I have often been hindered from coming to you. But now that there is no more place for me to work in these regions,'

(Paul must have been banished from all the synagogues at that time, because the word of God has no end and is an every day duty.)

'And since I have been longing for many years to see you, I plan to do so when I go to Spain. I hope to visit you while passing through and to have you to assist me on my journey there, after I have enjoyed your company for a while.'

(There are two things here. First, the one who speaks preaches the one who speaks. This is again the, 'I, I, I, I, me. me, me.' As many say; it is me, myself and I. The other thing is; there is no way that a Jesus' disciple would have planed a trip to the Romans in Rome. Not even Peter, the man to whom the Messiah gave the keys of the kingdom of heaven and to whom the same Messiah said not to go among the Gentiles.)

'Now, however, I am on my way to Jerusalem in the service of the saints,'

(Paul must be the one who started this business to call men, 'saints,' because the Messiah said that only One is good, and he was not even talking about himself, but about the Father who is in heaven. And isn't he, Paul, who would have written this here in this same gospel;)

Romans 3, 23. 'For all have sinned and fall short of the glory of God.'

(So, how could he say there were men who were saints then? This is because he is one of the worse kind of diabolic liars. See again;)

John 8, 44. 'He was a murderer from the beginning, not holding to the truth, for there is no truth in him. When he lies, he speaks his native language, for he is a murderer, a liar and the father of lies.'

(I think this is clear enough.)

'Now, however, I am on my way to Jerusalem in the service of the saints there. For Macedonia and Achaia were pleased to make a contribution (under Paul's orders) for the poor among the saints in Jerusalem.'

(Never an apostle or a Jesus' disciple has reported a gift coming from Paul to the Church of Jerusalem. And if this was the case, the Jesus' apostles wouldn't have managed to get rid of him as quick as they did, and I think they really are the ones who planned Paul's trip to Rome. See for yourselves by reading Acts 21, 18-21.

Then the apostles set up the trap for Paul, and it worked. Paul was put on his way to Rome; there where he built the roman church, and this is something that none of Jesus' disciples could have done.)

'They were pleased to do it, and indeed they owe it to them. For if the Gentiles have shared in the Jews' spiritual blessings, they owe it to the Jews to share with them their material task and have made sure that they have received this fruit.'

(This is also contrary to the Messiah's teaching, who said, 'You have received freely, give freely.')

'So after I have completed this task and have made sure that they have received this fruit, I will go to Spain and visit you on the way. I know that when I come to you, I will come in the full measure of the blessing of Christ.'

(And then, the tone has changed again with what comes next.)

'I urge you, brothers, by our Lord Jesus Christ and by the love of the Spirit to join me in my struggle by praying to God for me. Pray that I may be rescued from the unbelievers in Judea and that my service in Jerusalem may be acceptable to the saints there, so that by God's will I may come to you with joy and together with you be refreshed. The God of peace be with you all. Amen.'

(Believe it, the money that Paul was collecting was not for the Jews of Jerusalem that he hated with passion, but it was going to Rome and this from the very first day. And this is still the way today with the churches that he has founded. It has to be someone else than Paul who brought the gifts to the saints of Jerusalem. What is next is proving this.)

'I command you our sister Phoebe, a servant (in my French Bible, instead of servant, the word is deaconess,) of the church in Cenchrea. I ask you to receive her in the Lord in a way worthy of the saints and to give her any help she may need from you, for she has been a great help to many people, including me.'

(This couldn't be coming from Paul either, because Paul said that women have no right to speak in churches, but a deacon or a deaconess is indeed a person who has something to say in churches. See Paul in;)

1 Corinthians 14, 33-34. 'For God is not a God of disorder, (contrary to the devil) but of peace. As in all the congregations of the saints, women should remain silent in the churches, they are not allow to speak, they must be in submission, as the Law says.'

(Paul must have been talking about a roman's law, because to him, the Law of God was, 'obsolete,' and, 'the old way of the written code.' See that abomination in Romans 7, 6. Paul didn't care one bit for the Law of God and I really think this is because the Law demand to love God with all of our heart. This is very far from being Satan's will, God's main enemy. See what James, Jesus' brother and the other Jesus' apostles had to say about Paul and this in his advanced ministry.)

Acts 20, 21. 'When they heard this, they (the Jesus' apostles) praised God. (They knew then that Paul was finally caught.) Then they said to Paul: 'You see, brother, (brother, I doubt) how many thousands of Jews have believed, and all of them are zealous for the Law. (But Paul was to teach only to the Gentiles, so what was he doing in all the synagogues?) They have been informed that you teach all the Jews who live among the Gentiles to turn away from Moses, (away from the Law of God, away from God's commandments and away from the circumcision,) telling them not to circumcise their children (an everlasting covenant between God and all of the Jews) or live according to our customs.'

(The customs of the Jews are indeed to obey God's commandments and to be circumcised.)

'Greet Priscilla and Aquila, my fellow workers in Christ Jesus. They risked their lives for me. Not only I but <u>all the churches</u> of the Gentiles are grateful to them.'

(But as we read in the book of the Acts; we can see that all Paul did was to enter in the synagogues of the Jews everywhere on his way; which is the opposite of what he was supposed to do. See Paul in;)

Galatians 2, 7-9. 'On the contrary, they saw that I (Paul) had been entrusted with the task of preaching the gospel to the Gentiles, just as Peter as been to the Jews. James, (Jesus' brother) Peter and John, those reputed to be pillars gave me (Paul) and Barnabas the right hand of fellowship when they recognized the grace given to me. (Why not a bit of boasting, when he's at it?) They agreed that we (Paul and company) should go to the Gentiles and they to the Jews.'

(The right hand of fellowship didn't mean much to James, to Peter and to John, as far as Paul was concerned, because they got rid of Paul as soon as the first opportunity showed up. They did this for a very good reason too, because Paul was preaching against the Law of God, against the God's commandments and against the circumcision to the Jews. James and the other apostles had understood by that time, just like I did, that Paul was rather sent by the devil. We have to remember too that this story was told by Paul and written by Luke and that they are both liars. The apostles did this with a very smart plan too, and you can read the rest of it in Acts 21, 22-26.

You'll be able to read also, as you keep reading on, Paul's problems and how he lied to get out of them. But the Jesus' apostles, guided by the Holy Spirit, got rid of Paul for a couple of years, because he was kept in prison and he lived in Rome after that.

During that time the Jesus' disciples could preach the word of God, the truth, the Jesus' messages a bit more with peace.

You will notice also that Paul has many churches and just about everywhere, contrary to Jesus, the Messiah, who has founded only One. Jesus' Church includes all of the Jesus' disciples, who are all brothers. So, we have no other father than the Father who is in heaven. Then we have no priests, no bishop, no cardinal, no archbishop, no pope and no other pastor than Jesus, the Messiah. This is because that we, the Jesus' disciples, are following Jesus, the word of God, the truth.)

'Greet also the church that meets at their house. Greet my dear friend Epenetus, who was the first <u>convert</u>'

(See what Jesus said in;)

Matthew 23, 15. 'Woe to you, teachers of the Law and Pharisees, (deacons, priests, pastors, bishops, archbishops, cardinals and popes,) you hypocrites! You travel over land and sea to win a single convert, and when he becomes one, you make him (or her) a son of hell twice as much as you are.'

(This is exactly what Paul has done. His disciples have done it too and they still do the very same thing.)

'To Christ in the province of Asia.

Greet Mary, who worked very hard for you.

Greet Andronicus and Junias, my relatives who have been in prison with me. They are outstanding (better than the apostles) among the apostles, and they were in Christ before me.

Greet Ampliatus, whom I love in the Lord.

Greet Urbanus, our fellow worker in Christ, and my dear friend Stachys.

Greet Apelles, tested and approved in Christ.

Greet those who belong to the household of Aristobulus.

Greet Herodion, my relative.' (Would this be Herod the tetrarch, who was brought up with Paul? Paul didn't seem to have anything good to say about this one in is whole litany of salutations. Maybe it is because Herod didn't lift a little finger to help Paul while he was in trial against the Jews. Who knows?)

'Greet those in the household of Narcissus who are in the Lord.

Greet Tryphena and Tryphosa, those women who work hard in the Lord.

Greet my dear friend Persis, another woman who has worked very hard in the Lord.'

Greet Rufus, chosen in the Lord, and his mother, who has been a mother to me, too.'

(In my French Bible and in another Bible; Paul didn't say, 'has been a mother to me,' but he said that, 'is my mother.' Was he ashamed of her or her of him?

Greet Asyncritus, Phlegon, Hermes, Patrobas, Hermas and the brothers with him.

Greet Philologus, Julia, Nereus and his sister, and Olympas and all the saints with them.

Greet one another with a holy kiss. All the churches of Christ send greetings.

(Jesus, who is the Christ, as Peter said he is, has founded only One Church and all the members are all brothers. It is a Church where there is only one Father and He is the One who is in heaven. There is also only one Master and this is Jesus, the Messiah.

The one who has all of those churches is Paul, the devil and his members are not all brothers, because their leaders are either their fathers or their pastors, which is the same thing, and they are positioned above the others. The fact is that, from the nuns and friars and deacons; all the way to the pope; this is a pyramidal system.

They are not then the Church that the Messiah has founded.

If you have noticed, at times the author wrote many times, 'Christ, Christ, Christ,' and at other times, he wrote, 'Lord, Lord, Lord.' I think he too thought that to write too many, 'Christs,' in a row, would hit the eye of the reader. I also think that the, 'Christ,' mentioned by this author, either it is Paul or someone else, he is the false Christ that we find in the Gospel of Mark, of Luke and in the gospel of the John of Paul, who has also wrote the Revelation. Remember what we can read in Matthew 24, 24.

One has to know also that at the time of Paul; the Antichrist was already in the world.)

See 1 John 4, 3. 'But every spirit that does not acknowledge Jesus is not from God. This is the spirit of the Antichrist, which you have heard his coming and even now is already in the world.'

(And yet, the world is waiting for the Antichrist, just as it is waiting for the coming of the Messiah. The Antichrist has already been in the world for almost two thousand years and it is he who is still leading all the churches and the religions, except Jesus' Church, of course. It is also he who contradicts the Jesus' messages. Then, which were the Messiah's last words?)

See Matthew 28, 20. 'And surely I am with you always, to the very end of the age.'

(And he, the Messiah, you can and you must believe, because he is not a liar. He is the word of God, he is the truth.)

'I urge you, brothers, to watch out for those who cause divisions and put obstacles in your way that are contrary from the (lying) teaching you have learned. Keep away from them.'

(This is the typical teaching of Paul and company, because Jesus, the Messiah, has taught the exact opposite. See to start with what the Jews had to say about Paul in;)

Acts 24, 5-6. 'We have found this man to be a troublemaker, stirring up riots (divisions) among the Jews, all over the world. He is a ringleader of the Nazarene sect and even tried to desecrate the temple.'

(One has to wonder who was causing more divisions than the other.??? See Paul in;)

Titus 3, 10-11. 'Warn a divisive person once, and then warn him a second time. After that, have nothing to do with him. You may be sure that such a man is warped and sinful; he is self-condemned.'

(This is what Paul did all along his so-called ministry, causing divisions. So, if his disciples had properly listened to Paul; they should have had nothing to do with him. And if we look at the number of Christian religions there are in the world; Paul is still doing it. It is ironic but Paul's churches have multiplied by their divisions.

Then let's see what Jesus came to do on the earth besides preaching the word of God in;)

Matthew 10, 34-36. 'Do not suppose that I (the word of God) have come to bring peace on the earth. I did not come to bring peace but a sword. For I have come to turn "'a man against his father, a daughter against her mother, a daughter-in-law against her mother-in-law—(these are divisions) a man enemies will be the members of his own household.'

(What was Paul saying about such a man like Jesus, the Messiah, and about such a divisive person? Ho yes, he said that, 'such a man is warped and sinful; and he is self-condemned.'

(When I was saying that Paul condemns everybody and this includes the Messiah and the God's angels! This is just another example among many others.

Jesus is the word of God, and the word of God is also a sharp sword that splits between the truth and the lies. And if it causes divisions; this is because some people believe in it and others don't. Those who were causing divisions around Paul's disciples were most likely some Jesus' disciples, who were telling them the truth. This was not pleasing Paul at all; he who was preaching against the Law of God, as we saw it.

This was a sure thing that having some Jesus' disciples around; those who were contradicting Paul by telling the truth; were not welcome to Paul. This is what the truth, the word of God does; causing divisions even among the members of the same family. I can assure you that this is a case in my own family.

If some men thought it was the right thing to say, and to teach to stay away from such man as the Messiah; this is because it is not good for Satan and his ministry.

Why it is that way and why the Messiah said it? This is very simple. There has been, there are and there will be people who believe the truth and this right to the end. There will also be others who will oppose the truth. This is too bad, but this is the way it is.)

'For such people are not serving our Lord Christ, but their own appetites. By smooth talk and flattery they deceive the minds of naïve people. Everyone has heard about your obedience,' (isn't that flattery???,) so I am full of joy over you; (isn't that smooth talk???,) but I want you to be wise about what is good, and innocent about what is evil.'

(Such a phrases as the next two cannot be coming from Paul or from Satan; otherwise his kingdom would have not subsisted to this day and seeing what is happening in his world today; Satan is always there and still at work.)

'The God of peace will soon crush Satan under your feet. The grace of our Lord Jesus be with you.

Timothy, my fellow worker, (and under Paul's orders) sends his greetings to you, as do Lucius, Jason and Sosipater, my relatives.

I, Tertius, who wrote down this letter, greet you in the Lord.

Gaius, whose hospitality I and the whole church here enjoy, sends you his greetings.'

(According to the beginning of this gospel; the Romans, these letters were from Paul. First his name was Saul, and then it was changed to Paul. But since Paul became all things to all men; maybe he became Tertius to continue his seduction. We also saw that Paul liked to give orders to his disciples. Which means then that he was not equal to them, but above them and as he said; he was their father.)

See also Acts 17, 15. 'The men who escorted Paul brought him to Athens and then left with instructions'

(Here in my French Bible, instead of, 'instructions,' it is written, 'orders.' And in the King James, it is written, 'commandment.')

'For Silas and Timothy to join him as soon as possible.'

See also Colossians 4, 10-11. 'My fellow prisoner Aristarchus sends you his greetings, as does Markus, the cousin of Barnabas. You have received instructions (orders, commandments) about him, if he comes to you, welcome him. Jesus, who is call Justus, (just us) also sends greetings. These are the only Jews (2) among my fellow workers for the <u>kingdom of God</u>, and they have proved a comfort to me.'

(This was said late in Paul's ministry. It is nice to find out that only two Jews were caught by this Antichrist. We saw that Gaius was also mentioned earlier.)

See Acts 19, 29. 'The people seized Gaius and Aristarchus, Paul's travelling companions from Macedonia, and rushed as one man into the theater.'

(And I continue with;)

Romans 16, 23. 'Erastus, who is the city's director of public works, and our brother Quartus send you their greetings.'

(We take the credit where we can, don't we?

Romans 16, 24, in the New International Version Bible. This verse doesn't exist at all. I couldn't help but to let a bad word out.

Romans 16, 24, in my French Bible. 'Que la grâce de notre Seigneur Jésus Christ soit avec vous tous! Amen!'

(This is the exact same thing then what is written in the King James Bible.)

Romans 16, 24, in the King James Bible 1976. 'The peace of our Lord Jesus Christ be with you all. Amen.'

(The Ten Commandments written in Exodus 20, 4 of the same Bible; it says not to make any image of what is above, down on earth or under the waters, but this Bible contains hundreds of them.)

Romans 16, 24, from an 1882 Bible. 'The peace of our Lord Jesus Christ be with you all. Amen.'

((This is not from Paul or from one of his disciples, but it is from a Jesus' disciple. Let's see the rest of Romans now.)

'Now to Him who is able to establish you by my gospel and the proclamation of Jesus Christ, according to the revelation of the mystery hidden for long ages past, but now revealed and made known through the prophetic writings by the command of the Eternal God, so all nations might believe and obey Him—(here in the French Bible and in the King James; it is rather written,) 'made known to all nations for the obedience of faith.'

(Jesus and one of his disciples would have rather said, 'for the obedience of the commandments, of the Law of God.' This is because they knew that faith without deeds is dead,)

'To the only wise God be glory forever through Jesus Christ.'

(And this whole gospel, if we can call it a gospel, ends like it has started, meaning with a declaration coming from a Jesus' disciple, and this to mislead people and to make the lies accepted. Those lies were put among the truth coming from the Jesus' disciples. There was a very serious reason why the Messiah spoke about the parable of the weeds. He knew what was coming and what the wicked intentions of the devil were.

The same thing was repeated in almost all of Paul's letters to his so-called children; he who is the father of many, according to his own testimony.

In conclusion about all of these lies written in these letters from Paul to the Romans; it is very clear to me that this whole relentlessness to make people believe, mainly the Gentiles, because the Jews didn't buy Paul's lies, that the Messiah died on the cross to save the sinners, or to justify them; was simply a lie to take the blame off the Romans for the death of Jesus.

It is a sure thing that it would have been a lot more difficult for Paul and the Romans to build their gigantic religious empire, by saying they are responsible for the death of the Messiah. But by saying that the Messiah was sacrificed by his heavenly Father, by God; this way there were washing their hands about it, just like Pilate did it.

The Romans most likely had already in mind this religious system, this diabolic empire they have built, Christianity, and to do it; they absolutely had to make others carry the odious of that crime on someone else than them. And what better for them than to blame this abomination on God, who would have sacrificed His only Son? God who said that to do such a thing is an abomination. He is crafty the enemy.

Some people will ask me why God would let such a thing happen. When God has created man and woman, He let them free to obey Him or not, but not before telling them what would be the consequences. When God rose up a prophet like Moses, the Messiah, to justify many with his knowledge about the word of God; again He let people free to believe him or not and to listen to him or not, but again; He made people know also what would be the consequences in either cases. Then people would be able either to blame themselves or to congratulate themselves about their own choices.

God let us know through his Messiah that to obtain eternal life; we have to obey his Laws, to obey his commandments.

Satan to the contrary said that to be justified we have to believe, to have faith in, 'Christ.'

We are all free to believe in whom we want to, but hopefully, now you know the consequences also.

I finally went through Romans, but I repeat it; this seemed to my endless, and just like Jesus said it; this was also desolation for me to see all of these abominations in the Holy Place. To see the desolation in the New Testament of the Holy Bible. See Matthew 24, 15.

CHAPTER 6

1 Corinthians

Paul's disguised letters headings.

How disguised, will you ask me? By some letters that Paul used and made it look they were from him, while in reality, they actually are from a Jesus' disciple or from a Jesus' apostle. I know for example and this is because I paid attention to what I read, as Jesus, the Messiah, asked me to do, that Paul could not say, "Our Lord Jesus Christ,' just as he could not say; 'loving God with all of his heart.' And this is something that all of the Jesus' disciples could do and still do with pride and joy in their heart. When Paul was speaking about the Messiah; he was saying just, 'Christ,' as we can see in all of his letters, including these ones here in Corinthians.

Another thing that is very typical and distinct with Paul is that he said being the father of his disciples and he called them; 'my children.' Just as God has many children; Satan too has many demons. I am sure that this is a thing none of the Jesus' disciples or apostles have done, because they were listening to the Messiah who said this here in;)

Matthew 23, 8-9. 'But you (my disciples) are not to be called 'Rabbi,' for you have only one Master and you are all brothers. And do not call anyone on earth 'father,' for you have one Father, and He is in heaven.'

(So yes, I am sure that the Jesus' disciples, even those of nowadays, as they were in the time of the Messiah; they didn't let anyone call them, 'father,' and they don't call anyone, 'father or pastor,' other than their biological father or father-in-law or step-father.

From 1 Corinthians 1, 1-13, we can see the two versions, the one from a Jesus' disciple, who can say, 'Our Lord Jesus Christ,' and the other version from Paul, who spoke about the Messiah by just saying, 'Christ or Christ Jesus.' This is Jesus Christ backward. Do you know what Christian read backward is? It is an-ti-chris.

1 Corinthians 1, 1-13. 'Paul called to be an apostle of Christ Jesus by the will of God, and our brother Sosthenes. To the Church of God in Corinth to those sanctified in Christ Jesus and called to be holy, together with all those everywhere who call on the name of our Lord Jesus Christ—their Lord and ours: Grace and peace from God our Father and the Lord Jesus Christ.

I always thank God for you because of his grace given to you in Christ Jesus. For in him you have been enriched in every way—in all your speaking and in all your knowledge—because our testimony about Christ (this is from Paul) was confirmed to you. Therefore you do not lack any spiritual gift as you eagerly wait for our Lord Jesus Christ (this is from a Jesus' disciple) to be revealed. He will keep you strong to the end, so that you will be blameless on the day of our Lord Jesus Christ. God, who has called you into fellowship with his Son Jesus Christ our Lord, is faithful. I appeal to you, brothers, in the name of our Lord Jesus Christ, that all of you agree with one another so that they may be no divisions among you and that you may be perfectly united in mind and thought. My brothers, some from Chloe's household have informed me that there are quarrels among you. What I mean is this: One of you says, "I follow Paul;" another, "I follow Apollos;" another, "I follow Cephas (Peter);" still another, "I follow Christ." Is Christ divided?'

(As you can see for yourselves, it has been a very long time now since the word of God, the truth, is dividing people, just as Jesus, the Messiah said it. Since his coming there are people who follow the Messiah and others who are following Paul, his enemy.)

'Was Paul crucified for you?'

(No, but many are following him anyway. And if they were baptized by Paul; they were baptized by the spirit of the devil, by lies. Contrary to the Jesus' disciples; we are baptize by the Holy Spirit, by the word of God, by the truth and this makes a very big difference.)

'Were you baptized in the name of Paul?'

(We have seen already that Paul didn't really like baptism and he said himself that he was not sent to baptize, contrary to the Jesus' disciples.

All of us can read one of the last messages from Jesus, the Messiah, in Matthew 28, 19. All of us also know that the devil doesn't like much the holy water. The Jesus' baptism is the baptism of the Holy Spirit and the baptism of his disciples is the Baptism of the Holy Spirit also. This means they baptize with the word of God; we are baptizing with the word of God, with the Jesus' messages.

But do we really see Jesus' messages in Paul's writings? Can we read in Paul's writings about repentance; he who said his conscience was cleared after having killed Jesus' disciples. Paul, a murderer, a blasphemer, who forced others to blaspheme to have their lives saved. Can we read in Paul's writings about forgiveness; he who handed over people to Satan; those who didn't want to buy his lies and his teaching? Did Paul ever mention the Lord's Prayer, the One who is in heaven? Did Paul ever mention one of Jesus' parables? The answer to all of these questions is, never!

I will now write down a few comparisons to help you to better understand. In another word; I do this to open your eyes. This is something Jesus, the Messiah, particularly likes to do; especially to those who want to see, of course.

See Jesus in Matthew 5, 17. 'Do not think that I (Jesus) have come to abolish the Law or the <u>prophets</u>;

(who came before the Messiah) I have not come to abolish them but to fulfill them.'

(See now Paul in;)

Ephesians 2, 15. 'By abolishing in his flesh the Law with its commandments and regulations.'

Jesus, in Matthew 5, 18. 'I (Jesus) tell you the truth, until heaven and earth disappear, not the smallest letter, not the least stroke of a pen, will by any means disappear from the Law until everything is accomplished.'

See Paul in Hebrews 8, 13. 'By calling this covenant, 'New,' He (God) has made the first one obsolete and what is obsolete and ageing will soon disappear.'

(Let me make one thing straight here; it is not mainly the old covenant that Paul wanted to see disappear, but the Law of God in its entirety with its commandments and regulations, as it is written in Ephesians 2, 15. No I'm sorry, he would have keep:) 'Love your neighbour as yourself.'

(He needed a love one to play with. And this had to be a man, because he could not touch a woman, the most perfect and beautiful creature in the world.)

And if you want to know the real reason as why many peoples on this earth, mainly Paul, Rome and the Romans wanted to see Israel disappear from this world; you will find the answer in Jeremiah 31, 36.

The Romans would have killed more than a million and a half of Jews from the years 67 to 73 A.D.

This is also what Hitler, with the help of Rome tried to do with his world war from the years 1939 to 1945. And again, this was for the very same reason; to eliminate the Jews from the face of the earth. Who else than Satan could be so madly against the people of God? Six millions Jews, one third of the Jew's population on earth was killed that time.

Hitler was a big fan of Paul and he has actually repeated to his people the very same huge lie that Paul has told and this was to convince his people that the Jews must die. And his people blindly followed him. Here is the huge lie these two monsters have told in;)

1 Thessalonians 2, 14-15. 'You suffered from your own countrymen (the Jews) the same things those (Paul's) churches suffered from the Jews, who killed the Lord Jesus and the prophets and also drove us out.'

(This is also what Russia and its allies are getting ready to do against Israel as I am writing these lines. This is not for the pretty eyes of the Syrian president, Bashar al-Assad that Puttin and his army have installed themselves in Syria, closer to Israel. But what will happen to them is already prophesied in Ezekiel 38 and 39.

All the inhabitants of the earth are on the verge to see the super power of the Almighty one more time again; all of those who believe in Him and also those who don't.

Paul was so convinced that Rome and the Romans will succeed to eliminate the Jews that he had started to say the Law of God has disappeared, was abolished and this is what we can read in Ephesians 2, 15.

The Law of God is much different for a just man, for a righteous man than it was for Paul.)

See Psalms 19, 7-9. 'The Law of the Lord is perfect, reviving the soul. The Statutes of the Lord are trustworthy, making wise the simple. The precepts of the Lord are right, giving joy to the heart. The commands of the Lord are radiant, giving light to the eyes. The fear of the Lord is pure, enduring forever.'

(I said it before; the Law of God is the perfect guide to please God. See Paul now in;)

Hebrews 8, 7. 'For if there had been nothing wrong with the first covenant, no place would have been sought for another.'

(Who else than Satan would be arrogant enough to say that God did something wrong?

A new covenant doesn't necessarily mean a new Law, or at least; it doesn't abolish the Law. And it is evident too that this new covenant God has spoken about and said He will make with the house of Israel is to come to realization only after the end of this infamous world we are living in.

See again Jeremiah 31, 33. 'This is the covenant I will make with the house of Israel after that time," declares the Lord. "I will put my Law in their minds and write it in their hearts. I will be their God, and they will be my people.'

(One thing is very sure; it is not done yet. See Jesus in;)

Matthew 5, 19. 'Anyone who breaks one of the least of these commandments, (Paul broke or eliminated them all) and teaches others to do the same (Paul has done just that) will be called least in the kingdom of heaven, but whoever practices and teaches them will be called great in the kingdom of heaven.'

(This certainly didn't mean that Jesus, the Messiah, wanted to eliminate the God's commandments, as Paul said Jesus has done.

Paul's message, and there are many of them, but I chose this one here in;)

1 Corinthians 9, 20. 'To the Jews I became like a Jew, to win the Jews. To those under the Law I became like one under the Law, though <u>I myself (Paul) am not under the Law</u>, so as to win those under the Law.'

(Isn't that what we call hypocrisy nowadays? See this about Paul on the same subject, concerning breaking one of the least commandments. Paul didn't only suppress the least of the commandments, but he suppressed more than half of the first and greatest God's commandment of the Law, and this is to love God with our whole heart. See Jesus in;)

Matthew 22, 37-40. 'Love the Lord your God with all your heart and with all your soul and with all you mind. This is the greatest commandment. And the second one is like it; love your neighbour as yourself. All the Law and the Prophets hang on these two commandments.'

See Paul in;)

Galatians 5, 14. 'The entire Law is summed up in a single command: "Love your neighbour as yourself.'

(This is quite a false statement and here Paul has suppressed the greatest God's commandment and this is because he is the lawless one, the one who is not under the Law of God, and this is why he said being without sin. See Paul in;)

Romans 6, 14. 'For sin shall not be your master, (sin have no power over you) because you are <u>not</u> under Law, (like Paul is not) but under grace.'

(Paul said the sin has no power over them, because they are not under the Law, but he said also that they all have sin. What kind of grace is this? He is confusing the man.

See also Jesus in;)

Matthew 5, 23-24. 'Therefore, if you are offering your gift at the altar and there remember that your <u>brother</u> has something against you, leave there your gift in front of the altar. First go and be reconciled to your brother; then come and offer your gift.'

See Paul in;)

Acts 15, 37-39. 'Barnabas wanted to take <u>John</u>, also called <u>Mark</u>, with them, but Paul did not think it wise to take him, because he had deserted them in Pamphylia and had not continued with them in the work. (There was no forgiveness from Paul.) They had such sharp disagreement that they parted company. Barnabas took Mark and sailed for Cyprus.'

(Was that a way to reconciled? Paul was calling the scribes and the Pharisees, 'brothers,' but he was saying that he was the father of his disciples.

See also Jesus in;)

Matthew 5, 33-34. 'Again, you have heard that it was said, 'Do not break your oath, but keep the oaths you have made to the Lord.' But I (Jesus) tell you. <u>Do not swear at all</u>.'

(We should all know, don't we, that to swear is to take God as a witness? See Paul in;)

2 Corinthians 1, 23. 'I (Paul) call God as my witness that it was in order to spear you that I did not return to Corinth.'

(See also Paul in;)

Romans 1, 9. 'God, whom I serve with my whole heart in preaching the gospel of his Son, <u>is my witness</u> how constantly I remember you.'

(There are many more, but that should be enough for you to understand that Paul has acted contrary to Jesus' teaching, contrary to Jesus' messages.

See, and this is very important, because Jesus, the Messiah, said that this was from the devil, and Paul has proved this more than one way and more than once.

Matthew 5, 37. 'Simply let your 'Yes' be 'Yes,' and your 'No' be 'No;' <u>anything beyond this comes from the evil one</u>.'

(See also Jesus in;)

Matthew 5, 39. 'You have heard that it was said, 'Eye for eye, and tooth for tooth.' But I (Jesus) tell you. Do not resist an evil person. If someone strikes you on the right cheek, turn to him the other also.'

(See Paul in;)

Acts 23, 2-3. 'At this the high priest Ananias ordered those standing near Paul to strike him on the mouth. Then Paul said to him, (to the judge) 'God is going to strike you whitewashed wall!'

(This is not quite what I would call, 'turn to him the other cheek also.' If only Paul would have turned his head around, he might have got a slap behind it, because he greatly deserved it and even more. I would even say that in those days; he deserved death.)

See Matthew 5, 22. 'But I (Jesus) tell you that anyone who is angry with his brother will be subject to judgement. Again, anyone who says to his brother, 'Raca,' is answerable to the Sanhedrin. But anyone who says, 'You fool.' will be in danger of the fire of hell.'

(Then, Paul, who called them brothers, deserved all of this at once. So, a slap on the mouth was not too bad after all; depending of who gave it, of course.

(See Jesus in;)

Matthew 5, 43-45. 'You have heard that it was said, 'Love your neighbour and hate your enemy.' But I (Jesus) tell you: Love your enemies and pray for those who persecute you, that you may be sons of your Father in heaven.'

(Then, Jesus was not destined to be God's only Son, and to say that Jesus is God's only Son; this is to say that the other men are sons of the devil. This, I don't take it.

See Paul in;)

Galatians 1, 8-9. 'But even if we or <u>an angel from heaven</u> should preach a gospel other than the one we (Paul and company) preached to you, (full of lies, contradictions and abominations) let him be eternally condemned!'

(This again is for Paul to sit himself above God's angels and to condemn them is to take God's place.)

'As we have already said, so now I (Paul) say again, if anybody is preaching to you a gospel other than what you accepted, let him be eternally condemned.'

(Far from praying for those who contradicted him; Paul was cursing them and handing them over to Satan. Will Paul be blessed or damned or condemned for these wicked words, for this abomination? God will judge him, as He will judge me and as He will judge the rest of the world.

I have discovered that Paul has contradicted Jesus, the Messiah, about many, many subjects, and this is enough for me to understand that he is a bad tree and he distributes bad fruits.

See Jesus again in;)

Matthew 5, 48. 'Be perfect therefore, as your heavenly Father is perfect.'

(See Paul in;)

1 Corinthians 4, 14-16. 'I (Paul) am not writing this to shame you, but to warn you, as my dear children. Even though you have ten thousand guardians in Christ, you do not have many fathers, for in Christ Jesus I became your father through the gospel. Therefore I urge you to imitate me.'

(May God spear me from this! But this was not the first time that Paul proclaimed to be above all. I would even say more; I would say that this was claiming to be God.

Remember what was said in;)

Acts 26, 29. 'Paul replied, "Short time or long—I pray God that not only you but all who are listening to me today may become what I am, except for these chains."'

(This was said without any pretension, will you tell me? This bring us back to;)

2 Thessalonians 2, 1-4. 'Concerning the coming of our Lord Jesus Christ (this was not at all the way of Paul to speak or to write) and our being gathered to him, we ask you brothers, not to become to easily unsettled or alarmed by some prophesy, report or letter supposed to have come from us (the Jesus' apostles) saying that the day of the Lord has already come. Don't let anyone deceive you in any way, for that day will not come until the rebellion occurs and the man of lawlessness is revealed, the man doomed to destruction. (We know him now, he is revealed.) He will oppose and he will exalt himself over everything that is called God or is

worshipped, so that he sets himself in God's temple, proclaiming himself to be God.'

(And don't you go think that this was written by Paul, because this was written by one of Jesus' apostles to the Jesus' disciples.

To be Paul's imitator is to be the imitator of the man of lawlessness, imitator of the man doomed to destruction. It is also to be a murderer, a blasphemer and a liar from the beginning. There is not the smallest doubt in my mind, because Paul did and said everything contrary to what Jesus, the Messiah that God sent to us to save us with his knowledge. See Isaiah 53, 11.

See Jesus in;)

Matthew 6, 5-6. 'And when you pray, do not be like the hypocrites, for they (priests, pastors, rabbis) love to pray standing in the synagogues (in churches) and on street corners (the J……Witnesses,) to be seen by men. I (Jesus) tell you the truth; they have received their reward in full. But when you pray, <u>go into your room</u>, close the door and pray to your Father, who is unseen. Then your Father, who sees what is done in secret, will reward you.'

(See Paul now in;)

2 Timothy 2, 8. 'I (Paul) want men <u>everywhere</u> to lift up holy hands in prayer, without anger or disputing.'

(I lift my hands clean and I don't think they are holy, but they are also without anger and without disputing, to say that Paul has contradicted Jesus, just like the Messiah said it in his parable of the weeds.

See again Jesus in;)

Matthew 6, 6. 'But when you pray, go into your room, close the door and pray to <u>your Father</u>, who is unseen. Then your <u>Father</u>, who sees what is done in secret, will reward you.'

(Jesus, the Messiah, told us to pray the Father who is in heaven. From whom then comes the fact that millions of Christians and others are praying others than God? This is certainly not coming from the Messiah. You know what I mean; those who pray the Virgin Mary, who is not a virgin anymore for more than two thousand years, and also those who pray the false saints without any power. They are dead and resting in the dust. Don't they know what the Almighty has done to those who pray other god than He? 'Give to God what belongs to God,' and leave the dead rest in peace. Is this too much to ask for them?

See Jesus in;)

Matthew 6, 7-8. 'And when you pray, do not keep babbling like pagans,'

(See the rosaries, the novenas and the ways of the cross; there where a multitude of Christians are bowing before images made by men's hands; which oppose the second God's commandment.)

'For they think they will be heard because of their many words. Do not be like them (pagans) for <u>your Father</u> knows what you need before you ask Him.'

(And if Jesus, the Messiah, said that God is the Father of his disciples; this means that they too are the sons of God.

From whom then so many people have learned endless prayers, like rosaries and novenas? Yes, they have learned this from Paul's churches that contradict the Messiah, like Paul, their founder has done it.

See Jesus in;)

Matthew 6, 9-13. 'This, then, is how you should pray: "'Our Father <u>in heaven</u>, hallowed be your Name, your kingdom come, your will be done on earth as it is in heaven. Give us today our daily bread. Forgive us our debts, <u>as</u> we also have forgiven our debtors. And lead us not into temptation, but <u>deliver us</u> from the evil one.'

(Oups, there are two lines missing here in the New International Version Bible. I have then to go get them in the King James Bible. I wonder a bit why, but I do have a little idea about the reason it was deleted.

Here there are.)

'For thine is the kingdom, and the power, and the glory, for ever. Amen.'

(And why Paul has never mentioned the Lord's Prayer? This is because Paul's father is not the One who is in heaven. It is also because Paul didn't care one bit about God's will, he was incapable to forgive, and he proved it by handing people and God's angels over to Satan. What is more wicked than this and how can he allow this power to himself? This is because he is the one who, 'opposed and exalted himself over everything that is called God or is worshipped, so he has set himself up in God's temple, proclaiming himself to be God.'

(See Jesus in;)

Matthew 6, 19. 'Do not store up for yourself treasures on earth, where moth and rust destroy, and where thieves break in and steal.'

(What Paul and his multiple churches have done all over the world? We only have to look at Rome and in just about all towns and villages everywhere to see what they have accumulated through people's back. If I don't mistaking; this business is the sixth richest in the world. This is certainly not what I would call not to store up treasures on earth.

See Jesus in;)

Matthew 6, 21. 'For where your treasure is, there your heart will be also.'

(Where was Paul's heart and the mind of his churches? It is there where Paul preached Paul and there where it is the most evident is written in 2 Corinthians 11, 1-31. You will be able to see by the same occasion if Paul has preached Jesus, the Messiah, or if he has preached Paul.

See Jesus in;)

Matthew 7, 1-2. 'Do not judge, or you will be judged. For in the same way you judge others, you will be judged, and with the measure you use, it will be measured to you.'

(See now Paul in;)

1 Corinthians 5, 3. 'Even though I am not physically present, I am with you in spirit. And I have already passed judgement on the one who did this, just as if I was present.'

(But not only Paul judged others, and this contrary to the teaching of the Messiah; he also taught and incited his disciples to do it too, not to say this was most likely orders from him.

See also Paul in;)

1 Corinthians 6, 2-3. 'Or do you not know that the saints will judge the world? If the world is judge by you, are you not competent to constitute the smallest law courts? Do you not know that we will judge the angels? How much more matters of this life?'

(This though shows me in some way that there were some of those listening to Paul who knew the massages of the Messiah, for Paul to argue this way with them. They might have been handed over to Satan after that discussion though. We also know that Paul was not shy to judge an angel of heaven either, and to do so; this means that he put himself above them.

Peter spoke about those arrogant as Paul was, about someone who dares to slander the celestial beings.

2 Peter, 2. 10-11. 'This is especially true of those who follow their corrupt desire of the sinful nature and despise authority. Bold and arrogant, these men are not afraid to slander celestial beings; yet even angels, although they are stronger and more powerful, do not bring slanderous accusations against such beings in the presence of the Lord.'

(The God's angels won't do it, but Paul, the arrogant, did it. The judgement that Jesus talked about to his disciples is for the end of this actual world and they will be sitting on a throne with him to judge the twelve tribes of Israel. This has absolutely nothing to do with judging our neighbours now or then like Paul did it and has proposed it. Knowing Paul a bit better now; I think he most likely ordered it.

I don't think that Jesus talked to his disciples about judging God's angels either, because he told them not to judge.

The judgement that Paul proposed or ordered to his disciples was for his time and on and neither Paul nor his disciples were sitting on a throne to do it. Paul's churches have followed well Paul and his teaching by continuing to judge people through their confessional; which is also Antichrist. See what God said about it in;)

Jeremiah 17, 5. 'Cursed is the man who trusts in man.'

(This is the one who confesses his sins to another man, to a father who is not a father and even less the Father who is in heaven.)

'Who depends on flesh for his strength and whose heart turns away from the Lord.'

(So, God does not blame only those who call another man, 'father,' other than his biological father, but He also blames those who rely on another man for his strength. So, God blames all of those who confess their sins to another man instead of turning to God. I have the impression that this is concerning millions and millions of people and maybe billions. If all of them would follow Jesus, the Messiah, instead of following Paul; they wouldn't be in that position.

See also Jesus in;)

Matthew 19. 28. 'Jesus said to them, (his apostles) "I tell you the truth, at the renewal of all things (at the end time, not before) when the Son of Man sits on his glorious throne, you (Jesus' disciples) who have followed <u>me</u> (the Messiah) will also sit on twelve <u>thrones</u>, judging the twelve tribes of Israel."'

(This is not for Paul nor for his disciples, and not for their time either, but it is for the end time. There were people of Paul's time, who had reasons to argue against him.

See Jesus in;)

Matthew 7, 3. 'Why do you look at the speck of sawdust in your brother's eye and pay no attention to the plank in your own eye?'

(But Paul saw it without even be present.)

See 1 Corinthians 5, 3. 'Even though I am not physically present, I am with you in spirit. And I have already passed judgement on the one who did this, just as if I was present.'

(Why did Paul see or has pretended he could see without being present? This is because Paul has pretended he was the Counsellor, the supposedly Spirit of truth that the false Christ, who is in the gospel of John spoke about and said he will send after his departure. Read what is next and be careful when you read.)

John 14, 16-17. 'And I (the false Christ who is in the gospel of this John,) will ask the Father, and he will give you another Counsellor to be with you forever—the Spirit of truth. The world cannot receive Him, because it neither sees Him nor knows Him. (Who can see a ghost?) But you know Him, for He lives (present) with you and will be (future) in you.'

(This is another contradictory phrase in itself, just like Paul wrote many of them.

See also John 14, 26, John 15, 26, John 16, 7, and John 16. 13. Note also that the true Jesus, the true Messiah, who is in the Holy gospel of Matthew, has never mentioned this. This means everything to me.

Just note also that the gospel of this John is not from the John, Jesus' apostle nor from the John, Jesus' brother, but from the John, Paul's disciple. And I sincerely think that this gospel is from Paul himself. The John, Jesus' apostle was a man without any education;

so, he could not write this long gospel of John nor the Revelation.

See for your own reference;)

Acts 4, 13. 'When they saw the courage of Peter and John and realized that they were unschooled ordinary men, they were astonished and they took note that these men had been with Jesus.'

(When the true Jesus spoke about the Holy Spirit; he didn't say that He will be with us only after his own death, or when he is gone, but that it will be He who will be in us as we need it, just as He did it with Peter. And for sure, Jesus was not gone yet.

See Jesus in;)

Matthew 16, 17. 'Blessed are you, Simon son of Jonah, for this was not revealed to you by man, but my Father in heaven.'

(And yet, Jesus was still in the world and Peter didn't have to wait that Jesus was gone to his Father who is in heaven before the Holy Spirit, the Spirit of the Father speaks to men. Besides, the Holy Spirit was communicating with the Messiah continually to put in his mouth the words of God.

See also;)

Matthew 10, 19-20. 'But when they arrest you, do not worry about what to say or how to say it. At that time you will be given what to say, for it will not be you speaking, but the Spirit of your Father speaking through you.' (the Holy Spirit.

See Jesus in;)

Matthew 7, 15. 'Watch out for the false prophets, they come to you in sheep's clothing, but inwardly, they are ferocious wolves.'

(Some people were talking about them this very evening on T.V., on a show called, 'Enquête,' which means, 'inquiry.' These pedophiles, children abusers, are for most of them officials of Paul's churches. One of them got five years in jail for having abused six children during many years. When we know that a family father can get ten years for abusing one child, one has to wonder. This priest and all of them alike should be executed for the wrong they have done. Many criminals were executed for doing less harm to others. But who are those ferocious wolves in sheep's clothing? They are those who preach Paul instead of preaching Jesus. They serve Satan instead of serving God.

See Jesus in;)

Matthew 7, 16. 'By their fruits you will recognize them.'

(I did recognize them because I know the word of God. I know the truth and those who contradict the word of God are liars; they are bad trees and they have bad fruits. They are antichrists.

See Matthew 7, 21. 'Not everyone who says to me, 'Lord, Lord,' will enter the kingdom of heaven, but only he who does the will of my Father in heaven.'

See now Paul in;)

Romans 10, 13. 'For, "Everyone who calls on the name of the Lord will be saved.'

(And this is again the opposite of what the Messiah has taught. Remember the message of the Messiah who said this here in;)

Matthew 6, 24. 'No one can serve two masters. Either he will hate the one and love the other, or he will be devoted to the one and despise the other. You cannot serve both God and money.'

(One is the master of lies and the other one is the master of truth. And of course, Jesus is right and this is the reason why I cannot love Paul nor serve him, not him and not his churches, because not only he is the enemy, but he incarnates the lies and the evil one.

I Love Jesus, I love God, I love his word and I love the truth. When I decided to accept Jesus as my personal Saviour; this is the exact question I asked myself; do I want to serve God, or do I want to serve the devil? We cannot serve two masters.

See what Jesus said in;)

Matthew 12, 30. 'He who is not with me is against me, and he who does not gather with me scatters.'

(Believe it; he knows and I am on his side. Who were scattering the Jesus' disciples?

Some people will tell me: 'Yes, but didn't Jesus also say: 'I have come to call the sinners?'

(Yes, Jesus came to call the sinners to repent for their sins, to turn away from them. And those who haven done so, like Paul, who said his conscience was clear and also said he is not under the Law of God, will be told what Jesus said he will tell them. There is not much simpler then this.

So all of those who say they all have sin; you better begin to sincerely repent, because God knows the hypocrites, who believe they are saved by their faith and grace preached by the ferocious wolf.

This here is what the Messiah said he will tell them in;)

Matthew 7, 23. 'Then I (Jesus) will tell them plainly, 'I never knew you. Away from me, you evildoers.'

(The evildoers are those who have one or more sins, but the sincere repentance can erase them all. This is the Messiah's message to save us. This is how he bears our sins. This is also how he justifies many.

It will be good for you to read this again;)

Matthew 13, 41-42. 'The Son of Man (Jesus, the Messiah) will send out his angels, and they will weeds out of his kingdom (of heaven, because there is no weeds in the kingdom of God,) everything that causes sin and all who do evil. (These include the forceful men who laid hold on his kingdom, and shut it down in people's faces and all who say they all have sins.) They will throw them in the fiery furnace, where there will be weeping and gnashing of teeth.'

(See Jesus in;)

Matthew 7, 24. 'Therefore everyone who hears these words of mine (Jesus' messages) and puts them into practice is like a wise man who built his house on the rock.'

(The one who listens to Jesus' messages will be unshakable, solid facing the temptations from the devil. He will recognize the truth, and he will do what the Jesus' apostles did with Paul; he will tell him that he is a liar.

See Jesus in;)

Matthew 7, 26. 'But everyone who hears these words of mine and does not put them into practice is like a foolish man who built his house on sand.'

(No one has to be a scientist genius to understand these words and to understand that Paul didn't listen to the words of the Messiah. In any case, if Paul has listened to Jesus; he didn't put his words into practice, because he preached the opposite and this several times. But could we expect anything else from the enemy of the truth? His goal is to mislead people and for what I can see in this world; he has succeeded.

See Jesus in;)

Matthew 12, 25-26. 'Jesus knew their thoughts and said to them, "Every kingdom divided against itself will be ruined, and every household divided against itself will not stand. If Satan drives out Satan, he is divided against himself. How then can his kingdom stand?"'

(And his kingdom, we know that it is the world with all of its scandals and its corruption. We also know that the devil's kingdom is still standing, because the wickedness is spread out more than ever. If Satan would have drove out Paul; he wouldn't have seduced so many people and his kingdom would not stand anymore. His kingdom would be destroyed, it would be ruined, but this is not the case, at least not yet.

The biggest part of the people of this world is afraid of the end of it. They are right to be afraid too, especially those who all have sin. But the Jesus' disciples like I am, on the contrary, can only apprehend it, and only eagerly wish for it, because it means the end of Satan's reign and the beginning of the kingdom of God.

See Jesus in;)

Matthew 12, 36-37. 'But I tell you that men will have to give account on the day of judgement for every careless word they have spoken. For by your words you will be acquitted, and by your words you will be condemned.'

(This, by the way, was told by the one who will judge every man. Paul has also contradicted Jesus about this matter.

See Paul in;)

Romans 3, 28. 'For we (Paul and company) maintain that a man is justified by faith apart from observing the Law.'

(See Jesus in;)

Matthew 12, 40. 'For as Jonas was three days and three nights in the belly of a huge fish, so the Son of Man will be three days and three nights in the heart of the earth.'

(The Messiah, who did not lie; said he will be three days and three nights in the heart of the earth, then, who lied about that one, and said he resurrected on the third day instead of on the forth day? This was certainly not done by one of his apostles or his disciples. This was done by the enemy of the truth, the liar, who has contradicted the Messiah so many times, and we know who he is now.

See Jesus in;)

Matthew 12, 46-50. 'While Jesus was still talking to the crowd, his mother and brothers stood outside, waiting to speak to him. Someone told him, "Your mother and brothers are standing outside, wanting to speak to you. He replied to him, "Who is my mother, and who are my brothers?" Pointing to his disciples, (those who follow him and receive his words) he said, "Here are my mother and my brothers. For whoever does the will of my Father in heaven is my brother and sister and mother."'

(This was not too flattering for the brothers and the mother of Jesus that thousands of people are praying to get favours from. Listening to Jesus is not only hearing what he has to say, but it is also to put in practice his words, which is to do the will of the Father who is in heaven.

When Jesus was pointing to his disciples; he was pointing to some people who were listening to him and were putting in practice what he was preaching. This was the word of God and this is still what Jesus expects from his disciples today. Though, no one can say without lying that this was what Paul did.

There is one more thing to note in the Messiah's messages; this is that he was never shy to say that his Father is the One who is in heaven, and this is something that the false Christ who is in the gospel of John has never done.

Jesus, who is in Matthew 13, 3-23, spoke to the crowd in parables and he explained them to his disciples afterward. With this one here; he tells them that the one that received the word of God and put it in practice will make many disciples with his work.

There is no way for me to know how many sincere disciples my books will produce, and it is not important for me to know. But I know that the One who asked me to write for Him didn't do it for nothing. I am sure of one thing though; He will sooner or later make them cross all the borders.

This won't be for my glory either, but for His, because I think that I will be recognized for my work maybe, but long after my death. So I don't do it for myself, but for Him and for my neighbours.

The Messiah's parable of the weeds, written from Matthew 13, 24 to 13, 30, and explained in Matthew 13, 36 to 13, 43, is what I think the key of all the humanity. Meaning, life, death, salvation, condemnation, life on earth in the kingdom of heaven, hell and what the devil did, and finally the Kingdom of God for the righteous, the God's elected, then eternal life. This is the story of Jesus, the story of the Messiah and what he has done; which means, sowing the truth on earth, and while men were sleeping, not paying attention, his enemy, the devil came to sow the weeds, the lies.

The Messiah was so afraid that the angels could pull out the smallest part of the truth that he asked them to leave the truth and the lies together until the end of time and it will be at that time only that he will ask them to throw the devil and his angels in the fire forever. It will be then only and not before that the righteous will make their entry in the kingdom of God.

There where it will be weeping and gnashing of teeth will certainly not be a place of joy. On the other hand; knowing my God who is in heaven; I am not worry at all about the joy and the good wine I will get in his kingdom.

See what Jesus said in Matthew 13, 32.

The mustard seed is maybe the smallest of all, but when it is planted well in the good soil; it grows straight up towards the heaven. The very smallest part of the truth about the word of God can become the greatest, because it can produce one Jesus' disciple, who could produce a hundred, who could produce thousands and this is most likely the reason why Jesus, the Messiah, didn't want the angels to pull out anything before the time of the harvest.

Where and when did you see or read where Paul talked about Jesus' messages to tell the truth? No matter how much I have read and read again and again, no matter how much I have searched; I didn't see it. Even the false Christ who is in the gospel of John didn't repeat the Messiah's messages. This is kind of strange isn't it, since they are both in the New Testament of the Bible?

See Jesus in;)

Matthew 13, 43. 'Then the righteous will (future) shine like the sun in the kingdom of their Father.'

(This really means that the kingdom of God is to come, and this will be only after the end of this world. The kingdom of heaven is present since the Messiah came in the world and on earth, and see what he said in;)

Matthew 11, 12. 'From the days of John the Baptist until now, (that was then, not in the future) the kingdom of heaven has been forcefully advancing, and forceful men lay hold of it.'

(This was at the present time of the Messiah and it is still for our present time to us. I am sure that all of the Jesus' disciples have talked about it; all of the Messiah's disciples have talked about the Master's kingdom of heaven, but neither Mark, or Luke, nor the John of the gospel of John, nor Paul, nor any of Paul's disciples have mentioned it.

This is simply because none of them are or were the Messiah's disciples and remember one important message from the Messiah written in;)

Matthew 12, 30. 'He who is not with me (Jesus) is against me, and he who does not gather with me scatters.'

(Is there anything simpler than this? We have already seen the one who was scattering the Jesus' disciples in;)

Acts 8, 3-4. 'But Saul (Paul) began to destroy the Church. (Jesus' disciples) Going from house to house, he dragged off men and women and put them in prison. Those who had been <u>scattered</u> preached the word wherever they went.'

(The scattering of Jesus' disciples by Paul and the Romans didn't stop them to preach the Messiah's messages and to preach the good news about the word of God and about the kingdom of heaven.

See Matthew 14, 1-4. 'At that time Herod the tetrarch heard the reports about Jesus, and he said to his attendants, "This is John the Baptist; he has risen from the dead! That is why miraculous powers are at work in him." Now Herod had arrested John (the Baptist) and bound him and put him in prison because of Herodias, his brother Phillip's wife, for John had been saying to him, "It is not lawful for you to have her."'

(According to this, Herod the tetrarch believed in the resurrection of the dead. He is also the one who made John the Baptist beheaded and who also have James, the brother of the apostle John put to death by the sword. But according to Paul, it would have been God who put Herod in place. We should not forget that the world is the kingdom of Satan.)

See Acts 12, 1-2. 'It was about this time that King Herod arrested some who belonged to the Church, <u>intending</u> to persecute them. He had James, the brother of John put to death by the sword.'

(But the John of the gospel of John has never mentioned this. This is kind of strange, isn't it? It seems to me that this would be an event not to forget, mainly because James too was a Jesus' apostle just like his brother John.

Another thing that is quite strange is the fact that Herod the tetrarch has started to persecute the Jesus' disciples just as soon as Paul pretended to become a Jesus' apostle, meaning his entry in the sheep pen. The two of them knew each other pretty good, since they were brought up together. So the persecution had to keep going on no matter what, and Paul couldn't keep at it and at the same time pretending to have become a Jesus' disciple.

Then the killing weapon had just moved from one hand to another, but the persecution from Rome against the Jews and against the Jesus' disciples had to continue, and Herod had the proper position to keep it on.

See for your references;)

Acts 13, 1. 'In the church at Antioch there were prophets and teachers; Barnabas, Simeon called Niger, Lucius of Cyrene, Manaen, who had been brought up with Herod the tetrarch and Saul (Paul).'

(What a church! What has James done wrong, other than just to be a Jesus' apostle? Yet Paul has never spoken a single word against Herod and he was not without knowing what Herod has done. On the contrary, Paul said that Herod was put in place by the will of God. See Paul in;)

Romans 13, 1. 'Everyone must submit himself to the governing authorities, for there is no authority except that which God has established. The authorities that exist have been established by God.'

(This equals blaming God for the death of Jesus' disciples instead of blaming the wicked. He is crafty the enemy. They have done the same thing concerning the death of the Messiah as well. Paul's god has to be either Caesar in those days or Satan, but certainly not the true God.

Matthew 13, 44. 'The kingdom of heaven is like a treasure hidden in the field. When a man found it, he hid it again, and then in his joy went and sold all he had and bought that field.'

(The treasure hidden in the field the Messiah talked about here is the so precious word of God. All the

Jesus' apostles left everything to receive it, and as far as I think, the one who had the most to lose is Matthew. He left behind a very good job, a very good salary and everything he owned to follow Jesus. Who among us can brag about haven done as much?

Paul has collected money and gold and his successors have continued to do the same. The result of that can be seen mainly in Rome and just about everywhere else. This is not Jesus' Church founded by the Messiah, started in Israel with his apostles and his disciples.

Paul's churches have started in Antioch; there where Paul called Peter a hypocrite, the one to whom Jesus gave the keys of his kingdom of heaven. Just that declaration in itself should be enough to wake up thousands of people who are sleeping.

See Acts 11, 25-26. 'Then Barnabas went to Tarsus to look for Saul, (Paul) and when he found him, he brought him to Antioch. So for a whole year Barnabas and Saul met with the church and taught great numbers of people. The (Paul's) disciples were called Christians first at Antioch.'

(Just make sure that you understand that these were Paul's disciples who were called Christians, not the Jesus' disciples and this is still the same nowadays.

So yes, Jesus, the Messiah, has founded his Church, his one and only Church in Israel with his apostles and his disciples who preach the word of God, and as he said it; 'The gates of Hades will not overcome it.'

See Jesus in Matthew 16, 16-19. 'Simon Peter answered, "You are the Christ, the Son of the living God." Jesus replied, "Blessed are you, Simon son of Jonah, for this was not revealed to you by man, but my Father in heaven. And I (Jesus) tell you that you are Peter and on this rock I will build my Church, (only one) and the gates of Hades will not overcome it. I will give you the keys of the kingdom of heaven; whatever you bind on earth will be bound in heaven, and whatever you loose on earth will be loosed in heaven."'

(These words were said to one of Jesus' apostles by the Messiah, and not at all to those who are not. Then all of those who let other people call them, 'father and holy father or pastor,' in Paul's churches are not Jesus' disciples. Do I have to add anything to this?

Paul has founded his first church in Antioch. Paul has founded Christianity with its whole hierarchy of deacons, priests, worthless shepherds, pastors, bishops, archbishops, cardinals and popes, in churches and cathedrals, who preach Paul and accumulate money.

Money that is been used nowadays to pay for their scandals of pedophilia and homosexuality and all kind of abuses.

There is a very strict message from the Messiah for them in;)

Matthew 13, 41-42. 'The Son of Man (Jesus, the Messiah) will send out his angels, and they will weeds out of his kingdom (of heaven) everything that causes sin and all who do evil. (These include the forceful men who laid hold on his kingdom, and shut it down in people's faces and all who say they all have sins.) They will throw them in the fiery furnace, where there will be weeping and gnashing of teeth.'

(None of them will succeed in making me believe they are not instructed about these messages from the Messiah, and they won't be able to play hypocrite before the Almighty either.

See what Jesus said about them in;)

Matthew 15, 14. 'Leave them; they are blind guides. If a blind man leads a blind man, both will fall into the pit.'

(And this is exactly what happened and still is happening in Paul's churches. Their congregations are blindly guide by worthless shepherds who guide them in darkness; making them believe they are saved by their faith and grace and they are brainwashed into not to receive the truth. What a shame!

This will take a superb miracle to open their eyes, but I just know that God can and will do it in His own time. I also know that Jesus, the Messiah, was opening the eyes only of those who wanted to. They don't seem to be too easy to find nowadays.

The story of Adam and Eve is the story of the entire world. It is the story of a world that has preferred listening to Satan instead of listening to God. It is a world that has preferred serving Satan instead of serving God. And almost all of the nations of this world are jealous of

Israel, because Israel is a people who are serving God. And I think this is the reason why God let the world be put to sleep by Satan, just like He did it in the Garden of Eden. But let me tell you one thing; the wake up time will be brutal.

Just as Jesus said it; the people of Israel are preaching to observe the God's commandments, but Rome, Paul and his churches are preaching just the opposite. They are preaching the lies. See Jesus again in;)

Matthew 23, 3. 'The scribes and the Pharisees have seated themselves in the chair of Moses; therefore all they tell you, do and observe.'

(And if Jesus, the Messiah, told us to listen to the Jews for our salvation; this is certainly not to listen to their enemies, Rome and Paul's churches. I hope for your own sake that you understand all of this.

Jesus said it in his parable of the weeds; 'But while everyone was sleeping.'

See Matthew 13, 25. 'But while everyone was sleeping, (not paying attention) his enemy came and sowed weeds among the wheat, and went away.'

(I just know that God chose me to ring the bell, to open your eyes, to make you understand that you are serving another god than the true God, and He doesn't like that at all. Than he has manifested Himself again, as He has always did in the pass, before His temper explodes again.

By serving Paul and his churches, you are serving another master than the Messiah, but this was the Messiah that God asked us to listen to.)

See Matthew 17, 5. 'While he was still speaking, a bright cloud enveloped them, and a voice from the cloud said, "This is my Son, whom I love; with him I am well pleased. Listen to him."'

(Yes, listen to him before it is too late. It is time to toll the knell with no stop to wake up the dead, meaning the sinners, to wake up those who are sleeping, programmed and conditioned not to hear the truth and I don't speak about my truth, even though it is the same, but the truth that is coming out from the mouth of God through the mouth of the Messiah.

CHAPTER 7

The very same stratagem was used at the beginning of 2 Corinthians, in the sense that it is started in the ways of the Jesus' apostles and continues in the ways of Paul. To better understand this; read with me;)

2 Corinthians 1, 1-4. 'Paul, an apostle of Christ Jesus (note that Paul has claimed this himself) by the will of God, and Timothy our brother. (Note also that somewhere else and according to Paul; Timothy is not the brother of Paul but his son.) To the church of God in Corinth, together with all the saints throughout Achaia: Grace and peace to you from God our Father and the Lord Jesus Christ. Praise be to God and Father of our Lord Jesus Christ, the Father of compassion and the God of all comfort, who comforts us in all our troubles, so that we can comfort those in any trouble with the comfort we ourselves have received from God.'

(And already the ways of Paul to write is showing up in what is next.)

2 Corinthians 1, 5. 'For just as the sufferings of Christ flow over into our lives, so also through Christ our comfort overflows.'

(As supplementary examples for you; I will write down the rest of 2 Corinthians 1 from verse 5 to 24; so you can see for yourselves if Paul has preached Jesus' messages and Jesus' sufferings or Paul and his sufferings.

2 Corinthians 1, 5-24. 'For just as the sufferings of Christ flow over into our lives, so also through Christ our comfort overflows. If we are distressed, it is for your comfort and salvation; if we are comforted, it is for your comfort, which produces in you patient endurance of the same sufferings we suffer. And our hope for you is firm, because we know that just as you share in our sufferings so also you share in our comfort. We don't want you to be uninformed, brothers, about the hardship we suffered in the province of Asia. We were under great pressure, far beyond our ability to endure, so that we despaired even of life. (If that had been the case, they would be dead.) Indeed, in our hearts we felt the sentence of death. But this happened that we might not rely on ourselves but on God, who raises the dead. He has delivered us from such a deadly peril, and He will deliver us. On Him we have set our hope that He will continue to deliver us, as you help us by your prayers. Then many will give thanks on our behalf for the gracious favour granted us in answer to the prayers of many. Now this is our boast: Our conscience testifies that we have

conducted ourselves in the world, and especially in our relations with you, in the holiness and sincerity that are from God. We have done so not according to worldly wisdom but according to God's grace. For we do not write you anything you cannot read or understand. And I hope that, as you have understood us in part, you will come to understand fully that you can boast of us just as we will boast of you in the day of the Lord Jesus. Because I was confident of this, I planned to visit you first so that you might benefit twice. I planned to visit you on my way to Macedonia and to come back to you from Macedonia, and then to have you send me on my way to Judea. When I planned this, did I do it lightly? Or do I make my plans in a worldly manner (not if he placed himself above all) so that in the same breath I say, "Yes, yes" and "No, no?" But as surely as God is faithful, our message to you is not "Yes" and "No." (But where is Jesus' message in all of this? No where,) For the Son of God, Jesus Christ, who was preached among you by me (Paul) and Silas and Timothy, (where, when and how?,) was not "Yes" and "No" but in him it has always been "Yes." For no matter how many promises God has made, they are "Yes" in Christ. And so through him the "Amen" is spoken by us to the glory of God. Now it is God who makes both us and you stand firm in Christ. He anointed us, set his seal of ownership on us, and put his Spirit in our hearts as a deposit, guaranteeing what is to come.

I (Paul) call God as my witness' (Jesus, the Messiah, told us not to do this at all and he said that the one who does it listens to the devil. Is that clear enough for you?,) 'that it was in order to spare you that I did not return to Corinth. Not that we lord it over your faith, but we work with you for your joy, because it is by faith you stand firm.'

(I agree to say that if Paul didn't return to Corinth; the Corinthians would have been spared.

Who Paul preached in all of these verses from 2 Corinthians 1, 5-24? Paul preached the, 'me, myself and I.' He preached Paul and company, he preached the, 'we, we, we,' the 'I, I, I,' the 'us, us, us,' and the 'our, our, our.'

What Jesus has suffered to bring us the word of God, what Jesus has preached to us; we don't find it in Paul's writings. No matter what the sons of Paul, the Christians are saying; they are not with the true God and neither with the Messiah, and for as long as they will have Paul in their hearts; they will also have the lies.

From 2 Corinthians 2, 1 to 17, Paul again only preached Paul and I counted 5 times where Paul spoke about Jesus by saying only, 'Christ,' which I consider is without any consideration or respect for his name.

Then came one verse that is a bit troubling; especially for someone who thinks that Paul was really a Jesus' disciple. It is written in;)

2 Corinthians 2, 12-13. 'Now when I (Paul) went to Troas to preach the gospel of Christ and found that the Lord had opened a door for me, I had no peace of mind,

because I did not find my brother Titus there. So I said good-by to them and went to Macedonia.'

(Isn't this what God has described as a worthless shepherd, a shepherd who abandon his sheep, no matter what the reason is? See, read and understand what is written in Zachariah 11, 17.

Contrary to Paul; when the Lord opens a door for me; I feel joy and happiness, and yes, a peace of mind too.

2 Corinthians 3, 2-3. 'You yourselves are our letter, (our Law) written in our hearts, known and read by everybody. You show that you are a letter from Christ, the result of our ministry, (Paul's deed) written not with ink but with the Spirit of the living God, not on tablets of stone but on tablets of human hearts.'

(This is from Paul an unspeakable mockery pointing against God, pointing against Moses, and pointing mainly against the Law of God and his commandments. It is a direct point to the time when the Almighty wrote his commandments on tables of stone before giving them to Moses.

God said that He will make a new covenant after that time, after the end of this actual world, but Paul and, or the devil, didn't have the patience to wait until then to pretend he is God (our, 'Paul's', ministry) and that he is the one who wrote on people's hearts. There is a reason why the devil is called the evil one.

See Jeremiah 31, 33. 'This is the covenant I will make <u>with the house of Israel</u> after that time," declares the Lord. "I will put my Law in their minds and write it in their hearts. I will be their God, and they will be my people.'

(This was said by God to the people of Israel, not to the people of Rome. This was said to Jeremiah, one of God's prophets, not to the devil.

I have to admit though that in the heart of many people; Paul is their god. He certainly found a way to seduce them and this despite all of the Messiah's warnings.

Writing on people's hearts; this is what Paul said he has done in 2 Corinthians 3, 2-3. What is written about the lawless one, about the man doomed to destruction again? Ho yes!

'Don't let anyone deceive you in any way, for that day will not come until the rebellion occurs and the man of lawlessness is <u>revealed</u>, the man doomed to destruction. (We know him now, he is revealed.) He will oppose and he will exalt himself over everything that is called God or is worshipped, so that he sets himself in God's temple, proclaiming himself to be God.'

(The Jesus' apostles knew what Paul was, but it was only later that the rebellion occurred. There was more than one good reason for the apostles managing to get rid of this devil.

Paul was one of the most educated men of his time about the Holy Scriptures, but this was not for the glory of God and neither for the ministry of the Messiah, but this was to mislead people. He knew how to use his knowledge to seduce the uneducated Gentiles, because he didn't have much success with the Jews, and this is most likely why he hated and despised the Jews so much and also because they are God's people.

2 Corinthians 3, 6. 'He has made us (Paul and company) competent as ministers of the new covenant—not of the letter (Law of God) but of the Spirit; for the letter kills, but the Spirit gives life.'

(What an abomination it is to say such a thing! What boldness this is again! We know that Satan is arrogant and that he doesn't like the Law of God, but nevertheless, why so few people have seen this abomination? This is because they were put to sleep by the liars and their lies and brainwashed, conditioned not to see the truth and this even when the truth is obvious.

Paul dared saying this was God who established him as a minister for this new covenant; a covenant that God will make after this time, after the end of this world. But God said He will make this covenant with the house of Israel. This will not be with the devil and his pagans. And to say that the letter, the Law of God kills; this is to say another terrible abomination. It is the sin that causes the death of the soul. It is the sin that kills, but this is not done by God.

I hope you understand my disarray, because it is very demoralizing to see so many abominations in the Holy

Place, in the Holy Scriptures. Although, I console myself when I read Jesus' messages and they always bring me back to;)

Matthew 24, 15. 'Therefore, when you see the abomination that causes desolation, which was spoken of through Daniel the prophet— standing in the holy place—(in the Bible) let the reader understand.'

(My mom asked me once where was this written in Daniel and I couldn't answer her at the time, but today I know where it is written. I can also say that it is all related.)

See Daniel 11, 36-37. 'The king will do as he pleases. He will exalt and magnify himself above every god and will say unheard-of things against the <u>God</u> of gods. (We just saw that Paul did this.) He will be successful until the time of wrath is completed, for what has been determined must take place. (The rebellion) He will show no regard for the gods of his fathers or for the one desired by women, nor will he regard any god, but will exalt himself above them all.'

(No one can say that Paul with a missing eye and a dry arm was one desired by women and on top of all; he didn't want to touch a woman. But on the other hand; we can easily say that he has exalted himself above all. Paul has also said unheard-of things against the true God, against Peter, against Moses, against Israel, against the Jews, against an angel of heaven, and against the Messiah. He is also arrogant enough to say: 'Christ,' while speaking about Jesus; the one Paul said he is the

Son of God and has also said that Jesus is God. This is to be excessively arrogant and absolutely devilish.

I said it and I repeat it, not me and none of Jesus' disciples would dare call Jesus, 'Christ.'

Just remember the God's commandment that says this here in;)

Exodus 20, 7. 'You shall not misuse the Name of the Lord your God, for the Lord will not hold anyone guiltless who misuse his Name.'

(But Paul, the lofty, the arrogant, didn't care at all about God's commandments, because, as he was saying; he was not under the Law of God, but above it. What a BS! And he was saying that because, as he said; 'For sin shall not be your master, (sin have no power over them) because you are <u>not</u> under Law, (like Paul is not) but under grace.'

(But nevertheless, millions and billions have and do believe in Paul.)

2 Corinthians 3, 13. 'We (Paul and company) are not like Moses (they should have been for their own good) who would put a veil over his face to keep the Israelites from gazing at it while the radiance was fading away.'

(And of course what was fading away for Paul is the Law of God that as he said was about to disappear.

See what God had to say about Moses in Numbers 12, 6-8, and about those who dare mocking him.)

Numbers 12, 6-8. 'Listen to my word; when a prophet of the Lord is among you, I reveal Myself to him in visions, I speaks to him in dreams. (And this is the way God speaks to me and shows me what I must write.) But this in not true with my servant Moses; he is faithful in all my house. With him I (God) speak face to face, clearly and not in riddles; he sees the form of the Lord. Why then (Paul or Satan) were you not afraid to speak against my servant Moses?'

(Paul was not afraid to do it because he claimed to be above all, including Moses, the Messiah and even the angels of heaven. He has just proved it again in 2 Corinthians 3, 13.

By reading in 2 Corinthians; I have the impression to be sitting at a conference and in front of a speaker that makes me feel like screaming and get out of it after everyone of his sentences he had finished to pronounce. And if I was sitting on a windowledge and on the third floor; I too would have a reason to fear for my life. So I am sorry then to put you through all of this, because I have to bring light about all of these abominations.)

2 Corinthians 5, 13-21. 'If we (Paul and company) are out of our mind, (blessed are the poor in spirit) it is for the sake of God; if we are in our right mind, it is for you. For <u>Christ</u>'s love compels us, because we are convinced that one died for all, and therefore all died.'

(God is the God of the living; so it is not true that all died. But maybe that all of those who are with Paul, those who are with the devil are dead. This is a great possibility.)

'And he (Jesus) died for all,'

(The Messiah died assassinated by the Romans like Paul, because he was spreading the truth, the word of God, and this is something Paul has never mentioned. But Jesus lives and he lives for me and for all of his disciples.)

'That those who live,'

(Paul knew how to write contradictory phrases like that one. He said that all died and also said those who live.)

'Should no longer live for themselves but for him who died for them and was raised again. So from now on we regard no one from a worldly point of view. Though we once regarded Christ in this way, we do no longer. Therefore, if anyone is in Christ, he is a new creation.'

(In the French Canadian language; this also means he is mad.)

'The old has gone, the new has come!'

(Paul here meant the new covenant, the one he has pretended having established through his ministry.)

'All this is from God, who reconciled us to Himself through Christ and give us (Paul and company, sons of the devil) the ministry of reconciliation; that God was reconciling the world to Himself in Christ,'

(We can see the very same lie in Ephesians 2, 14-16. God too must be getting very mad to see all of those abominations concerning Him. But his day of wrath is at the door.)

'Not counting men's sins against them.'

(All of these are lies from Paul and they are connected with what is still to come and that we can read in Jeremiah 31, 31-34, and this has absolutely nothing to do with the death of the Messiah. Almost two thousand years later, as of today and until the judgement comes; the sins will be counting against men, just as the Messiah said it. See for yourselves in;)

Matthew 7, 23. 'Then I (Jesus) will tell them plainly, 'I never knew you. Away from me, you evildoers.' (Sinners, those who commit sins. See also;)

Jeremiah 31, 31-34. 'The time is coming, declares the Lord, when I will make a new covenant with the house of Israel and with the house of Judah. (This is not with the house of Rome and neither with the sons of the devil.) It will not be like the covenant I made with their forefathers when I took them by the hand to lead them out of Egypt, because they broke my covenant, though I was their Master, declares the Lord. This is the covenant I will make with the house of Israel after that time," declares the Lord. "I will put my Law in their minds and write it in their hearts. I will be their God, and they will be my people. No longer a man will teach his neighbour or a man his brother, saying, 'Know the Lord,' because they will all know Me, from the least of them to the greatest, declares the Lords.'

(Who can say without lying that this is done and this almost 2000 years after the lying declaration of Paul?

'For I will forgive their wickedness and will remember their sins no more.'

(Paul has lied, he has misled and he has kept his people in darkness; forbidding it to know and to see the truth and worse yet; he has used the word of God to do it. He is, and there is no doubt at all in my mind, the worthless shepherd mentioned in Zachariah 11, 17. Paul is the one who sowed the weeds and Jesus, the Messiah, said about him that he is the devil. He is also the one of those who shut down the marvellous kingdom of heaven in his disciples' faces.

And I continue in 2 Corinthians 5, 19.)

'And He (God) has committed to us (sons of the devil) the message of reconciliation. We are therefore Christ's ambassadors, as though God were making his appeal through us. (Right????) We implore on Christ's behalf: Be reconciled to God.'

(Which for? There is no reason to do that, because according to Paul; God is not counting men's sins against them. More yet, according to Paul and company; Jesus, the Messiah, has taking all the sins in the world on him.)

'God made him (Jesus) who has no sin to be sin for us.'

(What an abomination it is to say such a thing about the Messiah, and it is the same abomination than to say that the Messiah has become a curse for us. This abomination is coming out of the mouth of Paul. The

Messiah didn't become a sin and neither a curse for us, on the contrary; he is a blessing for us. Jesus became our Saviour.)

'So that in him we might become the righteousness of God.'

(This might be a little too much to ask from the devil and his angels. Paul said that Jesus has become sin and a curse, has also said that Jesus is God. Then Paul also said that God is sin and a curse. Do you see the abominable? Do you see the abomination in the holy place, in the Holy Bible? It is about time, but good for you if you did.

From 2 Corinthians 6, 1-13, this seems to be another endless litany from Paul, but the word, 'Christ,' by itself is not mentioned, but things change in the next three verses.)

See 2 Corinthians 6, 14-16. 'Do not be yoked together with the unbelievers. For what do righteousness and wickedness have in common? Or what fellowship can light have with darkness? What harmony is there between Christ and Belial? What does a believer have in common with an unbeliever? What agreement is there between the temple of God and Idols?'

(What light has to do with darkness, Paul asked? Isn't it nice to see the light at the end of a tunnel? Isn't it nice to have a good working flashlight to walk with in total darkness in the night when there is no moon and no stars?

What Jesus, the Messiah, had in common with the publicans and all the sinners?

This is it; the Messiah came to call the sinners to repent. He wanted and he still wants to pull out the sinners from the devil's claws and to do it; he sat down with them. He will still do it and so will all of his true disciples. But this was not interesting to Paul. To Paul or to the devil; it is best not to have anything to do with those who might have a chance to turn to God. In another word, if someone is with the devil; leave him there where he is and the devil will be happy. That's Paul's policy. No wonder so many Christians are saying: "The hell with him."

See another reference in;)

Matthew 9, 10-13. "While Jesus was having dinner at Matthew's house, many tax collectors and sinners came and ate with him and his disciples. When the Pharisees saw this, they asked his disciples, "Why does your teacher eat with tax collectors and sinners?" On hearing this, Jesus said, "it is not the healthy who need a doctor, but the sick. But go and learn what this means: 'I desire mercy, not sacrifice.' (Not the mass) For I have not come to call the righteous, but sinners.""

(It is the sinners who need to hear the word of God the most, to hear the truth and fast is not fast enough, so they too can have the hope to get out of the devil's trap. Loving sex doesn't take away from anyone the right to love God with all of his heart. Loving liquor doesn't take away from anyone the right to love God with all of his heart. And this is also true for all of the other kind of slavery in this wild world.

To be a slave of sin doesn't forbid anyone for wanting to become a God's child, but listening to Paul's lying speeches won't help anyone to become one. Turn to the Messiah and listen to him. Do what he said; repent and turn to God and you will have a hard time counting all of your blessings. Remember this that the Messiah said and is written in;)

Matthew 11, 28-30. 'Come to me, all of you who are weary and burdened, and I will give you rest. Take my yoke upon you and learn from me, for I am gentle and humble in heart, and you will find rest for your souls. For my yoke is easy and my burden is light.'

(What I have just written is something that you will not find in Paul's writings and if Paul or one of his descendants, one of his imitators is your father or your pastor in one of Paul's churches; then the God of heaven is not your Father. So yes, the truth hits hard, but it splits also. The truth is the very sharp sword that slices between the truth and the lies and I understand that this could be very painful to those who don't know it. The truth is the sword that Jesus, the Messiah, brought to this world. See again;)

Matthew 10, 34. 'Do not suppose that I have come to bring peace on the earth. I did not come to bring peace but a sword.'

(This sword will be present at the last judgement and it would be best for anyone to be on the truth's side then, to obtain eternal happiness. No one will be able to say, 'I didn't know it,' because the Messiah said this that is also written in;)

Matthew 24, 14. 'And this gospel of the kingdom (of heaven that I preach) will be preached in the whole world as a testimony to all nations, and then the end will come.'

(The Almighty is the just God and all without any exception would have had the choice between the truth and the lies before going through the judgement; then there will be no possible excuse for those who have chosen the lies instead of the truth. There is another very important message that is written in;)

2 Thessalonians 2, 10. 'And in every sort of evil that deceive those who are perishing. They perish because <u>they refuse to love the truth</u> and so be saved.'

(Those are the ones who are listening to Paul instead of listening to Jesus, to the Messiah. Do you know that 99, 9% of those to whom I speak about this truth are rejecting it? Sad, but true!

I was saying that Satan is using the word of God to mislead people and what is following is another example of this fact;)

2 Corinthians 6, 16-17. 'What agreement is there between the temple of God and idols? For we (Paul and company) are the temple of the living God. As God has said: "I will live with them and walk among them, and I will be their God, and they will be my people."

(God said this will happen after that time, the end time, but Paul made them believe he was the one waking among them. In reality, Paul is the one who set himself in God's temple and proclaimed himself to be God.)

'"Therefore come out from them and be separate, says the Lord. Touch no unclean thing, and I will receive you."'

(This is most likely why Paul told men not to touch women, because they are unclean a few days each month.

I might be mistaking, but despite intensive searches; I didn't see in the God's prophets' writings what Paul has mentioned earlier, at least not as it is??????? On the other hand, see what we can read in Paul's writings.)

Romans 14, 14. 'As one who is in the Lord Jesus, I am fully convinced that no food is unclean in itself. But if anyone regards something as unclean, then to him it is unclean.'

(Now the manipulating of the Holy Scriptures is still showing up here. In my French Bible and in the King James Bible; there is no question of food at all in Romans 14, 14. Here how it is in the King James.)

Romans 14, 14. 'I know, and I (Paul) am persuaded that there is nothing unclean in itself. But to him that esteemeth anything to be unclean, to him it is unclean.'

(Go tell this to God Paul and see what He says. And why did Paul has treated women as if they are dirt? Rats, mice, pork, shit and all of the vermin is unclean no matter if you believe it is unclean or not. But again, Paul used the name of the Lord Jesus to lie and to mislead.

The children of God are God's temple; not the liars, not the sons of the devil. It is among the God's children that God stands.

Let me show you what the Almighty was talking about, when He mentioned not to touch something unclean, but this was not at all the sinners that the Messiah sat with to heal them, get them to repent, turn to God, and at the same time got out of the devil's trap. This was not about women either; the nicest creature God has ever made.

See Leviticus 11, 6-8. 'The (wild) rabbit, though it chews the cud, does not have a split hoof; it is unclean for you. And the pig, though it has a split hoof completely divided, does not chew the cud, it is unclean for you. You must not eat their meat or touch their carcasses; they are unclean for you.'

(Billions of Christians eat the pork and there are more recipes made out of the pig than from any other kind of animals. They even use the pig's blood to make sausages; which is against the will of God, and they want to give the Japanese life's lessons to them who eat the dogs.

Besides, we can speak to the sinners without touching them, I mean physically, of course.)

2 Corinthians 6, 18. '"I will be a Father to you, and you will be my sons and daughters, says the Lord Almighty."'

(This was taking out of its context again by Paul. This was not said to Paul and neither to his disciples from God, but to the Messiah and I think this was said also to the people of Israel.

See Jeremiah 31, 1. '"At that time," (in the kingdom of God) declares the Lord, "I will be the God of all the clans of Israel, and they will be my people."'

(Can you see that God was speaking about all the clans of Israel and not about Rome, or about Paul or about the Corinthians and even less about the sons of the devil? We have to keep in mind also what Paul himself said about who is the father of the Corinthians, the father of his disciples and that Satan too has many sons and daughters. See again;)

1 Corinthians 4, 15. 'I (Paul) am not writing this to shame you, but to warn you, as my dear children. Even though you have ten thousand guardians in Christ, you do not have many fathers, for in Christ Jesus I became your father through the gospel.'

(What a misfortune for them! It is for his disciples that Paul became their father and this without touching a woman. This might be just what he has called a miracle and a great sign.

We can see again in 2 Corinthians 2, 1-8 that Paul preached Paul and company and he has used a bit of flattery to smooth things out with the Corinthians, to seduce them.

Then we can see another contradictory phrase like Paul has made many of them.)

See 2 Corinthians 7, 8. 'Even if I caused you sorrow by my letter, I do not regret it. Though I did regret it.'

It is a bit different again in the King James Bible.

2 Corinthians 7, 8. 'For though I made you sorry with a letter, I do not repent, though I did repent.'

(I feel sorry for what Paul's disciples had to go through with him, because no kidding; he was very confusing. One thing is sure; Paul was not the type of men to repent, because he felt guilty of nothing, as he said it himself.

2 Corinthians 7, 15. 'And his affection for you is all the greater when he remembers that you were all <u>obedient</u>, receiving him with <u>fear</u> and <u>trembling</u>.'

(If not the Corinthians would have had to deal with Paul. Jesus has preached the fear of God, but Paul has preached the fear of those who can kill the body and we can see in these last lines that the Corinthians were living in terror. The Romans were extremely dangerous in those days anywhere in the world. See Jesus in;)

Matthew 10, 28. 'Do not be afraid of those who kill the body, but can't kill the soul. Rather, be afraid of the One who can destroy both soul and body in hell.'

2 Corinthians 8, 6-8. 'So we (Paul and company) urged Titus, since he had earlier made (a good scaring) beginning (to them) to bring also to completion this act of grace (with the whip) on your part. But just as you excel in everything—(with fear and trembling) in faith, in speech, in knowledge, in complete earnestness and in your love for us—see that you also excel in this grace of giving. I (Paul) am not commanding you (of course not)

but I want to test the sincerity of your love by comparing it with earnestness of others.'

(Why not a bit of flattery and create a bit of competition to boost things up a little when we are at it? This certainly cannot hurt when we want to pick up money. Isn't he, Paul who bragged about not using flattery with his disciples?

And this is how the church of Rome has started its enrichment; meaning with flatteries, and the fear of the poor people, who were ignoring the truth that was coming from the Messiah. The truth that was saying this among so many other things, but things we don't see in Paul's writings.)

Matthew 10, 8. 'You have received freely, freely give.'

(This certainly doesn't mean to take the money from the poor to get richer. But we already know that Paul was not preaching the Messiah and neither the word of God, but was preaching Paul and company. If we consider all of the Christian churches and others that are in the world today; anyone can tell that it is a good enough business, but this is not for the glory of God, and not for the Messiah either, who didn't want to have anything to do with this diabolic hierarchy.

Remember; 'And do not call anyone on earth, 'father.'

(And why not create a little competition between two regions that are jealous from one another. He is crafty the devil.)

2 Corinthians 8, 1-3. 'And now, brothers, we want you to know (of course) the grace that God has given the Macedonian churches. Out of the most severe trial, their overflowing joy and their extreme poverty'

(He should have been ashamed to take their money. This reminds me of two nuns who came to our place and took the only money we had to buy butter to put on our bread, and this for the rare time we had some bread.)

'Welled up in rich generosity.'

(Which really meant for Paul to say: Shut up Corinthians and give generously. Do you see that in Paul's mission, his goal was more to enrich his diabolic empire than to preach the real word of God? Who can argue that taking the money from the poor to build an empire is devilish? They are sons of the devil and the devil himself.

I do have serious questions about what is next really meant that we can read in;)

2 Corinthians 8, 5. 'And they did not do as we expected, but they gave themselves first to the Lord and then to us in keeping with God's will.'

(When a woman gives herself to a man; we know what this means, but here in 2 Corinthians, I just wonder.

With Paul we go from one lie to another.)

See 2 Corinthians 8, 9. 'For you know the grace of our Lord Jesus Christ, that though he was rich, (where did Paul get this?,) yet for your sakes he became poor, so that you through his poverty might become rich.'

(For a rare time that Paul spoke about Jesus; he did it to lie, not to preach to word of God. According to what is written in Matthew; Jesus didn't have what it takes to pay his entrance and we know that he left everything behind him to accomplish the will of God.)

See Matthew 17, 24-27. 'After Jesus and his disciples arrived in Capernaum, collectors of the two drachma tax came to Peter and asked, "Doesn't your Teacher pay the temple tax?" "Yes, he does, he replied. When Peter came into the house, Jesus was the first to speak. What do you think, Simon (Peter)?" He asked. "From whom do the kings of the earth collect duty and taxes—from their own sons or from others?" "From others," Peter answered. "Then the sons are exempt," Jesus said to him. "But so that we may not offend them, go to the lake and throw out your line. Take the first fish you catch; open its mouth and you will find a four-drachma coin. Take it and give it to them for my tax and yours.'

(Remember I was saying that the four and the five thousand men, beside women and children, who were following Jesus everywhere were not paying for the temple anymore and the tax collectors were losing money. Besides, they were fed freely. This was enough for the Pharisees and the Sadducees to be jealous and to hate Jesus. This is one thing the religions do and this is more than enough for God and for the Messiah to be against them.

Some people will also say that Jesus must have also made his own wine with water, since he could not afford to buy it. The question is that I have never seen anywhere than in Paul's writings that Jesus was rich; he who said it is hard for a rich man to enter his kingdom of heaven. Jesus has not made himself poor; he was poor money wise and without a place to rest his head. Though, if the story of water changed to wine was true; Jesus could have got rich just by selling his wine and from precious stones out of the mouths of fish. Most men without the Spirit of God would have done it and this without wondering about entering the kingdom of heaven or not.

When flattery is not enough anymore to collect money from the poor; then it is time to use insistence.)

See 2 Corinthians 8, 10-11. 'And here is my advice about what is good for you in this matter: Last year you were the first not only to give but also to have the desire to do so. Now finish the work, so that your eager willingness to do it may be matched by your completion of it, according to your means.'

(I apologize to the ones who are still sceptical about Paul and company, but to insist this way to influence people to give their money; this is not in any way, shape or form near the Holy Gospel of the Messiah. According to the Gospel of the Messiah, people had to supply the needs of the apostles, but not to buy them cathedrals. And the insistence continues.)

2 Corinthians 8, 13-14. 'Our desire is not that others might be relieved while you are hard pressed, but that there might be equality. At the present time your plenty will supply what they need, so that in turn their plenty will supply what you need. Then there will be equality.'

(There was equality alright; they both got equally robbed. The equality would have been that each of them keeps their plenty, if plenty was there. But since Paul mentioned their poverty earlier; I doubt very much there was plenty. But Paul robbed them both and he was gone with the pile of money and it is the very same way that the imitators of Paul and company robbed billions of people to build the huge diabolic empire that is spread out all over the world.

But even before Jesus, the Messiah, has started his ministry; while he was tempted by Satan; he had already said, 'no,' to all of these kingdoms of this world. They have so much money nowadays that they have to do money laundry. They rather hide their money than to pay their victims compensation and some people still think they are God's peoples.?????????????

See Matthew 4, 8-10. 'Again the devil took him (Jesus) to a very high mountain and showed him <u>all</u> the kingdoms of the world and their splendour. "All this I will give you," he said, "if you will bow down and worship me." Jesus said to him, "Away from me, Satan! For it is written: 'Worship the Lord your God, and serve Him only.'"

(This demonstrates two important things. First, this is demonstrating that all without any exception can be tempted by Satan. But this demonstrates also that when we leave God, when we leave the Spirit of God live in us and guide us; we are capable to say what Jesus told the devil: 'Away from me Satan!' And he will go away.

Did you know that the exact opposite happened to Paul? See Paul in;)

2 Corinthians 12, 7. 'To keep me from becoming conceited because of these surpassingly great revelations, there was given me a thorn in my flesh, a messenger of Satan, to torment me.'

(Oups, the manipulation shows up here again and one important line is missing. So one more time I have to get it from the King James Bible. In fact, it is another line that proves that Paul is from the devil.

From the King James Bible, 2 Corinthians 12, 7. 'And lest I should be exalted above measure through the abundance of the revelation, there was given me a thorn in the flesh, the messenger of Satan to buffet me, (Paul) <u>lest I should be exalted above measure</u>.'

(That's a good one. As if Satan, who is the king of false pride and the most conceited being, would send a messenger or one of his angels to stop anyone from exalting himself above measure. Come on!??????????

God or one of his angels can force someone to humiliation, but never Satan or one of his angels would do that. We can see also that the lord of Paul didn't listen to him and he didn't help him either.)

See 2 Corinthians 12, 8-9. 'Three times I pleaded with the lord to take it away from me. But he said to me, "My grace is sufficient for you, for my power is made perfect in weakness." Therefore I will boast all the more gladly about my weakness, so that Christ's power may rest on me.'

(It is true that Satan's power rest on the weakness and ignorance of people and it is also a sure thing that Satan will not pull away one of his angels from anyone and even less from one of his children; either he prays three times or more.

It seems to me though that Paul's crafty stratagem has worked for him, because his harvest is abundant.)

See 2 Corinthians 8, 20. 'We want to avoid any criticism of the way we administer the liberal gift.'

(Of Course; the money he has collected is just about all he has talked about until now in his gospel of 2 Corinthians and it continues. Some people might say that I have a bad spirit; I who is against wickedness, against sin, against the abominations and mainly against all the messages that contradict God and the Messiah.

And with humility Paul claimed that he and his imitators are saints and all of this by continuing to boast the competition between the two regions and this to get more money out of them. What did the Messiah say? 'You cannot serve both God and money.')

See 2 Corinthians 9, 1-2. 'There is no need for me to write to you about this service (donation) to the saints. For I know your eagerness to help, and I have been boasting about it to the Macedonians, telling them that since last year you and Achaia were ready to give; and your enthusiasm has stirred most of them to action.'

(To have created competition seems to have worked out for Paul.)

2 Corinthians 10, 1-2. 'By the meekness and the gentleness of Christ, I appeal to you—I, Paul, who am "timid" when face to face with you, but "bold" when away! I beg you that when I come I may not have to be bold as I expect to be toward some people who think that we live by the standards of this world.'

(There were a few among them anyway that figured Paul right, but it is also very clear that they put their lives on the line before this monster of the devil.

Who could read what is next without believing or understanding that Paul and company have set themselves above others, contrary to what the Messiah has taught; that all of his disciples are all brothers, then all equal. This is something we can read in Matthew 23, 8-9.

See 2 Corinthians 10. 5-6. 'We (Paul and company) demolish arguments and every pretension that sets itself up against the knowledge of God, and we take captive every thought to make it obedient to Christ. And we will be ready to punish every act of disobedience, when your obedience is complete.'

(According to what Paul is saying here; the obedience was due to him and his company. I think that Paul thought he was talking in parables when he was making contradictory phrases like that one, because when the obedience is complete, like it is with my dogs; there is no more disobedience and there is no need for punishment, since their obedience is complete. I also think that if no one has killed Paul; it is because they were all better than him, who is a murdered and a liar from the beginning.

Then the comparison about him, Paul, and the Jesus' apostles and the Jesus' disciples has started and this shows that Paul didn't like to have Jesus' disciples near his own disciples.)

2 Corinthians 10, 7. 'You are looking only at the surface of things. If anyone is confident that he belongs to <u>Christ</u>, he should consider again that we belong to <u>Christ</u> just as much as he.'

(There have been more manipulations of the Scriptures here too, and one, 'Christ,' was taken off. Someone might have thought too that three times in the same phrase were a bit too much. But in the French Bible and in the King James; 'Christ' is written three times in the same verse. But this proves again that some people are not shy at all to manipulate the Holy

Scriptures that are not all holy as you too can see for yourselves.

Here how it is written in the King James Bible.)

2 Corinthians 10, 7. 'Do ye look on things after the outward appearance? If any man trust to himself that he is Christ's, let him of himself think this again, that, as he is Christ's, even so are we Christ's.'

(Paul has done it three times in the same verse, but I said it before; none of the Jesus' disciples would have done this, I mean speaking about the Messiah this way. But all of this demonstrates that the competition was present against Paul and company and Paul didn't like that one bit. There were some who were from Jesus and others who pretended they were. Certainly that some of them belong to the Antichrist.)

2 Corinthians 10, 8-9. 'For even if I boast somewhat freely about the authority the Lord gave us (Paul and company) for building you up rather than pulling you down, I will not be ashamed of it. I do not want to seem to be trying to frighten you with my letters.'

(We have seen that there was no intimidation at all in his letters. No, a dream! And the only authority that Jesus gave to his disciples was not to be over people to whom they were to preach, but to chase demons like Paul and this is what they have done. We can read about it in Acts 21, 21.

But let's read again Jesus' instructions to his apostles that we can read in;)

Matthew 10, 7-8. 'As you go, preach this message: 'The kingdom of heaven is near.' Heal the sick, raise the dead, cleanse those who have leprosy, <u>drive out demons</u>. Freely you have received, freely give.'

(And Paul and company have done none of this, on the contrary; we have just seen it and it is the same thing in all of Paul's writings. All of this has continued with Paul's imitators in all of his churches that he has founded. His imitators have imitated him well.

It is written no where in Jesus' instructions to his apostles and to his disciples that they were to punish anyone or that anyone had to obey them. Jesus sent his disciples to instruct, not to command anyone. Paul was not sent by the same Lord than the Lord of the apostles and we know that the Lord of the apostles is the Messiah; the one who saves by his knowledge.

See now the way Paul was comparing himself to the true Jesus' disciples and Jesus' apostles in;)

2 Corinthians 10, 12. 'We do not dare to classify or compare ourselves with some who command themselves. When they measure themselves and compare themselves with themselves, they are not wise.'

(Nevertheless, Paul was comparing himself to them anyway and if they were without intelligence, how was he himself, who said he didn't dare to compare himself to them?

Let's see now two messages from Paul that are apparently in the same letter and tell me that this is not enough to be confused about him, at least for the poor Corinthians.)

2 Corinthians 10, 1. 'By the meekness and the gentleness of Christ, I appeal to you—I, Paul, who am "timid" when face to face with you, but "bold" when away!

(Here Paul is different when he is in one place than when he is in another, meaning with them versus away from them. This is what we say about someone that he is: 'A two faces person.' See now the exact opposite from the same man;)

2 Corinthians 10, 11. 'Such people should realize that what we are in our letters when we are absent, we will be in our actions when we are present.'

(Paul was not happy with contradicting God, with contradicting Jesus the Messiah and with contradicting the Jesus' disciples; he managed to contradict himself. He was wise and crafty enough to build one of the biggest religious empires in the world, but not enough to untangle himself with his lies. But this is it; the problems with the liars; they get tangled up in their own traps. 'We will recognize the tree by its fruits.' The Messiah said.

2 Corinthians 11, 1. 'I hope you will put up with a little of my foolishness; but you are already doing that.'

(They had no choice, I think. It was this or death, or at least the whip, but this is again a contradictory phrase in itself.

I talked about Paul's competition earlier and that he didn't like that at all, but we get another proof of it in what is next. We also find out that this competition was Jesus' apostles and Jesus' disciples.

2 Corinthians 11, 3. 'But I (Paul) am <u>afraid</u> that just as Eve was deceived by the serpent's cunning, your mind may somehow be led astray from your sincere and pure devotion to <u>Christ</u>.'

(The fact was that Paul was afraid that his disciples turn to the Jesus' disciples and to Jesus' apostles, who were telling them the truth without taking their money. We will also see later on what is written about fear.)

2 Corinthians 11, 4. 'For if someone comes to you and preaches a Jesus other than the Jesus we preached, or if you receive a different spirit from the one you received, or a different gospel from the one you accepted, you put up with it easily enough.'

(By his own words in these last lines, Paul himself has proved that he was preaching a different Jesus than the true Messiah, that he had a different spirit than the Holy Spirit and that he was preaching a different gospel than the one of the true Jesus' apostles.

And yes, the Corinthians were putting up with Paul easily enough not to be killed by the Romans, or at least, they tried. This was Paul who had a hard time to put up with the Jesus' apostles and disciples, who could speak with Paul's disciples. But Paul was even more arrogant, more bold with those who were preaching a different gospel than his. See again the one who attacked the Celestial Beings;)

Galatians 1, 8-9. 'But even if we or an angel from heaven should preach a gospel other than the one we (Paul and company) preached to you, (full of lies, contradictions and abominations) let him be eternally condemned! As we have already said, so now I (Paul) say again, if anybody is preaching to you a gospel other than what you accepted, let him be eternally condemned.'

(But Paul by mouthing this much as he did about his so-called own gospel, consisting in a huge part in picking up money from the poor people and by scaring and influencing them, by denigrating the Jesus' disciples; he himself has proven that he was preaching a different gospel than the one of the true disciples and apostles of the Messiah. He has proven that he was preaching a different Jesus than the Messiah and a different Christ. He proved at the same time that he was preaching a different god than the true God and because he was doing such things; the Spirit of God could not be with him.

And for the first time, I think, Paul, in what is following has clearly named those who were in competition with him, those he was denigrating, and this with the only goal to build up his reputation.)

2 Corinthians 11, 5. 'But I do not think I (Paul) am the least inferior to "those super-apostles.'

(At least Paul knew that the Jesus' apostles were super- apostles and as he said it and thought; he was not the least inferior to them. Who can still say that Paul didn't have a good opinion of himself? Paul has demonstrated himself that he is the weed, the lie that the Messiah spoke about in his parable of the weeds and Jesus said this was the devil.)

2 Corinthians 11, 6. 'I may not be a <u>trained speaker</u>, but I have knowledge. We have made this perfectly clear to you in every way.'

(And this was by quoting some messages from the Old Testament to better mislead them; he who was the most educated in the Law. As for Paul to be ignorant about languages; let's see what he said in another occasion.)

See 1 Corinthians 14, 18-19. 'I thank God that I speak in tongues more than all of you. But in the church I would rather speak five intelligible words to instruct others than ten thousand words in a tongue.'

(Paul, just like Satan, wanted to know what people had in their hearts, but God doesn't need us to speak to know our hearts and thoughts, because He can see what is done in secret. Remember what is written in Matthew 6, 6.

Paul also said he is not a trained speaker. In the French Bible he rather said that he was ignorant when comes to the languages. But let's see his super sermon in front of an uproar in Jerusalem.)

Acts 21, 40. 'Paul stood on the steps and motioned to the crowd. When they were all silent, he said to them in Aramaic.'

(Then you can read his long sermon from Acts 22, 1-21, and judge for yourselves if he is a trained speaker or not. The least you can find is that he is a liar.

2 Corinthians 11, 7. 'Was it a sin for me to lower myself in order to elevate you by preaching the gospel of God to you free of charge?'

(We all know now that this is false as we saw it a bit earlier. The gospel of God is free; it is the gospel of Paul that costs money. We will see also a bit farther how much Paul has lowered himself.)

2 Corinthians 11, 8. 'I (Paul) robbed (robbing someone is stealing and this is a sin, but not to Paul, because sin has no power on him,) other churches by receiving support from them so as to serve you.'

(This is another point shot directly at the Jesus' apostles to whom the Messiah said this in;)

Matthew 10, 9-10. 'Do not take along any gold or silver or copper in your belts; take no bag for the journey, or extra tunic, or sandals or a <u>staff</u>; for a worker is worth his keep.'

(But Paul was in a different camp than the Jesus' apostles and he didn't know much about the Messiah's instructions to them and this is most likely for that reason he did everything contrary to those instructions. One thing remains very evident though; this is that if Paul was sent by someone, this was certainly not by the same Jesus who is the Messiah.

In 2 Corinthians 11, 9, Paul has insisted again to contradict the instructions the Messiah gave to his apostles.)

2 Corinthians 11, 9. 'And when I was with you and needed something, I was not a burden to anyone, for the brothers who came from Macedonia supplied what I needed.'

(Who then was talking about the liberal gift? In other Bibles, instead of liberal gift; it is written; 'abundance.' See 2 Corinthians 8, 20.)

'I (Paul) kept myself from being a burden to you in any way, and I will continue to do so.'

(And again here, this is the opposite of Jesus' instructions to his apostles. Satan is the master of the false pride.

Don't forget that in what is following, Paul held this conversation against the true Jesus' apostles again and this is not funny at all."

2 Corinthians 11, 10-12. 'As surely as the truth of <u>Christ</u> is in me, (Paul) nobody in the region of Achaia will stop this <u>boasting</u> of mine. Why? Because I do not love you? God knows I do!'

(Of course he did; they were a cash cow for him.)

'And I (Paul) will keep on doing what I am doing in order to cut the ground from under those (Jesus' apostles) who want an opportunity to be considered equal with <u>us</u> (Paul and company) in the things <u>they</u> (Jesus' apostles) boast about.'

(What were the Jesus' apostles boasting about, if they were boasting about anything at all? To have received freely the teaching from the Messiah and in turn they were giving it freely to their disciples.

Were they boasting about only taking from people what they needed to survive each day, as the Messiah told them, contrary to Paul who was taking their money to build the empire that he did?

If there is one thing that we all can be sure about; this is that none of the Jesus' apostles and none of the Jesus' disciples wanted to be like Paul in any way, shape or form. And I am also sure of another thing; this is that none of them were teaching the word of God for a monetary gain. I just know it because I am like they were; I am a Jesus' disciple.

And the tone was elevated badly in what is following; which makes me think that Paul was losing some ground and at the same time; he was losing it, maybe even his mind. I mean that he acted as a fool. One can tell that Paul was not too happy anymore.)

2 Corinthians 11, 13-15. 'For such men (Jesus' apostles and disciples) are false apostles, deceitful workmen, masquerading as apostles of Christ. And no wonder, for Satan himself masquerades as an angel of light. (This is something that Paul knows more than anyone.) It is not surprising, then, if his servants masquerade as servants of righteousness. Their end will be what their actions deserve.'

(Ho, I see, because for Paul now, actions are accountable. Ho yes, I forgot. It is true that the Jesus' apostles were Jews, so, they were under the Law of God, which means that their actions count. It was different for Paul; he was not under the Law. He is the lawless one. See one more time what Paul said about deeds, actions in;)

Romans 3, 28. 'For we (Paul and company) maintain that a man is justified by faith apart from observing the Law.'

(We, Jesus' disciples, know that we will be justified by what we have done and this with or without faith, because this is what God and Jesus told us. See Jesus in;)

Matthew 16, 27. 'For the Son of Man is going to come in his Father's glory with his angels, and then he will reward each person according to what he has done.'

From 2 Corinthians 11, 16 to 11, 33, you will be able to see for yourselves if Paul preached our Lord Jesus Christ or if he preached Paul. You will see at the same time that Paul complained a lot about his misfortune for a man that his lord said no Jew or no one will put his hands on him to harm him. See this false prophet in;)

Acts 18, 9-10. 'One night the lord spoke to Paul in a vision: "Do not be afraid; keep on speaking, do not be silent. For I am with you, and no one is going to attack and harm you, because I have many people in this city."'

(This was the second false prophet who predicted something to Paul and has lied and if this lord is the one who stopped Paul on the road to Damascus; then, this is the second time. How you or anyone can believe anything that is coming from Paul or from Luke? It is good to believe, yes, but the truth.

2 Corinthians 11, 16-33. 'Again I say; let no one think me (Paul) foolish; but if you do, receive me as foolish, so that I also may boast a little. What I am saying, I am not saying as the Lord would, but as in foolishness, in this confidence of boasting. Since many (apostles) boast according to the flesh, I will boast also.'

(Paul spoke against the Jesus' apostles, but as he said; he did the very same thing. This must have been by foolishness.)

'For you, being so wise, tolerate the foolish gladly.'

(Was that arrogance or a bit of humility from Paul that won't last very long?)

'For you tolerate it if anyone enslaves you, anyone devours you, anyone takes advantage of you, anyone exalts himself,'

(Was that bragging about how he, Paul, was treating them?

'Anyone hits you in the face. To my shame I must say that we (meaning Paul alone, see Acts 23, 3) have been weak in comparison. What anyone else dares to boast about—I am speaking as a fool—I also dare to boast about.'

(Who wants to listen to someone who is speaking as a fool to learn something, especially about the word of God? Then Paul cannot accuse me or blame me for saying he is senile, because he speaks in foolishness and he is speaking as a fool and he asked his listeners to receive him as foolish. So I did. Paul also said that he is out of his mind. But he is the one the Christians are following.)

'Are they (Jesus' apostles) Hebrews? So am I. Are they Israelites? So am I. Are they Abraham's descendants? So am I. Are they servants of Christ? I am out of my mind to talk like this. I am more. (Arrogant, yes.) I have worked harder, been in prison more frequently, been flogged more severely and been exposed to death again and again.

(I guess there is no more weakness and no more humility here. Now people; understand that Paul here is comparing himself to the true super-apostles of Jesus. I wonder when and where he had the time to investigate what happened to the true apostles and about what they were doing. So here is more.)

2 Corinthians 11, 24. 'Five times I received from the Jews the forty lashes minus one.'

(195 lashes, but Paul's lord told him the Jews will not attack or harm him. I wonder who lied about this one, Paul or his lord, or both. In the French Bible his lord said that no one will lay hand on him, and I thought, maybe just the whip.)

'Three times I was beaten with rods, once I was stoned, (apparently no one can survive this) three times I was shipwrecked. I spent a night and a day in open sea; I have been constantly on the move. I have been in danger from rivers, in danger from bandits, in danger from my own countrymen,'

(These must be the Jews, because Paul was living in peace in Rome,)

'In danger from Gentiles, in danger in the city, in danger in the country, in danger at sea and in danger from false brothers.'

(The false brothers that Paul was talking about here were the Jesus' apostles and Jesus' disciples. It's not over yet, but I couldn't help bringing in a comment here. No one can kill the devil. It was a good thing, for him I mean, that he was a Roman after all. What was Jude saying about people like Paul yet? Oh yes, see;)

Jude 1, 16. 'These are grumblers, faultfinders, following after their own lusts; they speak arrogantly, flattering people for the sake of gaining an advantage.'

(And I continue.)

'I have laboured and toiled and have often gone without sleep, I have known hunger and thirst have often gone without food. I have been cold and naked.'

(I don't know why, but this last one I kind of believe it.)

'Besides everything else, I face daily the pressure of my concern for all the churches.'

(See, Jesus has only one Church; the devil has many of them. Jesus didn't have so many problems; at least, he didn't complain as much as Paul did.)

'Who is weak and I do not feel weak? Who is led into sin, and I do not inwardly burn? If I must boast, I will boast of the things that show my weakness."

(To boast about his weakness, he, Paul, who just said that he did more than any apostle? I rather think that he has boasted about his toughness and endurance in all of this, don't you?)

'The God and Father of the Lord Jesus,'

(At least Paul didn't say; 'our Lord Jesus' here and I know that the Lord Jesus is not his lord.)

'Who is to be praised forever knows that I'm not lying.'

(And one more time here, Paul swore by taking God as his witness; which my Lord Jesus said not to do, not to swear by anything and the Messiah said that the one who does; that was coming from the devil. Only the liars need to do this, trying to be believed by others. See Matthew 5, 34-37.)

'In Damascus the governor under king Aretas had the city of the Damascenes guarded in order to arrest me.

But I was lowered in a basket from a window in the wall and slipped through his hands.'

(And we know it; this was done with the help of a little roman army. Wasn't he Paul, who said we have to summit to the governor's authorities? See again;)

Romans 13, 1. 'Everyone must submit himself (this includes Paul) to the governing authorities, for there is no authority except that which God has established. The authorities that exist have been established by God.'

(More yet, Paul said that the ones who fear the authorities are the wicked ones, the outlaws. There you are.

But one fact remains; this is that in Paul's writings, we learn and we hear a lot about Paul, but very little, at least about something good from Jesus and his disciples and mainly very little, if not nothing about the Messiah's messages.

Do you still believe the Messiah would have sent a man to preach Paul and his misfortunes to the Gentiles, instead of preaching the word of God; meaning all of the Jesus' messages to his disciples?

Well, not me! I said it before; it is good to believe, yes, but to believe the truth.

Just like a hypnotist, the devil has put the world to sleep with his lies. See for yourselves Matthew 13, 25. But contrary to this spectacular specialist of the stage; he didn't wake it up after the show, but he made it incapable to receive the truth. This is at least what the world seems to be to me. I am very happy for having escaped it and I thank God with all of my heart.)

2 Corinthians 12, 2-4. 'I know a man in Christ who fourteen years ago was caught up in the third heaven. Whether it was in the body or out of the body I don't know—God knows. And I know that this man—whether in the body or apart from the body I don't know, but God knows—was caught up in paradise. He heard inexpressible things, things that a man is not permitted to tell.'

(In my opinion, if Paul has heard inexpressible things, things that a man is not permitted to tell; he didn't go to paradise or up in the third heaven, but he went in hell.

This strangely resembles also a lot of the revelations from the so-called John of the Revelation, who has seen terrible monsters and spoke about the Paul's seven churches. This is something the true Jesus' apostle John wouldn't have done. Not only because the true John, Jesus' apostle, wouldn't tell some abominations like these, but also because he was an unschooled man.

We will see in what is following that Paul rather has a close relation with an angel of Satan and he even found a way to lie about that one too.'

2 Corinthians 12, 6-7. 'Even if I should choose to boast, I would not be a fool, because I would be speaking the truth. But I refrain,'

(From telling the truth, of course. What's new?)

'So no one will think more of me than is warranted by what I do or say.'

(It is always the same thing in Paul's writings, 'Me, myself and I.'

'To keep me from becoming conceited because of these surpassingly great revelations, there was given me a thorn in my flesh, a messenger of Satan, to torment me.'

(Do you really believe that a messenger of Satan, who is the most conceited being ever, could keep whomsoever from becoming conceited about whatsoever? Not me! I say this because a messenger of Satan would do the exact opposite. One of God's angels, especially the one that Paul said he would be eternally condemned, lost, if he was preaching a different gospel than Paul's lying gospel, could do it, but a God's angel knows very well that nothing can be done or said to bring Satan to God; not even God could do it. A God's angel wouldn't waste his time with Paul either, because the word of God put in the mouth of the Messiah teaches us to drive out such demons. See Matthew 10, 8.)

2 Corinthians 12, 8. 'Three times I pleaded with the Lord to take it away from me.'

(Again, who would pray to the Lord, to God, three times to take away from him someone who keeps him from becoming conceited? Only the devil or a son of the devil could do such a thing. The least he should have done is not to mention this. I do believe that Paul's lord, Paul's god is Satan.)

2 Corinthians 12, 9-10. 'Therefore I will boast all the more gladly about my weakness, so that Christ's power may rest on me. That's is why, for Christ's sake, I delight in weakness, in insults, in hardship, in persecutions, in difficulties. For when I am weak, I am strong.'

(It is always the same thing with Paul; the, 'me, myself and I.' It is the, 'I, the, 'me,' the 'us,' the, 'we,' the, 'myself,' and the, 'I am.' And this constitutes the biggest part of his so-called gospel. But if he delighted so much in his weakness; why was he complaining so much earlier while comparing himself with the Jesus' apostles and at his trial?

2 Corinthians 12, 11. 'I have made a fool of myself, but you drove me to it.'

(Why not for Paul to blame the Corinthians for his misfortunes and for his sins; this way his conscience is always clear and he can feel guilty of nothing.)

'I ought to have been commended by you, for I am not the least inferior to the "super-apostles," even though I am nothing.'

(This was for Paul a way to say to his disciples that the Jesus' super-apostles were nothing to him and this was also what he wanted his disciples to think. This was a way for him to put down the apostles and to elevate himself to their level as well.

2 Corinthians 12, 12. 'The things that mark an apostle—signs, wonders and miracles—were done among you with great perseverance.'

(This was said without any pretension, would you say? This was also exactly what Jesus, the Messiah has prophesied in;)

Matthew 24, 24-25. 'For false Christs and false prophets will appear and perform great signs and miracles to deceive even the elect—if that were possible. See, I have told you ahead of time.'

(One of Jesus' apostles has mentioned it too and this was not Paul.)

See 2 Thessalonians 2, 8-10. 'And then the lawless one will be revealed, whom the Lord Jesus will over throw with the breath of his mouth (the word of God) and destroy by the splendour of his coming. The coming of the lawless one will be in accordance with the work of Satan displayed in all kinds of counterfeit miracles, signs and wonders, and in every sort of evil that deceive those who are perishing. They perish because they refuse to love the truth and so be saved.'

(They perish because they believe in lies, because they believe the lawless one. They believe the one who introduced himself in the sheep pen, to the one for whom the Jesus' super-apostles are nothing, to the one who has contradicted Jesus' messages, to the one for whom the Law of God and the God's commandments are ageing and about to disappear. In short, they believe in the false Christ, in the false prophet who sat himself in God's temple. They believe in the one who has seduced way too many and it is time to stop this.)

2 Corinthians 12, 13-14. 'How were you inferior to the other churches, except that I was never a burden to you? Forgive me this wrong! Now I am ready to visit you for the third time, and I will not be a burden to you, because what I want is not your possessions but you.'

(This is scarier yet. But if Paul didn't want their possessions, why was he insisting so much to get their money earlier, in the same gospel? We have to see again;)

2 Corinthians 8, 7. 'But just as you excel in everything—in faith, in speech, in knowledge, in complete earnestness and in your love for us—see that you also excel in this grace of giving.'

(They had to give their possessions, either from smooth talk or flattery and if this was not working, then this was the whip and his little roman army and from that came fear and trembling.)

2 Corinthians 12, 15. 'So I (Paul) will very gladly spend for you everything I have and expend myself as well. If I love you more, will you love me less?'

(This too is quite scary, since we already know that Paul had money. See an example of that in;)

Acts 24, 26. 'At the same time he was hoping that Paul would offer him a bribe, so he sent for him frequently and talked with him.'

(We also know that in those days the money could be used to buy slaves. So when Paul said that he wanted them; then yes, this could have been very scary for them. And yes, a rich man with a bad temper, with a whip and a little roman army could very well send them in hell on earth. From that thought then came the fear and trembling.

Then the confession came from the very mouth of the crafty one in 2 Corinthians 12, 16, and it cannot be clearer than this.)

2 Corinthians 12, 16. 'Be that as it may, I have not been a burden to you. Yet, crafty fellow that I am, I (Paul) caught you by trickery!'

(Then the pride of the arrogant won over the simplicity of a disciple. Paul caught them by trickery. The Corinthians were caught just like Adam and Eve have been, by the same devil and by the same trick. It is through lies and from a few messages from the ancient prophets that Paul used to mislead people, letting them think he is telling the truth. The devil is crafty, but he also knows the Holy Scriptures.)

2 Corinthians 12, 17-19. 'Did I exploit you through any of the men I sent you? (Yes) I urged Titus to go to you and I sent our brother with him. Titus did not exploit

you, did he? (Yes) Did we not act in the same spirit and follow the same course? (Yes) Have you been thinking all along that we have been defending ourselves to you? (Yes) We have been speaking in the sight of God (God doesn't need money) as those in <u>Christ</u>; and everything we do, deer friends, is for your strengthening.' (False! And I know it.

When have you read anything like that coming out of the Messiah's mouth? The answer is never. The strengthening that Paul was talking about here was about his empire that is Christianity, the total of the diabolic religions that we know about today. Those that enriched themselves with the money from the poor ignorant people, who think they could buy a place in heaven with their money. But how could we blame these poor people who have learned the lies from the liars instead of the truth from God through his children?

2 Corinthians 12, 20-21. 'For <u>I</u> (Paul) am <u>afraid</u> that when <u>I</u> come <u>I</u> may not find you as <u>I</u> want you to be, and you may not find <u>me</u> as you want <u>me</u> to be. <u>I</u> <u>fear</u> that there may be quarrelling, jealousy, outbursts of anger, (against Paul, it is very possible,) factions, slander, gossip, arrogance and disorder. <u>I am</u> <u>afraid</u> that when <u>I</u> come again <u>my</u> God will humble me.'

(For sure, it is terribly scary for the devil, who is the king of false pride, or for his son, to be humbled, especially before his disciples.)

'Before you, and I will be grieved over many who have sin earlier and have not repented of the impurity, sexual sin and debauchery in which they have indulged.'

(Do you see? Paul who has preached that it was best for a man not to touch a woman, had a hard time accepting the real nature of human kind and he was doing everything he could possibly do to change God's plan. For this very reason, two thousand years later; the earth is still not filled. I sincerely believe that Paul's satanic work, the clergy and the empire of all his churches are responsible for that.

I don't say that I am for impurity or for sexual sin of any kind, but unlike Paul; I am on God's side who said: 'Be fruitful, multiply and fill up the earth.'

(Paul has mentioned earlier those who fear and I, personally, like better those who do what they preach. Jesus said the same thing when he mentioned those in;)

Matthew 23, 2-3. 'The teachers of the Law and the Pharisees sit in Moses' seat. So you must obey them and do everything they tell you. But do not do what they do, for they do not practice what they preach.'

(This was Paul too; he who was a Pharisee, as he said anyway. But Paul could not be a Pharisee and preach against the Law of God or against Moses either.

See what John, Jesus' brother had to say about fear in;)

1 John 4, 18. 'There is no fear in love. But perfect love drives out fear, because fear has to do with punishment. The one who fears is not made perfect in love.'

(All of the Jesus' brothers have seen through Paul, and as I do; they knew he was the Antichrist.

See that I am not the only one, apparently, to question where Paul is coming from or to whom he belonged. I said it before and I repeat it; if none of the Corinthians have kill Paul; this is because they were all better than him. Or yet, maybe, because they all have believed that Paul was God as Paul, himself, has pretended he was.

2 Corinthians 13, 1-2. 'This will be my third visit to you. "Every matter must be established by the testimony of two or three witnesses. I already gave you a warning when I was with you the second time. I now repeat it while absent: On my return <u>I will not spare</u> those who sinned earlier or any of the others.'

(Hello gentleness! And were there two or three witnesses each time someone was having sex? And if this is not pretending being God, to whom retribution is due; then tell me what that is. It is true too that Paul said he could see and judge someone without even be present. It is not surprising then that the Corinthians were expecting Paul or anyone from Paul with fear and trembling.)

2 Corinthians 13, 3. 'Since you are demanding proof that <u>Christ</u> is speaking through <u>me</u>. He is not weak in dealing with you, but is powerful among you.'

(It is not easy for anyone to make people swallow the lie once they know the truth. There is one thing that my mom saw and she brings it up quite often. It is written in;)

Luke 14, 26. '"If anyone comes to me and does not <u>hate</u> his father and mother, his wife and children, his brothers and sisters—yes even his own life—he cannot be my disciple."'

(This is a declaration worthy of the Antichrist and of Satan, but as far as I think; it is from the false Christ, and then, it makes really some sense. Because Jesus, the true Messiah came to preach love for God and for our neighbour, not hatred for anyone. To hate in all languages and in all the nations is the opposite of love.

Almost every verse is an abomination in this gospel of Paul and did I have to be very blind not to see this earlier. It is the very same thing for all the believers not to see it now. This is one of the reasons why I have to excuse the atheists; especially when we hear that everything in the Holy Bible is all inspired by the Holy Spirit. The Holy Spirit doesn't incite anyone to lie about anything, especially not about the word of God.

Read more to see a couple more abominations in;)

2 Corinthians 13, 4. 'For to be sure, he was crucified in weakness,'

(False, Jesus was crucified because of the wickedness in the world, mainly the one of the Romans, but this, Paul would not say.'

'Yet he lives by God's power. Likewise, we are weak in him.'

(False again! It is quite the opposite; because in Jesus I find the strength to continue to denounce and to expose this demon.)

'Yet by God's power we will live with him (Jesus) <u>to serve you</u>.'

(There was manipulation of the Scriptures here again. In the French Bible and in the King James, instead of: 'To serve you,' the meaning is more: 'To acts against you, or, 'to act toward you with the power of God.'

(Paul again used the word of God to use the whip against them. Paul, the father, gave himself the authority on others, but this didn't come from God or from the Messiah, but from the devil. And Paul would have not succeeded to disturb so much shit, if only the Romans weren't almost controlling everything and everywhere in those days. They wouldn't have succeeded to kill Jesus either.)

2 Corinthians 13, 5. 'Examine yourselves to see whether you are in the faith; test yourselves. Do you not realize that <u>Christ Jesus</u> is in you—unless, of course, you fail the test?'

(This clearly means: 'Unless, of course I, Paul, force you to it.'

(And this didn't necessarily mean having faith in Jesus or in God, but to have faith in Paul, in his ministry and in his gospel. And as we can see it now; this was done by the whip, by force that Paul was saying was coming from God. How many believed in Paul and how many still do? To me this is not a gospel at all, and if this is one, then it is worthy of Satan.)

2 Corinthians, 13, 10. 'This is why I write these things when I (Paul) am absent, that when I come I may not have to be harsh (to use the whip and or the army,) in my use of authority—the authority the lord gave me for building you up, not for tearing you down.'

(This whole letter from Paul to the Corinthians is 99.9999 % about Paul, himself and he, and the rest is about, 'Christ,' and God.

What is surprising me the most, is that no one has kill him, but we have seen it earlier, no one can kill the devil, especially when he has an army to protect him. And this is how the Roman Catholic Church and Christianity were founded. What a shame!

And Paul has finished his letter to the Corinthians the same way he has started it, meaning with some words that are coming from a Jesus' disciple. This way all the suspicions are erased and Paul had a much better chance to be believed.

2 Corinthians 13, 14. 'May the grace of the Lord Jesus Christ and the love of God, and the fellowship of the Holy Spirit be with you all.'

(Finally, I went through it all, but not without any pain, I have to admit it. It is very desolating to see so many abominations in the holy place. I wish you all to have the courage too to go through it, to better know whom you are dealing with. But it is over due time for you Christians to be born again and to begin believing the truth, and this is for your own salvation.)

See again 2 Thessalonians 2, 10. 'And in every sort of evil that deceive those who are perishing. They perish because they refuse to love the truth and so be saved.'

Chapter 8

To help you understanding all of this; I will continue to put my words and commentaries between parentheses.

Again here at the beginning of Galatians, Paul has mixed up his writings, his venom, with the writing of some of the Jesus' apostles, and he most likely thought it was worth it, otherwise; he wouldn't have done it.)

Galatians 1, 1-5. 'Paul, an apostle—sent not from men nor by man, but by Jesus Christ.'

(I know it now; Paul was sent by Satan, not by man. Jesus was a man, and we have to see one of John's messages, from Jesus' brother's in;)

1 John 4, 2-3. 'This is how you can recognize the Spirit of God: Every spirit that acknowledges that Jesus Christ has come in the flesh is from God, (Paul has not done that here) but every spirit that does not acknowledge Jesus is not from God. This is the spirit of the Antichrist, which you have heard his coming and even now is already in the world.'

(Paul was already in the world in those days.)

'And God the Father, who raised him from the dead—and all the brothers with me, to the churches (more than one) of Galatia: Grace and peace to you from God our Father and the Lord Jesus Christ,'

(This last phrase is the way of a Jesus' disciple to speak about our Master; which Paul could not do.)

'Who gave himself for our sins to rescue us from the present evil age,'

(See, Paul and his churches don't teach that Jesus gave himself, but they say that God gave him, sacrificed his one and only own Son.)

'According to the will of our God and Father, to whom be glory for ever and ever. Amen.'

(Now, what is following has not at all the same tone.)

Galatians 1, 6-7. 'I am astonished that you are so quickly deserting the one (Paul) who called you by the grace of Christ'

(This is Paul's way to speak about the Messiah, but I rejoice anyway, to see that some of the Galatians have seen through this Antichrist and turned away from him.)

'And turning to a different gospel—.'

(Paul meant here, turning to the gospel of the Jesus' apostles.)

'Which is really no gospel at all. Evidently some people (Jesus' disciples) are throwing you into confusion and are trying to pervert the gospel of Christ.'

(This means, to pervert the lying gospel of Paul. Do you see that there is no; 'Our Lord Jesus Christ,' in Paul's speech?

And Paul's venom continues in all the rest of his writings. I think that you have seen enough now to continue by yourselves to see the difference between a Jesus' disciple and a Satan's disciple, between the truth and the lie, between what is good and what is bad.

If God does not exist, there wouldn't be anything good and if Satan does not exist, there would be nothing bad, but this is not the case, in one case or in the other.

As it is just about everywhere in his writings, Paul has started his letter with the words of a Jesus' apostle, to gave himself some credit, and as it is just about everywhere; he has put his venom, his lies between the beginning and the end of his letters. So Paul just had to intercept letters from the Jesus' apostles, because they were writing to the other dispersed Jesus' disciples regularly and in every region where they had gone.

But Paul, as we have seen it, was writing to his churches mainly to tell his disciples not to let themselves be seduced by another gospel than his, a gospel where Paul preached mainly Paul in all of his letters.

The Jesus' disciples, I am sure, were preaching the Messiah and his messages, and Jesus, contrary to Paul, was not at all against the circumcision or the Law of God.

But before going any farther, here is the end of Paul's letter to the Galatians that ends just as it was started; I mean with the true words of a true Jesus' apostle.)

See Galatians 6, 18. 'The grace of our Lord Jesus Christ be with your spirit, brothers. Amen.'

(I wanted to leave the most part of the Galatians off to spare you of this agony that is desolation, but this gospel from Paul is also so full of abominations that they have to be denounced and I felt after that it is my duty to do it.

You will see again many; 'I, I, I,' and some, 'we, we, we,' and some, 'me, me, me,' and some, 'my, my, my,' and some, 'us, us, us,' and also many times, 'Christ.'

As far as I know, Paul and his churches are saying that Jesus is God and that he is the, 'Christ.' This means then that Paul has taken the Name of God in vain and this many, many times. But Paul didn't care about that at all, because, as he was saying; he was not under the Law of God. So he could allow himself to do anything without sinning and without any conscientious problem.

There is one very importing thing here, one detail to note; this is that Jesus, the Messiah, has never allowed himself to pronounce the Name of God in his whole gospel written by Matthew. When Jesus was speaking about God; he was saying; 'My Father who is in heaven,' or: 'The heavenly Father,' and again: 'The Lord of heaven.'

There is a huge difference between the humble and gentle in heart Messiah and the most arrogant that the Antichrist is.

I have already spoken about the Paul's blasphemy and his repetition that is written in Galatians 1, 8-9. This was certainly not worthy of a Jesus' apostle to defend his gospel with a blasphemy this way.

Galatians 1, 10-12. 'Am I now trying to win the approval of men, or of God? Or am I trying to please men? If I were trying to please men, I would not be a servant of Christ. I want you to know, brothers, that the gospel I preached is not something that man made up.'

(His gospel is not from men, I know, it is from Satan and it is evident.)

'I did not receive it from any man, nor was I taught it; rather I received it by a revelation from Jesus Christ.'

(Paul, just like Satan, was very arrogant and he was not shy at all to mix his lies with the name of Jesus and with the Holy Name of God, but Satan has already done it in the Garden of Eden with Adam and Eve, so he just continued to do it again, since he was successful the first time.

What is next is again Paul who preached Paul in;)

Galatians 1, 13-20. 'For you have heard of my previous way of life in Judaism, how intensively I persecuted the Church of God and tried to destroy it. I was advancing in Judaism beyond many Jews of my own age and was extremely zealous for the traditions of my fathers. But when God, who set me apart from birth and called me by his grace,'

(It is certainly not God who would set someone apart to kill the Jesus' disciples and to fight a war against them afterward.)

'Was please to reveal his Son in me so that I might preach Him among the Gentiles. I did not consult any man.'

(This is a lie again, but this is only for those who know the truth from the Holy Bible.)

'Nor did I go up to Jerusalem to see those who were apostles before I was, but I went immediately into Arabia and later returned to Damascus.'

(Yes, in Damascus, where, according to the Scriptures, a so-called disciple guided him by the hand because he could not see anymore. This is according to his love friend Luke, who wrote the story. Now take a look in Acts 9, 19, to see if it is true that Paul has not consulted any man.)

Acts 9, 19. 'Saul (Paul) spent several days with the disciples in Damascus.'

See Again Galatians 1, 13-14. 'For you have heard of my previous way of life in Judaism, how intensively I persecuted the Church of God and tried to destroy it. I was advancing in Judaism beyond many Jews of my own age and was extremely zealous for the traditions of my fathers.'

(Paul then was conscientious that this was God's Church that he tried to destroy, and yet; his conscience was clear and he felt guilty of nothing.

It is as Jesus said; Paul was one of those who were killing the prophets.

See Matthew 23, 31. 'So you testify against yourselves that you are the descendants of those who murdered the prophets.'

(But it was not only their fathers who were killing the God's children; Paul has done that too. And it was not because he didn't know God's Law that's says: 'You shall not kill,' because he was one of the most educated of his generation.

And why Paul had a clear conscience and that even after haven killed Jesus' disciples, after haven killed God's children? This is because he was happy for haven done the work of his father, the work of Satan.)

See 2 John 1, 7. 'Many deceivers, who do not acknowledge Jesus Christ as coming in the flesh, have gone out into the world. Any such person is the deceiver and the Antichrist.'

(And here we are; this is another Jesus' brother, who is telling us who really is the Antichrist.

Galatians 1, 18-20. 'Then after three years, I (Paul) went up to Jerusalem to get acquainted with Peter and stayed with him fifteen days.'

(Between you and me, I don't believe for one second that Peter could have put up with Paul and his lies during all of that time, and how could someone spend fifteen days with Peter and learn nothing from him? This is absolutely impossible.)

'I saw none of the other apostles—only James, the Lord's brother. I assure you before God that what I am writing you is no lie.'

(And one more time the arrogant swore again; which is to take God as a witness, and this to back up his lie and most likely because this was a lie. But the Messiah said not to do that.) See Matthew 5, 34-37. 'This comes from the evil one.'

(How could someone with a solid head on his shoulder and a bit of common sense to reflect about things believe that Paul spent fifteen days with Peter and met with James, Jesus' brother and have learn nothing from them? And how could Paul say he met these two and also say he has not consulted any man?

It is greatly possible that Satan has learned nothing from men, because he is crafty and bad enough to lie and to sin on his own will and to swear about his lies as well.

Let see again who Paul has preached in the rest of his letter to the Galatians.

Galatians 1, 21-24. 'Later I went to Syria and Cilicia. I was personally unknown to the churches (more than one) of Judea that are in Christ. They only heard the report:

"The man who formerly persecuted us is now preaching the faith he once tried to destroy. And they praised God because of me.'

(It seems to me that everything we heard about Paul came from Paul. And this is how the ferocious wolf tried to make his entry in the sheep pen. And if the churches of Judea were praising God because of Paul; this was because he had stopped for a time to persecute the Jesus' disciples and this was indeed to give himself a chance to enter the camp of the apostles. Paul had at that time delegated his mercenary duties to his friend Herod the tetrarch, who had imprisoned Peter and have James killed by the sword, the Jesus' apostle, John's brother. But the Jesus' apostles who were guided by the Holy Spirit didn't fall in the devil's trap.)

See Acts 9, 1. 'Meanwhile, Saul (Paul) was still breathing out murderous threats against the Lord's disciples.'

(Paul was not any better, according to the apostles more than fifteen year later.)

See Acts 21, 21. 'They have been informed that you (Paul) teach all the Jews who live among the Gentiles to turn away from Moses, (away from the Law, away from the God's commandments and away form circumcision) telling them not to circumcise their children (then against the circumcision) or live according to our customs.'

(Then, this was also against the people of God and this was several years after his so-called conversion to

Jesus. The devil had then just changed his tactical ways; since that when he was killing the Jesus' disciples; he was sending them directly to God. This is what Paul saw at the killing of Stephen. Paul knew then that he would do a lot more damages in the sheep pen if only he could make anyone believe he was also a Jesus' apostle, and this is what he has done.

Galatians 2, 1-2. 'Fourteen years later I (Paul) went up again to Jerusalem,'

(This was then seventeen year after his so-called conversion to Jesus.)

'This time with Barnabas. I took Titus along also. I went in response to a revelation and set before them (the apostles) the gospel I preach among the Gentiles.'

(But according to what is written in the Acts by Luke, Paul's loved friend and most likely also was his secretary; concerning the distance covered by Paul; all Paul has done was to enter in all the synagogues of the Jews, just as the false Christ who is in the gospel of John has done. Look and be careful as you read this in;)

Acts 13, 4-5. 'The two of them, sent on their way by the Holy Spirit, went down to Seleucia and sailed from there to Cyprus. When they (Paul and company) arrived in Salamis, they proclaimed the word of God in the Jewish synagogues. John was with them as a helper.'

(There are many more, but here is just another one; just to make sure that you have enough proofs.)

Acts 14, 1-2. 'At Iconium Paul and Barnabas went as usual into the Jewish synagogue. There they spoke so effectively that a great number of Jews and Gentiles believed. But the Jews who refuse to believe (in Paul's lies and contradictions) stirred up the Gentiles and poisoned their minds (with the truth) against the brothers.'

(To Paul those who didn't want to believe in his lies, his contradictions and his abominations were the bad Jews. Besides, the Gentiles, as always, had no right and still have no right to enter in the Jewish synagogues. Look and read carefully what some Jews had to say about Paul in what is next in;)

Acts 21, 28. 'Men of Israel, help us! This is the man (Paul) who teaches all men everywhere against our people (Israel) and our Law (of God) and this place.'

(This is the temple! See that I am not the only one and neither the first one to say that Paul is the lawless one.)

'And besides, he has brought Greeks (Gentiles) into the temple and defiled this holy place."

(Is that clear enough for you? And I continue.)

'But I did this privately to those who seemed to be the leaders,'

(Then this was to Peter, to James and John. In the French Bible and in the King James, Paul knew exactly who the leaders were among the Jesus' apostles. And trust me, if Paul wanted to speak to them in private; this is because he knew perfectly well who the leaders were.)

Galatians 2, 3-4. 'Yet not even Titus, who was with me, (Paul) was compelled to be circumcised, even though he was a Greek.'

(What a relieved this seemed to be for Paul! The Jesus' apostles, the most considerate among them, weren't that bad and authoritarians after all. The thing was, do you see, that Paul didn't want that any other man than he touches his Titus? Paul circumcised Timothy, so he was able by himself to circumcise Titus as well. But if Titus was not circumcised; this was because Paul was completely against the circumcision, just like he is against everything that is coming from God. Either this is the circumcision, the Law of God, the commandments and even the word of God.)

'This matter arose because some false brothers,'

(Paul here was talking about the group of the circumcision, who was working hand in hand with the Jesus' apostles to circumcise the baby boys at the age of eight days, and this according to the Jewish customs.)

'Had infiltrated our ranks to spy on the freedom we have in Christ Jesus and to make us slaves.'

(The freedom Paul was talking about here was not to be obligated to be under the Law of God, not to be obligated to obey the God's commandments and not to be obligated to be circumcised. In fact, Paul didn't want to have anything to do with the customs of the Jews, with the people of God. But the truth is that our Lord Jesus Christ, the Messiah, didn't come to abolish anything from the Law of God, nor anything that is coming from God. See again for yourselves Matthew 5, 17-18.)

Galatians 2, 5-6. 'We did not give in to them for a moment,'

(Why would they have to give in to them for anything, if they were not compelled to anything?

'So that the truth of the gospel might remain with you.' (The Galatians) As for those who seemed to be important—'

(Paul knew exactly who were the most important and this is why he said that he spent fifteen days with Peter and met with James.)

'Whatever they were makes no difference to me;'

(Paul, the arrogant, thought himself above them all)

'God does not judge by external appearance—those added nothing to my message.'

(The meaning is completely different than this in the French Bible. It says, 'Those who are the most considerate among them (the apostles) didn't impose anything to me.'

(Then, if nothing was imposed to Paul and company from the most important among the Jesus' apostles and that Titus was not compelled to be circumcised, why then Paul told the Galatians he did not give in to them and why was he so defensive? It is a bit contradictory, to say the least.

When someone doesn't care about the Law of God and about the covenant God made with Abraham and his people, then why would he care about the most important of the Jesus' apostles and what they had to say, or about the word of God?

Paul said more than once that he has learned nothing at all from men and we have to believe it in the sense that Satan has learned nothing from human kind, but many believed and still believe in him and still follow him anyway.

Paul said that he spent fifteen days with Peter. How anyone could spent even one day or even one hour with the most considerate of the Jesus' apostles; the one to whom Jesus gave the keys of the kingdom of heaven and learn nothing from him? To me the answer is very simple. He has to be God, or one of his angels, or Satan, or one of his angels, or one of devil's demons.

I am far from being Peter, but I am sure that you have learned something in the two first minutes you spent in this book of mine.

But believe it; Paul was not one of God's angels and he is not God either. What I personally think is that meeting has never taken place. And since Paul lied about so many things; he most likely lied about that one too. All of this just to give himself some credit, trying to be believed and to get some consideration from the ones he tried to convince. So lying, judging, swearing, blaspheming, using the word of God; everything and anything was allowed to him, since sin had no power on him. As he said anyway.)

See Romans 6, 14. 'For sin shall not be your master, (sin have no power over you) because you are <u>not</u> under Law, (like Paul is not) but under grace.'

(I don't think that Peter could have put up with Paul even one day. Besides, Peter and James, Jesus' brother, have done what had to be done to get rid of Paul, and I think that was only at Paul's second visit with them. All of the Jesus' apostles and James had more than enough of Paul then, and so do I now.

Galatians 2, 7-8. 'On the contrary, (contrary to be compelled to anything) they saw that I have been entrusted with the task of preaching the gospel to the Gentiles, just as Peter has been to the Jews. For God, who was at work in the ministry of Peter as an apostle of the Jews, was also at work in my ministry as an apostle to the Gentiles.'

(If this was the case, then what were Paul and company doing in all of the synagogues of the Jews; there where no Gentile has the right to enter? And if Paul and company entered the Jewish synagogues; this had to be done by force, so by Paul and his army, just like he was doing it before his so-called conversion. See Paul in;)

Acts 26, 11. 'Many a time I (Paul) went from one synagogue to another to have them punished, and <u>I tried</u> to force them to blaspheme. In my obsession against them, I even went to foreign cities to persecute them.'

(The Holy Scriptures are teaching us also that Paul was not welcome at all in the synagogues or in the temple, and this long after his so-called conversion. Read carefully Acts 21, 21-31.

And if this was the case for the temple; this was also the case in all of the Jewish synagogues, because the temple and all the synagogues were under the same rules and customs from the Jews.

Galatians 2, 9-10. 'James, Peter and John, those reputed to be pillars.'

(So now they don't just seem to be the most important for Paul, they are.)

'Gave me and Barnabas the right hand of fellowship when they recognized the grace given to me. They agreed that we should go to the Gentiles, and they to the Jews. All they asked was that we should continue to remember the poor, the very thing I was eager to do.'

(Let's us see how Paul remembered to poor in;)

1 Corinthians 11, 34. 'If anyone is hungry, he should eat at home, so that when you meet together it may not result in judgement. And when I (Paul) come I will give further directions.'

(This shows at the same time who was the bishop in Paul's churches. Paul remembered the poor alright, but he didn't feed them and he didn't want his churches to feed them either. Paul was among them to pick up the money, not to give and this is what all of his churches have done also.

Jesus' Church has a much different device: 'You have received freely, give freely.'

(Who wants to join me now in this wonderful Church of the Messiah? It is up to anyone to reach me in the beautiful kingdom of Jesus, in the kingdom of heaven. Not in when only God knows when, but now, immediately. All you have left to do is to follow Jesus and Jesus' teaching, not Paul and his lies.

What is next is the exact message from Paul that helped me to open my eyes about him. It is with that message that Paul proved to me that he was not a true Jesus' apostle or one of his disciples, because he has done the exact opposite of what Jesus taught his apostles.

And from there, as you can see for yourselves; I found hundreds of messages from Paul that contradict the teaching of the Messiah.

Galatians 2, 11-14. 'When Peter came to Antioch, I (Paul) <u>opposed him</u> to his face, because he was clearly in the wrong. Before certain men came from James, (Jesus' brother) he (Peter) used to eat with the Gentiles. But when they arrived, he began to draw back and separate himself from the Gentiles because <u>he was afraid</u> of those who belonged to the circumcision group. The other Jews joined him (Peter) in his <u>hypocrisy</u>, so that by their hypocrisy even Barnabas was led astray.

When I saw that they were not acting in line with the truth of the gospel, (that was not yet written in those days) I (Paul) said to Peter in front of them all, "You are a Jew, yet you live like a Gentile and not like a Jew. How it is, then, that you force Gentiles to follow Jewish customs?"'

(Let me show you now two things, two messages of truth from the Messiah's gospel that Paul didn't respect, but not at all. See Jesus in;)

Matthew 18, 15. 'If your brother sins against you, go and show him his fault, just between the two of you.'

(So, if Peter was truly in the wrong, as Paul said it, and if Peter was a brother to him, as Paul said it; and if Paul was a true apostle, as Paul said it; then he would have had to show him his fault just between the two of them and not before the whole assembly as he has done it.

Here is the second action that Paul did that doesn't agree with the Jesus' teaching in Paul's story of Antioch.)

See Matthew 5, 39. 'But I (Jesus) tell you. Do not resist an evil person. If someone strikes you on the right cheek, turn to him the other also.'

(Now, according to the Scriptures, Paul has not respected either one. I don't say that Peter was in the wrong, on the contrary, but Paul said it, at least in that story of Antioch. But according to Jesus, Paul should have not opposed Peter to his face or otherwise.

I don't think either that Peter would have done anything because he was afraid of the circumcision group or have forced anyone to follow the Jewish customs. I absolutely don't believe either that Peter would have acted as a hypocrite like Paul said he did.

And if all the other Jews and also even Barnabas pulled away from Paul; this was only a very good thing. But for Paul this was most likely the real reason why he was so upset, not to say, furious.

I am sure that Peter who was carrying the keys of the kingdom of heaven has obeyed our Master until the end, has obeyed Jesus, and this no matter what the devil wanted the world to believe. This story about Paul and Peter in Antioch is just another wile from the devil to discredit Peter. So, listen to Jesus, as God asked us to do, see Matthew 17, 5, and don't let yourselves be seduced by this liar of Paul.

This story of Antioch is also the one that opened my eyes about the false prophet. With that story Paul proved to me that he is not Peter's brother in Jesus, that he is not Jesus' brother and neither mine.

There is one thing that is very strange; this is that it is through a revelation that I received in a dream that God showed me who is the Antichrist. But contrary to the revelation that Paul received; the one I received happened to be truthful and well founded and everything I wrote about Paul in my books proves it.)

Galatians 2, 15. 'We who are Jews by birth (Paul and Peter) and not 'Gentile sinners."

(There are and there were sinners among the Jews also, since Jesus said this: 'Go rather to the lost sheep of Israel.'

There are also the reproaches the Messiah made against the scribes and the Pharisees that we can read in Matthew 23, 13-36. Being a Jew is not a good enough reason not to be a sinner.

Then came one of the biggest lies from Paul's mouth in what is next, but it seems that this didn't stop him to seduce many people anyway.

Galatians 2, 16. 'Know that a man is not justified by observing the Law, but by faith in Jesus Christ. So we, too, (the demons) have put our faith in Christ Jesus that we may be justified by faith in Christ and not by observing the Law, because by observing the Law no one will be justified.'

(What I just wrote down coming from Paul is completely contrary to the Jesus' messages and completely contrary of the word of God. Which one do you believe?

See Matthew 11, 19. 'The Son of Man (which means, God's Prophet) came eating and drinking, and they say, 'Here is a glutton and a drunkard, a friend of tax collectors and sinners, but wisdom is proved right by her actions.'

See also Matthew 16, 27. 'For the Son of Man is going to come in his Father's glory with his angels, and then he will reward each person according to what he has done.'

(Is that clear enough for you? This is not by faith alone, faith that is completely worthless without actions.

Do you want more proofs that Paul has lied? Here are some more of them.)

Job 34, 10-11. 'So listen to me, you men of understanding. Far be it from God to do evil, from the almighty to do wrong. He repays a man for what he has done; He brings upon him what his conduct deserves.'

(That too is clear enough.)

Psalm 62, 12. 'And that You, O Lord are loving. Surly You will reward each person according to what he has done.'

(See also Proverbs 24, 12, Ezekiel 7, 27 and 33, 20.)

Isaiah 59, 18. 'According to what they have done, so will He repay wrath to his enemies and retribution to his foes; He will repay the Islands their due.'

Jeremiah 17, 10. 'I the Lord search the heart and examine the mind, to reward a man according to his conduct, according to what his deeds deserve.'

Jeremiah 32, 19. 'Great are your purposes and mighty are your deeds. Your eyes are open to all the ways of men; You reward everyone according to <u>his conduct</u> and as <u>his deeds</u> deserve.'

Jeremiah 51, 56. 'For the Lord is a God of recompense, He will fully repay.'

Hosea 4, 9. 'I (God) will punish both of them for their ways and repay them for their deeds.'

(Jesus, the Messiah and a big number of God's prophets, who were there before him, and so did God, said that men will be judged according to their ways and their deeds. But God's enemies have said the exact opposite. So you, Christians of the whole world who have put your trust in Paul; you Paul's fans, will you continue to believe Paul, to believe Satan instead of believing the Messiah and all of the God's prophets, instead of believing in the Almighty?

Paul was bringing out all kind of messages from the Old Testament to keep people in darkness, to mislead them, then why did he has never mentioned the ones I just wrote down? And don't you think that he didn't know them, because he knew them more than anyone, just as he said it himself.

See how much saliva Paul deployed to make people swallow his lie in what is next;)

Galatians 2, 17-21. 'If, while we (the demons) seek to be justified in Christ, it becomes evident that we ourselves are sinners,'

(If you are a sinner, you are evidently a son of the devil, you are dead, but God is the God of the living.)

'Does that mean that Christ promotes sin? Absolutely not!'

(Jesus doesn't, but the devil does, by saying that all of his children have sins and by saying they are not under the Law of God.)

'If I rebuild what I destroyed, I prove that I am a lawbreaker. For through the Law I died to the Law so that I might live for God.'

(To live for God is to live to the Law, not die. The dead, the sinners live for Satan. It is not the Law that causes the death of the soul, but sin. Look at Ezekiel 18, 18 again, and the story of Adam and Eve.)

'I (Paul) have been crucified with <u>Christ</u> and I no longer live.'

(This is false again, unless he was one of the robbers crucified at the same time Jesus was. Jesus was resurrected by God, not Paul, even though he tried to make people believe he was resurrected too. And if he no longer lives; this means he is dead, but God is the God of the living.)

'But Christ lives in me.'

(This is false too, because Jesus lives in who preaches Jesus; so he lives in who preaches the word of God and not in the one who preaches Paul and his lies. The false Christ lives in the liar.)

'The life I live in the <u>body</u>,'

(In the flesh, as it is written in the King James Bible) 'I live by faith in the Son of God.'

(So do Satan, his angels and his demons.)

'Who loved and <u>gave himself</u> for me.'

(This is false again, because Jesus gave himself, this is true, but he gave himself for those, the sinners, who have at heart to repent; which is not at all Paul's case. And this is not all; Paul and his churches have said many times that this was God who gave his one and only Son to save the world.)

'I do not set aside the grace of God, for if righteousness could be gained through the Law, Christ died for nothing.'

(Jesus, in fact, has died for nothing concerning all of those who refuse to repent and to turn to God. And here is what he said he will tell them.)

See Matthew 7, 23. 'Then I (Jesus) will tell them plainly, 'I never knew you. Away from me, you evildoers.'

(I would like to add something to this, 'all of you evildoers who believed in me, Jesus.'

(Outch, yes outch, because this is the truth, no matter the size of your faith, and no one will be able to say that Jesus didn't tell us. This is why Jesus gave himself, so we can get the knowledge of the truth. He told us also what will be the blessings that come with listening to the word of God and what will be the consequences for listening to the liars, the deceivers. These are the ones I denounce in my books.

Then we can see in what is next how Paul treated those who have preferred listening to the truth from the Jesus' disciples and turned away from Paul, and this I think, by risking their lives.)

Galatians 3, 1-5. 'You foolish Galatians!'

(Do you remember Jesus in;)

Matthew 5, 22. 'But anyone who says, (to his brother) 'You fool.' will be in danger of the fire of hell.'

'Who has bewitched you? (My guess is, 'the Jesus' disciples.')

'Before your very eyes Jesus Christ was clearly portrayed as crucified. I would like to learn just one thing from you,'

(Come on now, 'they are foolish.' Besides, Paul, you already said that you have learned nothing from men.)

'Did you receive the Spirit by observing the Law, or by believing what you hear?'

(I would say that if they received the Holy Spirit; this was because they heard the truth from some of the Jesus' disciples, and this was why Paul called them foolish. It is very clear to me that Paul was teaching faith to the detriment of the obedience to the Law of God, to the detriment of the obedience in the God's commandments.)

'Are you so foolish? After beginning with the Spirit, are you now trying to attain your goal by <u>human effort</u>?

(This last phrase is written differently in the King James Bible. Here it is: 'Are ye now made perfect <u>by the flesh</u>?'

(Here Paul doesn't want the Galatians to return obeying to the Law of God, but just to believe in what he taught. This said in another word; would be to believe in his lies. He didn't want them to be justified by deeds, by flesh, but just by faith. But see again what he said just a page earlier in;)

From the King James, Galatians 2, 20. 'And the life which I now live in the flesh I live by the faith of the Son of God.'

(Well, let me tell you; the faith of the Son of God is not at all Paul's faith. There were manipulations here again. Here is how it is written in the International Bible.)

Galatians 2, 20. 'The life I live in the body, I live by faith in the Son of God.'

(The faith of someone and the faith in someone are two much different meanings.

The devil believes so much in the Son of God that he has deployed thousand of efforts and hundreds of lies to keep his world in darkness.

'Have you suffered so much for nothing—(Because of Paul) if it really was for nothing?'

(What is next was manipulated again. The one who gives the Spirit in the New International Version Bible is God, but in the French Bible and in the King James Bible, it is 'he,' and it really means, Paul, as you too will see with what comes next.

'Does God give you his Spirit and work miracles among you because you observe the Law, or because you believe what you heard?

(Paul's predication and his lies. See now the King James Version.)

Galatians 3, 5. 'He therefore that ministered to you the Spirit, (which is Paul) and worked miracles among you, doeth he it by the work of the Law, or by the hearing of faith?

(And who preached faith to the detriment of the obedience to the Law of God. This is Paul. This is certainly not God. Paul is also the one who pretended giving the Spirit to these poor people. This too was for Paul the claim he was God.

I have been writing about these things concerning Paul for quite some times, but I still wonder what miracle he has performed. I think they were some little magic tricks as a sorcerer could do. I remember though that Jesus, the Messiah, has mentioned something important about this kind of people.)

See Matthew 24, 24. 'For false Christs and false prophets will appear and perform great signs and miracles to deceive even the elect—if that were possible.'

(I believe here that the Galatians didn't believe in Paul's great signs and miracles more than I do myself and this was a good thing for them. They were not so foolish after all and they could make the difference between a little magic trick, as a sorcerer could do, and a true miracle. I also think they could make the difference between a true Jesus' disciples and a false one, a demon. The Galatians were not so foolish if they could resist to Paul's lies. This is the blessing for knowing the truth. One has to remember too that, as Jesus, the

Messiah said it, the false Christs have already appeared, and we can see them in the gospel of Mark, and Luke and in John.

And, as it is his habit and as Paul thought it necessary for him to influence those he believed were foolish; he brought back again another story from the Old Testament, but all he did with it is another lie to mislead people. Paul spoke;)

Galatians 3, 6-9. 'Consider Abraham: "He believed God, and it was credited to him as righteousness." Understand, then, that those who believe (like Satan and his demons) are children of Abraham. The Scripture foresaw that God would justify the gentiles by faith, and announced the gospel in advance to Abraham: "All nations will be blessed through you." So those who have faith are blessed along with Abraham, the man of faith.'

(All of this is a pile of lies again. It is not through the belief, or through the faith of Abraham that all the nations were blessed through Abraham, but because of his obedience to the Law of God.

Look and decide for yourselves by reading what is next:)

Genesis 26, 4-5. 'I will make your descendants as numerous as the stars in the sky and I will give them all these lands, and through your offspring all nations on earth will be blessed, because Abraham obeyed Me

(God) and kept my requirements, my commands, my decrees and my Laws.'

(What did God talk about in this declaration, the faith in God, the faith in Jesus, or about the obedience in his Laws? You can answer that for yourselves. I personally know the answer for a long time now. Besides, this was said longtime before God gave his commandments to Moses. God has made his will known to Adam and Eve right from the beginning.

What is next is another succession of abominations from Paul, from the lawless one.)

Galatians 2, 10-13. 'All who rely on observing the Law are under a curse,'

(To say such a thing is an abomination.)

'For it is written: "Cursed is everyone who does not continue to do everything written in the book of the Law."'

(What about those who continue to observe the Law? What about Zachariah and his wife Elisabeth? See Luke 1, 5-6.

This is not because Paul, Satan and all his angels and demons don't love God enough to observe the Law of God that the rest of the world can't or doesn't observe it. The one who misses can always repent, as the Messiah asked us to do to be forgiven. This is even his main message to save us.

Satan would like to see the whole world being cursed, but this is not the case. He would also like to see God's angels being condemned, but that is not the case either. It is not because Satan is the lawless one that the rest of the world followed him in his abominations.)

'Clearly no one is justified before God by the Law.'

(Again and as always, this is a lie and an abomination from Paul's part. We have just seen it; Abraham was justified by his obedience to the God's Laws and he is not the only one. And far from being cursed; all the nations of the earth were blessed and are blessed because of his actions. See also the Messiah in;)

Matthew 16, 27. 'For the Son of Man is going to come in his Father's glory with his angels, and then he will reward each person according to what he has done.'

(Just to play on words here; 'To Satan and to Paul is the faith without deeds, without the Law. Just like James, Jesus' brother said it; faith is dead and useless without deeds. See James 2, 17.)

'Because, "The righteous <u>will live</u> by faith." The Law is not based on faith; on the contrary, "The man who does these things will live by them."

(The Law had to be created before someone could believe in it. (The righteous live and feed on every word that comes out of God's mouth. See Matthew 4, 4. But that was not for Paul and it is not for Satan either. This is for the righteous.)

'<u>Christ</u> redeemed us from the curse of the Law,'

(Jesus redeemed nothing at all from the Law, not even the least stroke of a pen.)

'By becoming a curse for us,'

(What, but what an abomination that one is! Talking about the abomination in the holy place, in the Holy Bible, do you see it?

'For it is written: 'Cursed is everyone who is hung on a tree.'

(If Jesus was a curse, 'lost, condemned,' as the devil say he is; even God wouldn't want him. But there is worse yet. The same devil, by saying that Jesus is God is also saying that God is, 'cursed,' and this is also blaspheming. Be sure to note too that this was said by Paul long after his so-called conversion to Jesus. Blasphemer on day?????

Satan would like for Jesus to be a curse, as he has also wanted for a God's angel to be eternally condemned, but the Messiah is the greatest blessing the world has known to this day and this is far away from being a curse. Though, this is what disturbs Satan the most. The Messiah came to save the world that Satan believes it belongs to him, and this makes him mad as hell. If there is a curse coming from Jesus, the Messiah; it is a curse for Satan, for his angels and for his demons.

He will hate me just as much for denouncing him and he will send his demons to persecute me, but no matter what happens, God his my support; He is my shield.)

Galatians 3, 14-16. 'That the blessing of Abraham (the blessing came from God) might come on the

Gentiles through Jesus Christ; that we might receive the promise of the Spirit through faith.'

(This is not necessarily and only the Spirit that was premised, but God's blessing and not only to the posterity of Abraham, but to all the nations on the earth and this, because of Abraham's obedience to the Laws of God. These Laws that Paul didn't want to have anything to do with. This promise was not made to the demons.

'Brothers,'

(Sure, Paul talked to them as if they were brothers. The ones he called; 'foolish.')

'Let me take an example from everyday life.'

(This is how it is written in the New International Version Bible. Let's see now the one from the King James.)

'Brothers, I speak after the manner of men.'

(You have to admit that this is a bit different. But Paul claimed to be God here again, or at least someone else.)

'Just as no one can set aside or add to a human covenant that has been duly established, so it is in this case. The promises were spoken to Abraham and to his seeds.'??????????

(The promises were made to Isaac as well, and this because of Abraham's obedience to the Laws of God. Read carefully Genesis 26, 1-5, to see the truth.

'The Scriptures does not say, "and to seeds," meaning many people, but, "and to your seed," meaning <u>one person</u>, who is <u>Christ</u>.'

(There is still something false here in what Paul wrote. The posterity of Abraham is not only Jesus, far from it, but it is the entire nation of Israel and this because of Abraham and it is because of his obedience to the Laws of God that all the nations on earth are blessed through him. This is the truth. So we are all blessed because of the people of Israel; the Jews that Paul, the devil and the Romans kept busy denigrating.)

See again Genesis, 26, 4. 'I (God) will make your descendants as numerous as the stars in the sky.'

(There is a lot more than one star in the sky, just like there is a lot more than one person in the posterity of Abraham.

As you can see it for yourselves; there is something to contradict in just about everything Paul wrote. For what I see in Paul's writings; it seems to me that a liar can't stop lying, because one lie can't wait for another. This proves undeniably that Paul was not sent by Jesus, the Messiah. Jesus could not have sent someone in the world to mislead it and to preach everything contrary to his own teaching, contrary to the word of God. This is impossible. On the other hand, it is very possible that Satan sent one of his demons to oppose God's plan, or else, he came himself to do his dirty work.)

Galatians 3, 17-19. 'What I mean is this: The Law, introduced 430 years later, does not set aside the covenant previously established by God and thus do away with the promise.'

(This is abomination again, because this is to say that God didn't hold to his promise by establishing his ten commandments. What Paul has wrote here is completely abominable.

The Law of God can not be too old or obsolete, or disappear, or put aside, cancelled, as Paul said it is.)

See Hebrews 8, 13. 'By calling this covenant, 'New,' He (God) has made the first one obsolete and what is obsolete and ageing will soon disappear.')

(The Messiah said that not the least stroke of a pen will disappear from the Law of God. God said that his Laws will be in his people's hearts for the eternity, after this actual world, but Satan said that the Laws of God are obsolete and about to disappear. Who do you believe?)

'For if the inheritance depends on the Law, then it no longer depends on the promise; but God in his grace gave it to Abraham through a promise.'

(The inheritance came from God.)

'What then was the purpose of the Law? It was added because of transgressions.' until the Seed to whom the promise referred had come.'

(This is false again. We have just seen it. Abraham was obeying to the <u>Laws</u> of God and this is even the very reason why the promise was made to his posterity. When God wrote his commandments on stones in the presence of Moses on Mount Sinai; this was not the first time God has made his will known to the world, especially to Israel, his people. Besides, God wrote them twice and the first time was before one part of his people has committed idolatry against Him.)

'The Law was put into <u>effect</u> through angels by a mediator.'

(The promise made to the posterity of Abraham didn't start with the Messiah, but with Isaac, Abraham's son and it continues, because all the nations on earth are blessed because of Abraham's obedience. It is written in Genesis 26, 4-5.

The Law, which is the will of God, was put into effect by God Himself to Adam and Eve the first time and the punishment for failing to obey came because of their disobedience. They chose to listen to the charming devil, to the deceiver. And all who listen to Paul, to Satan, still today, as always, and this without repenting, will also receive the punishment. The blessings from the promise God has made to Abraham, or because of Abraham, will be for those who obey the Law, for those who obey the commandments. Listening to the devil was sad and harmful on earth for Adam and Eve, and it will be the same for all of those who listen to Paul; because he has done the very same thing the serpent did in the Garden of Eden. This was and is contradicting God.

The demons can make people believe just about all the lies to the people who know just about nothing about the truth. And this is, especially if these demons are highly educated and are speaking to the ones who don't know anything about the word of God. This is exactly what Paul has done.)

Galatians 3, 20-22. 'A mediator, however, does not represent just one party, but God is One. Is the Law, therefore, opposed to the promises of God? Absolutely not! For if the Law had been given that could impart (gives) life.'

(Well, this is exactly what obeying the Laws of God does to us. It keeps us alive. It is the sin, disobeying to the Laws that cause us to die spiritually. Let's see again one of the main messages form the Messiah written in;)

Matthew 19, 17. 'But if you want to enter into life, (to live) keep the commandments.'

(Then, to observe the Law.)

See also Ezekiel 18, 18-20. 'But his father will die (this is spiritually) for his own sin, because he practiced extortion, robbed his brother and did what was wrong among his people. Yet you ask, 'Why does the son not share the guilt of his father?' Since the son has done what is just and right and has been careful to keep all my decrees, he will surely live. (This by observing the Law.) The soul who sins is the one who will die. The son will not share the guilt of the father, nor will the father share the guilt of the son. The righteousness of the righteous man will be credited to him, and the wickedness of the wicked will be charged against him.'

(Then, the sin of Adam and Eve cannot be charged to the rest of the world.??????????? This is at least questionable. The world has already received the punishment for their sin.)

See also 2 Kings 14, 6. 'Yet he did not put the sons of the assassins to death, in accordance with what is written in the Book of the Law of Moses where the Lord commanded: "Fathers should not be put to death for their children, nor children put to death for their fathers; each is to die (again, spiritually) for his own sins."'

(The entire God's judgement and his entire justice begin with his Laws and they are the culminant point; which determines the will of God, but Satan spent incalculable efforts to make people believe that the God's Laws have no more values since Jesus died on the cross. This is nothing else than a desolating abomination. And I continue with Galatians 3, 21.

'Then righteousness would certainly have come by the Law. But the Scripture declares that the whole world is a prisoner of sin,'

(It is not the Holy Scripture that declares the whole world is prisoner of sin. Satan did and does that, so talk for yourself Paul. The weed among the wheat, the wolf in the sheep pen continues to lie, continues his contradictions and his abominations in the holy place, and they are right here in the Holy Bible. And the wicked world has given Satan a lot of room. I'd say at least 95% of the New Testament.

'So what was promised, being given through faith in Jesus Christ, might be given to those who believe.'

(What a lie this is again! It is obvious to me that Satan was preaching for himself and for his demons, which they too believe in Jesus Christ. The promise from God was received by his people long before Jesus came on this earth. We only have to think about Abraham, Isaac, Jacob, Joseph, Moses, David and all of those who had the will of God in their heart just like Jesus did and it is still the same.)

Galatians 3, 23-25. 'Before this faith came,'

(As if faith didn't exist before the coming of Jesus. This is completely ridiculous. Wasn't he, Paul, who was talking about the faith of Abraham, and the faith of Sarah and about the faith of many others, who were there long before Jesus? Remember; 'It is by faith that.....'

See Paul in Hebrews 11, 3, Hebrews 11, 4, Hebrews 11, 5, Hebrews 11, 7, Hebrews 11, 8, Hebrews 11, 9, Hebrews 11, 11, Hebrews 11, 17, Hebrews 11, 20, Hebrews 11, 21, Hebrews 11, 22, Hebrews 11, 23, Hebrews 11, 24, Hebrews 11, 27, Hebrews 11, 29, Hebrews 11, 30 and Hebrews 11, 31.

'We were held prisoners by the Law, locked up until faith should be revealed.'

(I just wonder if Paul was not talking about himself and his demons here.)

'So the Law was put in charge to lead <u>us</u> to <u>Christ</u> that <u>we</u> might be justified by faith. Now that faith has come, we (Paul and company, the lawless ones) are no longer under the supervision of the Law.'

(This is another way for Paul, for the lawless one, to say that the Law of God doesn't exist anymore, that it was abolished with the death of Jesus on the cross. But as always, he lies just as he breathes.

No one was or is locked-up and no one was or is prisoner of the Laws of God. All were and are free to follow them or not, but also, all were and are warned about the consequences as well.

Even Adam and Eve were warned right from the beginning and they too had their choices. And if Paul didn't have the choice, or if he was a prisoner of God's Laws; he wouldn't have been able to say so many lies nor so many abominations and to do so much wrong. But he too will have to face the consequences.)

There are more lies in;)

Galatians 3, 26-27. 'You are all sons of God through faith in <u>Christ Jesus</u>. For all of you who were baptized into <u>Christ</u> have clothed yourselves with <u>Christ</u>.'

(This too is completely false and this not only according to me, but according to the Messiah himself.)

See Matthew 12, 50. 'For whoever does <u>the will</u> of my Father in heaven is my brother, sister and mother.'

(God's will is certainly not for anyone to say that his Laws don't exist anymore; He who said they will be in our hearts forever.)

So, it is not necessarily only the one who believes in Jesus or not and the one who is baptize in Jesus or not that is saved, but it is the one who does the will of the Father in heaven. See again what Jesus said to those who believe in him and to those who are baptize in him and don't do the will of the Father in heaven, or are refusing to obey in the Laws of God or to recognize them.)

Matthew 7, 22-23. 'Many will say to me on that day, (of the judgement) "Lord, Lord, 'did we not prophesy in your name, and in your name drive out demons and perform many miracles? Then I will tell them plainly, 'I never knew you. Away from me, you evildoers.'

(This is just one of the consequences for listening to Paul and not been under the Law of God and not to live according to the Lord's commandments; but mainly not to have repented for his sins, like Paul, who always had a clear conscience, being guilty of nothing.)

Galatians 3, 28-29. 'There is neither Jew nor Greek,'

(If there is no more Greek; then why has Paul circumcised Timothy because his father was a Greek?

'Slave nor free, male nor female, (just demons) for you are all one in Jesus Christ. <u>If</u> you belong to <u>Christ</u>, (yes, if) then you are Abraham's seed, and heirs according to the promise.'

(If all the dogs had a saw instead of a penis; there would be a lot less trees out there.

Here again Paul didn't tell the truth. Those who are Abraham's posterity are those who like Abraham did it, are obeying to the Laws of God. So they are not like Paul and his disciples, who are not under the Laws of God, because, if they are not under the Laws of God; they can not be his children and neither heirs of the promise. Those who belong to Jesus are following Jesus; the same man and Messiah who said this here in;)

Matthew 19, 17. 'If you want to enter life, (if you want to be heirs of the promise and to be Abraham's posterity, then) obey the commandments.'

(Yes, obey God's Laws, which means, to be under God's Laws. Listen to the Messiah; he tells the truth, contrary to Paul. And here is one thing God had to say about his Laws in;)

Deuteronomy 7, 11-12. 'Therefore, take care to follow the commandments, decrees and Laws I (God) give you today. If you pay attention to these Laws and are careful to follow them, then the Lord your God will keep his covenant of love with you, (people of Israel) as He swore to your forefathers.'

(This means then that we are heirs of the promise only if we are following the Laws of God and his decrees; and if faith has something to do with it; it is only if it leads us to obey God's Laws, God's commandments. If not, then, faith his dead, worthless, just as James, Jesus' brother said it.

So many lies and lies again, abominations and contradictions to God's and Jesus' messages give me headaches, and it is only because the Messiah said not to pull out the weeds that I think they are still there in the Holy Bible. But please, let no one say anymore that everything written in the Bible is all inspired by the Holy Spirit, because then, you would make Jesus a liar and Satan an angel of light.)

Galatians 4, 1-5. 'What I (Paul) am saying is that as long as the heir is a child, he is no different from a slave, although he owns the whole estate. He is subject to guardians and trustees until the time set by his father.'

(Are the children slaves of their parents just because they owe them obedience? This is still non-sense from Paul.)

'So also, <u>when we were children</u>, we were in slavery under the basic principles of the world. But when the time had fully come,'

(To this day the time has not fully come yet, and if everything was accomplished with Jesus' death on the cross; he wouldn't have had to ask us to make disciples in all the nations.)

'God sent his Son, born of a woman,'

(Rare are those who are born of a man. Only Paul tried that, but it didn't seem to work for him either. See Paul in;)

Galatians 4, 19. 'My dear children, for whom I (Paul) am again in the pains of childbirth until <u>Christ</u> is formed in you.'

(Isn't that for Paul to pretend to be the father of his disciples? Or maybe it was to pretend he was their mother.

See what the Almighty is reserving for the wicked sinners of the earth; which is written in;)

Isaiah 13, 8. 'Terror will seize them, pain and anguish will grip them; they will writhe like a woman in labour. They will look aghast at each other, their faces aflame.'

(And I continue with;)

Galatians 4, 4. 'Born under Law, to redeem those under Law, that we might receive the full rights of sons.'

(What a pile of rubbishes these are again. First, Jesus redeemed no one who were or are under the Law of God. Leave me bring you back to;)

Matthew 5, 17-19. 'Do not think that I have come to abolish the Law or the <u>prophets</u>; I have not come to abolish them but to fulfill them. (He didn't come to release anyone from it either.) I (Jesus) tell you the truth, until heaven and earth disappear, (then for as long as the universe exist) not the smallest letter, not the least stroke of a pen, will by any means disappear from the Law until everything is accomplished. Anyone who breaks one of the least of these commandments, (Paul broke or eliminated them all) and teaches others to do the same (Paul has done just that abundantly,) will be called least in the kingdom of heaven, (this is lower than a pig) but whoever practices and teaches them will be called great in the kingdom of heaven.'

(The Jesus' apostles have done it and his disciples are continuing to do it, as you can see by reading this book. So, maybe you should join me in this beautiful kingdom of heaven, in Jesus' kingdom, because nothing could make you happier, and this despite the troubles and the headaches.

Remember this important message from the Messiah written in;)

Matthew 12, 30. 'He who is not with me is against me, and he who does not gather with me scatters.'

(But the Paul's children story written in Galatians 4, 3, is another point directed directly against Jesus who said this in;)

Matthew 18, 2-3. 'Jesus called a little child and had him stand among them. (The disciples) And he said to them: "I tell you the truth, unless you change (be converted) and become like little children, you will never enter the kingdom of heaven.'

See also Matthew 19, 14. '"Let the little children come to me, (to the word of God) and do not hinder them, for the kingdom of heaven belongs to such as these."'

Galatians 4, 6. 'Because <u>you are</u> sons,'

(This is not; 'we are sons.' Paul has kind of excluded himself by saying it this way.)

'God sent the Spirit of his Son into our hearts, the Spirit who calls out, "Abba, Father.'

(It is not the Spirit of the Son that God sent to his children, but his own Spirit. This is the same way God put his own Spirit on the Messiah, and it is with that Spirit, with the word of God that Jesus baptizes those that he touches with his messages to this very day. Jesus said it himself.)

See Matthew 28, 20. 'And surely I am with you (his disciples) always, to the very end of the age.'

(It is also written that he will not shout or cry out.)

See Isaiah 42, 1-2. 'Here is my servant, whom I uphold, my chosen one in whom I delight; I will put my Spirit on him and he will bring justice to the nations. He will not shout or cry out, or raise his voice in the streets.'

(Why did Paul said the opposite? You can answer that yourselves.)

Galatians 4, 7. 'So you are no longer a slave,'

(Slave of the Law of God. This is what Paul meant here,)

'But a son; and since you are a son, God has made you also an heir.'

(Paul has excluded himself in this last verse again. I just wonder why. What Paul doesn't say here, is that we cannot become an heir, God's sons and daughters only by the grace of God. His grace is for everyone, but not everyone is catching it. But it is mainly as the

Messiah said it, by repenting of our sins, walking away from the slavery of sins and by turning to God. This is what allows us to become God's children and this is what the Messiah has preached. The grace of God is given to all of those who obey Him. One other thing that Paul didn't say, is that even if we are heirs by the grace of God, or by any means; we are disinheriting ourselves by committing a sin that cause the death of the soul that is not followed by repentance. This is the truth, but it is not with Paul and evidently not with his teaching either.)

Galatians 4, 8-9. 'Formerly, when you did not know God, you were slaves to those who by nature are not gods. But now that you know God—or rather are known by God—'

(As if God didn't know them before Paul spoke to them. This is rubbish again.)

'How is it that you are turning back to those weak and miserable principles? Do you wish to be enslaved by them all over again?

(What Paul talked to them about being enslaved of here, are the God's commandments, the Laws of God.

And why not a bit of humility in what is next?)

Galatians 4, 11-12. 'I (Paul) fear for you, that somehow I have wasted my efforts on you. I plead with you, brothers, <u>become like me</u> (a blasphemer, a liar and a murderer,) for I became (I am) like you.'

(Paul was a specialist of contradictory phrases and he most likely thought these were parables. But the Messiah said something quite different like this here; 'Therefore, be perfect as your heavenly Father is perfect.')

Galatians 4, 13. 'As you know, it was because of an illness,'

(Yes, he was missing the right eye and he had a withered right arm.)

'That I first preached the gospel to you.'

(Didn't he say earlier that this was because the Lord hit him on the road to Damascus? I rather think he did it to have his revenge on the Almighty because of his illness. What he called: 'The thorn in his flesh.')

Galatians 4, 14-16. 'Even though my illness was a trial to you, you did not treat me with contempt or scorn. Instead, you welcomed me as if I were an angel of God, as if I were Christ Jesus himself. <u>What has happened</u> to all your joy? I can testify that, if you could have done so, you would have torn out your eyes and given them to me.'

(That was because Paul was missing one, but he called them foolish, then they found out he was the devil and they kept their eyes for themselves. They were not so dumb after all, and according to what Paul said about them; they were much better than he is.)

'Have I now become your enemy by telling you the truth?'

(I rather think this was because they realized that Paul was lying to them with full mouth of lies; and this after blaspheming against an angel of God and calling them, 'foolish.')

Galatians 4, 17. 'Those people (Jesus' apostles and disciples,) are zealous to win you over, but for no good. What they want is to alienate you from us, (that's a good thing) so that you may be zealous for them.'

(They were smart those Galatians, not so foolish.)

Galatians 4, 18. 'It is fine to be zealous, (for Paul) provided the purpose is good, and to be so not just when I am with you.'

(This was with a whip and his army. Paul's reputation was known just about everywhere and this is most likely why he had to go farther and farther to win a convert, and this even up to where the barbarians have figured out Paul rightly by saying he was a murderer. And this explains why Paul had to travel all over the world on ground and on sea. See Jesus in;)

Matthew 23, 15. 'Woe to you, teachers of the Law and Pharisees, you hypocrites! You travel over land and sea to win a single convert, and when he becomes one, you make him (or her) a son of hell twice as much as you are.'

(By reading in Galatians I can see that Paul has not always succeeded, but this is not because he didn't try.)

Galatians 4, 19-20. 'My dear children, for whom I (Paul) am again in the pains of childbirth until Christ is formed in you, how I wish I could be with you now and change my tone, because I am perplexed about you!'

(By reading this last lamentation from Paul, I kind of wonder now if he thought he was the father or the mother of his disciples. Although, he said before that he was their father. And if Paul was so perplexed about the Galatians; this was because he knew there were some of the Jesus' disciples around them, who were telling the truth and it was not corresponding with his lies. And wasn't that taking God's place or thinking he was the nostril of the world, by calling them his children? See Paul again in;)

1 Corinthians 4, 14-15. 'I (Paul) am not writing this to shame you, but to warn you, as my dear children. Even though you have ten thousand guardians in Christ, you do not have many fathers, for in Christ Jesus I became your father through the gospel.'

(Isn't this what we say about someone who wants to take God's place, or has taken it? See again 2 Thessalonians 2, 4.

The Jesus' disciples have only One Father and He is in heaven, and this is not Paul and neither Satan.)

Galatians 4, 21. 'Tell me, you who want to be under the Law, are you not aware of what the Law says?'

(Those who hear the Law of God are those who listen to it. The Galatians wanted to belong to God; to be under the Law of God, but this devilish man, this Paul tried all he could to dissuade them with all kind of lies. And this with no doubt in my mind is the work of the devil. We have to see one of the most important messages from the Messiah written in;)

Matthew 11, 12. 'From the days of John the Baptist until now, the kingdom of heaven has been forcefully advancing, and forceful men (like Paul) lay hold of it.'

See also Matthew 23, 13. 'Woe to you, teachers of the Law and Pharisees, you hypocrites! (Like Paul) You shut the kingdom of heaven in people faces. You yourselves do not enter, nor will you let those enter who are trying to.'

(This is exactly what Paul has done and continues to do it with his lying gospel written in the New Testament of the Bible. This is also what Paul successors, his imitators are doing.

This is also why God chose me, to open the eyes of the blinds and to thwart Satan's plans. But, O my God; they are so numerous.

But now the cat is out of the bag. Paul let people believe earlier, not far back in Galatians 4, 9 that he was talking about the weak and miserable principles and this without mentioning he was talking about the Laws of God. But I had figured it out already, but what a hypocrite! These were the God's commandments that Paul called weak and miserable principles. This is only worthy of Satan and of his angels; either they are disguised as angels of light or not.

Then, to influence them and to show them that he knows God's affairs and the Holy Scriptures; Paul brought to them another story of Abraham and his two sons from the Old Testament. But this time this was to put them to sleep while they were still standing up. All of this though was for Paul one and only goal; this was to make them swallow his lies, his venom that will keep them in the dark and to bring them in hell with him. Everything was good for Paul to keep his disciples as far as possible from the Law of God and away from the will of God that is for all of God's children to obey Him, to obey his Laws and that they are circumcised.)

Galatians 4, 22-31. 'For it is written that Abraham had two sons, one by the slave woman and the other by the free woman.'

(Sara was not a free woman, for she was married to Abraham, but that without being his slave.)

'His son by the slave woman (Ismaël) was born in the ordinary way; (through flesh) but his son by the free woman (Isaac) was born as the result of the promise.'

(What a pile of rubbishes this is again. Isaac too was born in the ordinary way and through the flesh, even if that was done as the result of the promise.)

'These things may be taken figuratively, for the women represent two covenants.'

(If you go back and read the story of Abraham and Sarah concerning Abraham's two sons; you too will see that God has made no covenant with Sarah or with Hagar, but He has made a covenant with Abraham. And as far as I could read, God has made no covenant with a woman.)

'One covenant is from Mont Sinai and bears children who are to be slaves: This is Hagar. Now Hagar stands for Mont Sinai in Arabia and corresponds to the present city of Jerusalem, because she is in slavery with her children.'

(Not only Jerusalem, but Israel too was dominated by the Romans in those days, but the slavery that Paul meant to speak about here was more the obedience of the Israelites, to the Laws of God, to God's commandments. Jerusalem, the people of Israel is God's first born and it is not Abraham first or second born. There was no one like Paul to mix up his disciples.)

'But the Jerusalem that is above is free, and she is our mother. For it is written: "Be glad, O barren woman, who bears no children; break forth and cry aloud, you who have no labour pains.'

See now Isaiah 54, 1. 'Sing, O barren woman, you who never bore a child; burst into song, shout for joy, you who were never in Labour.'

(She has never bore a child and she was never in labour, but Paul called her a mother. Paul also said the exact opposite of what the Almighty said. It is either

Paul or his churches that have manipulated the Holy Scriptures and this is disgusting.

One thing though, the French version of that verse is not the same than the English one. I'll translate it for you.)

'Rejoice O barren, you who don't bear children anymore! Shout out your joy, you who don't suffer the pains of childbirth anymore.'

(The meaning is totally different from one version to the other.

And who is the true barren one in that story, for Sarah was barren, Genesis 11, 30. Rebekah was barren, Genesis 25, 21. Leah was also a barren and so was Rachel, see Genesis 29, 31. But they all became fruitful by the will of God and they all have known the pains of bearing a child.

'Because more are the children of the desolate woman than of her who has a husband.'

(I just wonder where this information came from, because God said this to Abraham that we can read in;)

Genesis 13, 16. 'I (God) will make your offspring like the dust of the earth, so that if anyone can count the dust, then your offspring could be counted.'

(Wow, this is a lot of people, which is to me uncountable.)

'Now, you, brothers, like Isaac, are children of promise.'

(Pardon me! The children of the promise are children of Abraham, some Jews and they are like Abraham, Isaac and Jacob, then children of God and not no-repented pagans. Jesus, the Messiah, came to tell us, pagans, what we have to do to become God's children and this is to repent and to turn away from our sins; and this is something that Paul didn't do and didn't teach, on the contrary.)

'At that time the son born in an ordinary way persecuted the son born by the power of the Spirit. It is the same now.'

(This is rubbish again! The two sons were born in an ordinary way. In those days the nation of Israel was besieged by the Romans and the Israelites were persecuted by the Romans and not the other way around.)

'But what does the Scripture say? "Get rid of the slave woman and her son, for the slave woman's son will never share in the inheritance with the free woman's son." Therefore, brothers, we are not children of the slave woman, but of the free woman.'

(This is false. The children of the free woman, as Paul called her, are Jews and circumcised and this is not at all what Paul wanted for himself, or for the Galatians, or for any of his disciples.)

Galatians 5, 1. 'It is for freedom that <u>Christ</u> has set us free. Stand firm, then, and do not let yourselves be burdened again by a yoke of slavery.'

(What a liar this Paul is! The yoke of slavery that Paul talked about here is God's Laws, God's commandments. These commandments say that not the least stroke of a pen will by any means disappeared from them, as the Messiah said it. Jesus has set us free, this is true, but not from the Laws of God, but he set us free from the slavery of sins to whoever sincerely repents of them. Sins are what forbid people to belong to God and Jesus, the Messiah, saves many by telling us what to do to get rid of them.)

Galatians 5, 2. 'Mark my words! I, Paul, tell you that if you let yourselves be circumcised, <u>Christ</u> will be of no value to you at all.'

(Just think about it for a moment; who else than Satan would want to break, to abolish an everlasting covenant that God made between Himself and his children? For whoever doesn't know this; the circumcision is an everlasting covenant, forever, that God has made between Himself and Abraham and all of Abraham's descendants after him. See again;)

Genesis 17, 9-13. 'Then God said to Abraham, "As for you, you must keep my covenant, you and your descendant after you for the generations to come. This is my covenant with you and your descendants after you, the covenant you are to keep: Every male among you shall be circumcised. You are to undergo circumcision, and it will be the sign of the covenant between Me and you. For the generations to come every male among you who is eight days old must be circumcised, including those born in your household or bought with money from a foreigner—<u>those who are not your offspring</u>. Whether born in your household or bought with your money, they must be circumcised. My covenant <u>in your flesh</u> is to be an <u>everlasting</u> covenant.'

(There is nothing complicated in what we have just read. The people of Israel, the Jews have respected this covenant and still do.

Paul wanted his disciples to believe they were heirs of the promise God made to Isaac because of the obedience of Abraham, but he didn't want them to respect this covenant. What a devil!)

Galatians 5, 3. 'Again I declare to every man who lets himself be circumcised that he is obligated to obey the whole Law.'

(Pour Timothy, who let himself be circumcised by Paul. All the laws, either they are from God or from any of the governments on this earth are made to be obeyed entirely by all, and this, either we like them or not. There is also punishment for disobedience. But Paul, who was circumcised at eight days old, according to himself, of course, why didn't he practice all the God's Laws and why did he preach against them so much? Paul didn't tell us that, but the reason is very simple; this is because he rebelled against God and against everything that is from Him; either it is the Laws, the circumcision, the Jesus' disciples, God's words, and even God's people, Israel. To me it is very clear; Paul's description is written in 2

Thessalonians 2, 3-4. None other than Satan has been dead set against everything that is from God as much as Paul did.)

2 Thessalonians 2, 3-4. 'Don't let anyone deceive you in any way, for that day will not come until the rebellion occurs and the man of lawlessness is <u>revealed</u>, the man doomed to destruction. He will oppose and he will exalt himself over everything that is called God or is worshipped, so that he sets himself in God's temple, proclaiming himself to be God.'

(Does this remind you of someone introduced in the New Testament?)

Galatians 5, 4. 'You who are trying to be justified by Law have been alienated from <u>Christ</u>; you have fallen away from the grace.'

(I personally call this blasphemy, but this is not the first time that Paul practiced it. Read the same verse again and replace, 'Christ,' by Antichrist; you will see then how much this makes more sense. And those who alienate themselves from the Antichrist will have a much better chance to receive God's grace. The thing is that you are alienated from the false Christ if you obey the Law, the God's commandments, and even more, if you do, you will obtain eternal life. I'm not the only one to say this; the Messiah said it long before me. Read and meditate on what is written in;)

Matthew 19, 16-17. 'Now a man came up to Jesus (the true one) and asked, "Teacher, what good thing I must do (a deed) to get eternal life?" "Why do you ask me about what is good?" Jesus replied. "There is only One who is good. If you want to enter life, obey the commandments."'

(This is God's Law. If that was Jesus death; he would have said; 'wait for my death.'

Only one is good, but Paul's churches have made thousands of saints that are not, like st Paul, for example. And instead of saying that Jesus is a saint; they said he is a curse. How nice? Is this their gracious grace? The grace of those who say they all have sins; I can live without it.

See also Deuteronomy 7, 11-12. 'Therefore, take care to follow the commandments, decrees and Laws I (God) give you today. If you pay attention to these Laws and are careful to follow them, then the Lord your God will keep his covenant of love with you, as He swore to your forefathers.'

(This is the promise God made to Abraham and it is for those who listen to God and obey his commandments.)

See also 1 King 2, 3. 'Observe what the Lord your God requires: walk in his ways and keep his decrees and commands, his Laws and requirements, as written in the Law of Moses, so you may prosper in all you do and wherever you go.'

(This is a very nice promise.)

Galatians 5, 5-6. 'But by faith we (Paul and company) eagerly await through the Spirit, the righteousness for which we hope. For in Jesus Christ neither circumcision nor incircumcision has any value. The only thing that counts is faith expressing itself through love.'

(How arrogant is this demon of Paul to use the name of the Messiah and the name of the Holy Spirit to lie, to say an abomination again! But the Messiah said it himself that he didn't come to abolish the Law of God or the prophets. It is not Jesus, the Messiah, either, who would abolish an everlasting covenant established between God and his children, on the contrary and he said it.

Then we are getting another proof that the Galatians were not so foolish in what is next in;)

Galatians 5, 7. 'You were running a good race. Who cut in on you and kept you from obeying the truth?'

(I lift up my arm to answer him, because I know these were one or more Jesus' disciples who did it; and this was not to forbid them to obey the truth, but to forbid them to believe in this demon's abominable lies.)

Galatians 5, 8. 'That kind of persuasion does not come from the one who calls you.'

(No, this kind of persuasion does not come from Satan, but it comes from God and this tells me that God loved the Galatians; to warn them this way and delivered them from the evil one. God did the same with me and I am very grateful to Him with all of my heart. I am pretty sure the Galatians were grateful to Him too, at least when Paul, his whip and his army were away from them.

We cannot say that Paul didn't know the truth; we can only say that he was preaching against it.)

Galatians 5, 9. 'A little yeast works through the whole batch of dough.'

(See also Jesus in;)

Matthew 13, 33. 'The kingdom of heaven is like yeast that a woman took and mixed into a large amount of flour until it worked all through the dough.'

(This will be until all the truth is known by all. Then the end of the devil's kingdom will come, and the kingdom of God will finally be opened to the righteous.)

Galatians 5, 10-11. 'I (Paul) am confident in the Lord that you will take no other view. The one who is throwing you into confusion will pay the penalty; (watch out for his army) whoever he may be. Brothers, if I am still preaching circumcision,'

(Of course Paul was still preaching circumcision and abundantly too, but he was preaching against it. He was also preaching the truth abundantly, but he was preaching against it. What a hypocrite he is!)

'Why am I still persecuted? In that case the offence of the cross has been abolished.'

(The offence of the cross belongs to the Romans and it is far from being abolished, because it will follow them straight to hell. But the Romans, beginning with Paul, have attributed this odious crime to God and to God's people; by saying He has sacrificed his Son. The Romans have done all that was possible to attribute this crime to the Jews, while in reality; the Messiah was assassinated by the Romans. 'The abomination that causes desolation!' Do you see it?)

Galatians 5, 12. 'As for those agitators,'

(Those were the people of the circumcision group, who were promoting the circumcision, this everlasting covenant between God and his children. They were working with the Jesus' apostles and were causing Paul troubles, because Paul was against it. They had at heart to help the voluntary Gentiles; in this case here these were the Galatians, to obey God's wills. But Paul as you can see as I do was mouthing against it and tried to stop them.)

'I (Paul) wish they will go the whole way and emasculate themselves.'

(This is bad enough and is against the will of God, which is for men to be fruitful, to multiply and to fill up the earth, but in the French Bible and in the King James; Paul wish they would be cut off, meaning, put to death.

Under that verse of Galatians 5, 12 in the French Bible; we are referred to;)

Joshua 7, 25. 'Joshua said, "Why have you brought this <u>trouble</u> on us? The Lord will bring trouble on you today. Then all Israel stoned him, and after they had <u>stoned</u> the rest, they burned them.'

(So they were put to death; which was the same thing Paul wanted for those of the circumcision group.

It is a fact that Satan would want for all men to be emasculated, not to be fruitful and this way being unable to multiply and fill up the earth, because this is the will of God. Satan knows very well that the day when the earth will be filled to God's taste; this will be the end for him. God Himself said it and we can read it among others in;)

Isaiah 11, 9. 'They will neither harm nor destroy on all of my holy mountain for the earth will be full of the knowledge of the Lord as the waters cover the sea.'

(According to what I read in all of his writings, Paul worked none stop the slow down this process. This was Paul who created these churches where men were told it is best for them not to touch women; which is completely contrary to the will of God. Women and men who entered a group of monasteries have listened and still are listening to Paul; which makes them counter to nature and anti-productive and this too is the work of Satan.

I strongly believe that Paul by doing this has created the largest club of homosexuals and lesbians in this world, beside a club of pedophiles and he knew exactly what he was doing too.

According to what is written in Isaiah 11, 9; Satan, the bad, the wrong, the wickedness won't be part of this world anymore.)

Galatians 5, 13. 'You, my brothers, were called to be free. But do not use your freedom to indulge in sinful nature; rather, serve one another in love.'

(Which is to love one another, and this is the new commandment of the false Christ who is in the gospel of John.

Do you remember that Paul called the Galatians, 'foolish,' earlier in Galatians 3, 1? And now he just called them, 'brothers.' See what the Messiah said about such a person in;)

Matthew 5, 22. 'But I (Jesus) tell you that anyone who is angry with his brother will be subject to judgement. Again, anyone who says to his brother, 'Raca,' is answerable to the Sanhedrin. But anyone who says, 'You fool.' will be in danger of the fire of hell.'

(And Paul being one of the most arrogant of men was not at all the type of men to repent, believing himself to be above everything and above all.

Then comes one of the worse lies that is written in the New Testament of the Bible and it is from Paul's mouth and from Paul's writing's hand.)

Galatians 5, 14. 'The entire Law is summed up in a single command: "Love your neighbour as yourself."'

(In the entire Law of God, there is no question for Paul to love God with all of his heart, with all of his soul or with all of his thoughts. One has to believe that this was and still is way too hard for Satan to do; because he is the one who loves himself more than anything and more than anyone.

Do you remember how Satan acted in the Garden of Eden with Adam and Eve? Let me refresh your memory and bring you back to that story of our first parents, their sin and their disobedience to God; after being tempted be the craftiest of all. See Genesis 2, 16 to Genesis 3, 4.)

Genesis 2, 16. 'The Lord God took the man and put him in the Garden of Eden to work it and take care of it. And the Lord God commanded the man, (his first commandment) "You are free to eat from any tree in the garden; but you must not eat from the tree of the knowledge of good and evil, for when you eat of it <u>you will surely die</u>. (See, God was speaking about the spiritual death.) The Lord God said, "It is not good for the man to be alone. I will make a helper suitable for him." Now the Lord God had formed out of the ground all of the beasts of the field and all the birds of the air. He brought them to the man to see what he would name them; and whatever the man called each living creature, that was its name. So the man gave names to all the livestock, the birds of the air and all the beasts of the field.'

(So Adam was not without any intelligence or without knowledge if he could do all of this before tasting the fruit from the tree of knowledge and before having a woman.)

'But for Adam no suitable helper was found. So the Lord God caused the man to fall into a deep sleep; and while he was sleeping, He took one of the man's ribs and closed up the place with flesh. Then the Lord God made a woman from the rib He had taken out of the man, and He brought her to the man. The man said, "This is now bone of my bone and flesh of my flesh; she shall be called, 'woman,' for she was taken out of man."'

(It is amazing that after finding a name for all the living creatures on earth; Adam could find one for her. And this again, was done before he tasted the fruit from the tree of knowledge. I don't think I could, unless, of course, God inspires me the same way He did for me to write all of my books.)

'For this reason a man will leave his father and mother and be united to his wife, and they will become one flesh. The man and his wife were both naked, and they felt no shame.

Now the serpent was <u>more crafty</u> the any of the wild animals the Lord God had made. He said to the woman, "Did God really say, 'You must not eat from any tree in the garden?"

(Can you see that Satan was not shy at all to use the Holy Name of God to pass his messages, to trap people and he continues to do it?

'The woman said to the serpent, "We may eat from the trees in the garden, but God did say, 'You must not eat fruit from the tree that is in the middle of the garden, and you must not touch it, or you will die.'" "You will not surely die."'

(As it was then, as it is today and as always, the devil contradicted God and he continues to do so. The crafty one knew exactly what God said, but this was for Satan the beginning of his revolution against God and he lied to Eve by contradicting God, and she let herself be seduced by him. Satan continues to do the exact same thing and this is what we can see in Paul's writings.

The definition of the entire Law of God by the Messiah is quite a bit different for him than it is for Paul.)

See Jesus again in Matthew 22, 36-40. 'One of them, an expert in the Law, tested Jesus with this question: 'Teacher, which is the greatest commandment in the Law?' Jesus replied; 'Love the Lord your God with all your heart and with all your soul and with all your mind. This is the greatest commandment. And the second one is like it; love your neighbour as yourself. All the Law and the Prophets hang on these two commandments."

(Paul and the Messiah have not the same definition of the Law of God, but who do you believe?

Galatians 5, 15-18. 'If you keep on biting and devouring each other, watch out or you will be destroyed by each other. So I say, live by the Spirit, and you will not gratify the desires of the sinful nature.'

(The desires of the flesh were created by God to fulfil his will that is for men to be fruitful, to multiply and to fill up the earth. But as I have already said it; the day when this will be done; this will be the end for Satan, and he is not in a hurry for that. So Satan has done a lot to slow down this process and he has preached a lot for men not to touch women; which he called sinful nature. But what God has asked men to do is not sinful and it is not immoral, on the contrary; it is to do God's will.

'For the sinful nature desires what is contrary to the Spirit, and the Spirit contrary to the sinful nature. They are in conflict with each other, so that you do not do what you <u>want</u>.'

(The Spirit of God never was and is not at all opposed to the will of God. But I understand the Galatians wanted to obey God's commandments despite Paul's opposition, not to say, Satan's opposition.)

'But if you are led by the Spirit, you are not under Law.'

(This is true if you are led by Satan's spirit, because God's Spirit doesn't contradict God or God's will in anything.

But see what is written against those who like Paul don't want to have anything to do with God's Law. See what happened to those who have despised God's Law and have despised the word of God in;)

Isaiah 5, 24. 'Therefore, as tongues of fire lick up straw and as dry grass sinks down in the flames, so their roots will decay and their flowers blow away like dust; for they have rejected the Law of the Lord Almighty and spurned the word of the Holy One of Israel.'

(See also;)

Isaiah, 30, 8-9. 'Go now, write it on a tablet for them, inscribe it on a scroll, that for the days to come it might be an everlasting witness. These are rebellious people, deceitful children, children unwilling to listen to the Lord's instruction.'

(Is this reminds you someone? And the abomination continues.)

Galatians 5, 19-21. 'The acts of the sinful nature are obvious; sexual immorality, impurity and debauchery; idolatry and witchcraft; hatred, discord, jealousy, fit of rage, selfish ambition, dissensions, factions and envy; drunkenness, orgies, and the like. I warn you, as I did before, that those who live like this will not inherit the kingdom of God.'

(Might as well tell them that they all are going to hell, there where Paul wanted them to go anyway. Who was he to tell them where they are going to go? Wasn't this to judge people before the time of the judgement; something the Messiah said not to do? And again one more time; why Paul in is entire litany of sins didn't mention the blasphemy and the murder, which he was both guilty of, not mentioning the lies? Was there a better way for Paul to take all hope to be saved away from all of them?

Here, 'murders,' is not mentioned, but it is in the King James. Also, instead of factions like is it mentioned here, it is replaced by sects as condemnable in the French Bible. Let's see the one who was accused by the Jews to be a ringleader of the Nazareth sect and Paul has not deny it in;)

Acts 24, 5-6. 'We have found this man (Paul) to be a troublemaker, stirring up riots (divisions) among the Jews, all over the world. He is a ringleader of the Nazarene sect and even tried to desecrate the temple.'

(I would say he did more then just tried to desecrate it, he did it, because the Jews tried to stone him because of it. During the whole interrogation before Felix, from Acts 24, 6 to Acts 24, 21, Paul didn't deny being the ringleader of that sect, even though this was false.)

Galatians 5, 22-23. 'But the fruit of the Spirit is love, joy, peace, patience, kindness, goodness, faithfulness, gentleness, and self-control. Against those things there is no law.'

(This is very ironic, because these are all what Paul didn't have.)

Galatians 5, 24. 'Those who belong to Christ Jesus have crucified the sinful nature, (the desires of the flesh) with its passions and desires.'

(This is completely false, except maybe for Paul's followers, because Jesus, the Messiah, knows very well the will of God that is for men to be fruitful, to multiply and to fill up the earth; which means that men need passions, desires of the flesh to accomplish the will of

God. Besides, Jesus has done nothing and he has said nothing against the will of the Father who is in heaven, on the contrary.)

Galatians 5, 25. 'Since we live by the Spirit, let us keep in step (walk) with the Spirit.'

(These are words in the air and to speak to hear oneself, because when someone lives by the Spirit of God; it is an automatism, he walks with God. But why Paul didn't mention whose spirit he is talking about? The spirit of evil exists just as well as the Spirit of God. When I speak about the Spirit of God; I am not shy at all the mention God.

See what is written from Jesus' brother in;)

1 John 4, 6. 'We are from God, and whoever knows God listens to us; but whoever is not from God doesn't listen to us. This is how we recognize the Spirit of truth and the spirit of falsehood.'

(Not to say, 'the spirit of lies.'

Remember I was saying that Satan too knows the messages of the Messiah; we can see a proof of that again in what is following in;)

Galatians 5, 26. 'Let us not become conceited, provoking and envying each other.'

See now Jesus in;)

Matthew 12, 25-26. 'Jesus knew their thoughts and said to them, "Every kingdom divided against itself will be ruined, and every household divided against itself will not stand. If Satan drives out Satan, he is divided against himself. How then can his kingdom stand?"'

(Of course, Satan didn't want to see his kingdom divided, because he wants it to live on. 'Love one another,' is good for all the kingdoms. Than to love one another is just as good for Satan's kingdom as it is for the kingdom of heaven. When it comes to the kingdom of God; there is not even a reason to ask, because all will know the will and the Law of God and will obey Him.)

Galatians 6, 1-2. 'Brothers, if someone is caught in a sin, you who are spiritual should restore him gently. But watch yourself, or you also may be tempted. Carry each other's burdens, and in this way you will fulfill the law of Christ.'

(I have already said it, the Messiah's ministry was not consisting in making or remaking the Laws of God and he said it himself that he didn't come to abolish them, not even the least stroke of a pen.

If an individual became a man; this is because he was raised by his parents normally, and it is no one else's business to restore him. If he has committed a crime, it is the law of men to take care of him; which is usually done. If he has committed a sin that is not the law of men's business; then it is a thing that concerns this man and God.

Paul knew how to restore people's spirit by bringing them to the lowest level, less than nothing.

Galatians 6, 3. 'If anyone thinks he is something when he is nothing, he deceives himself.'

(The Messiah had way more consideration for us than Paul had. See Jesus in;)

Matthew 10, 29-31. 'Are not two sparrows sold for a penny? Yet not one of them will fall on the ground apart from the will of your Father. And even the very hairs of your head are all numbered. So don't be afraid; you are worth more than many sparrows.'

(Even the dust of the earth is something and apparently, this is what we are, but still, this is better than nothing. Nothing doesn't exist.

See Genesis 2, 7. 'The Lord God formed the man from the dust of the ground and breathed into his nostrils the breath of life, and the man became a living being.'

(Then, if the man was formed with the dust of the ground; let no one say he is nothing. This was even an exceptional deed, executed with an exceptional substance, and by an exceptional Being, by the Highest Being and this is my God.

In the same way and just as easy, God will resurrect those He wants for the eternal life and the others for the eternal shame.

See Daniel 12, 2. 'Multitudes who sleep in the dust of the earth will awake; some to everlasting life, others to shame and everlasting contempt.'

(There where it will be weeping and gnashing of teeth. This will be a place that will certainly not be too joyful.)

Galatians 6, 4-5. 'Each one should test his own actions.'

(What for, if the deeds don't count, at least according to Paul?

'Then he can take pride in himself, without comparing himself to somebody else. For each one should carry his own load.'

(Is that what we call; 'Love your neighbour as yourselves? Then see what Paul has just said in;)

Galatians 6, 2. 'Carry each other's burdens.'

(I don't really know if Paul was mixed up or not, but one thing is sure; he is confusing.)

Galatians 6, 6. 'Anyone who receives instruction in the word must share all good things with his instructor.'

(Paul wanted to pick up everything he could, but the Messiah has never taught this way, on the contrary, because he said this; 'You have received freely, give freely.' What have the Jesus' disciple received freely? This is the teaching of the Messiah. The one who wants your goods is a thief; just don't let him do it.)

Galatians 6, 7-8. 'Do not be deceived: God cannot be mocked. (This is false again, because Paul did it. The truth is that God cannot be mocked without consequences.)

'A man reaps what he sows. The man who sows to please his sinful nature, from that nature will reap destruction.'

(This is false. The man who sows his seed with his wife will reap posterity, and that was not a risk for Paul, because he didn't want to touch a woman. The woman, one of the greatest marvels of this world, created by God and came out of a man. There is nothing in this corrupted world that is made more marvellously than a woman, who is a genial instrument of reproduction. Man and woman were made in the image of God, creators; this is not little to say.)

See again Genesis 1, 27. 'So God created man in his own image, in the image of God He created him; male and female He created them.'

(But Paul didn't want her, not for him and not for the other men.)

'The one who sows to please the Spirit, from the Spirit will reap eternal life.'

(And again here, Paul didn't dare say which spirit he was talking about, just like him and the false Christ who is in the gospel of John could not say where his father was from. The true Messiah was able to say that his Father is in heaven and to say his heavenly Father.)

Galatians 6, 9-10. 'Let us not become weary in doing good, for at the proper time we will reap a harvest ($) if we do not give up. Therefore, as we have the opportunity, let us do good to all people, especially to those who belong to the family of believers.'

(We know that now, the family of believers instead of those who are under the Law of God; meaning, Paul's enemies.)

Galatians 6, 11-12. 'See what large letters I (Paul) use as I write to you with my own hand.'

(I even doubt the Galatians read it entirely, because so many abominations causing desolation is very desolating alright. And if this was as desolating for the Galatians as this was for me; then this would have been preferable for them to burn these letters on reception. But Paul's letters have a good beginning and a good ending, that I'm pretty sure are from someone else than from Paul.)

'Those who want to make a good impression outwardly,'

(Those were the Jesus' apostles and disciples and the circumcision group that Paul was talking about here and he wanted them dead.)

'Are trying to compel you to be circumcised. The only reason they do this is to avoid being persecuted for the cross of Christ.'

(Then what was the reason for Paul to circumcise Timothy? Jesus had absolutely nothing against circumcision and nothing to do with it; except the fact he said to do what the scribes and the Pharisees are telling us to do. See Jesus in;)

Matthew 23, 2-3. 'The teachers of the Law and the Pharisees sit in Moses' seat. So you must obey them and do everything they tell you.'

(And this includes being circumcised; which the group of the circumcision was doing and whose Paul wanted dead. But Paul contradicts himself and this in the same latter to the;)

Galatians 2, 3. 'Yet not even Titus, who was with me, (Paul) was compelled to be circumcised, even though he was a Greek.'

(Then why Paul was complaining so much against the group of the circumcision? Let's see now whom, by whom and why one man was compelled to be circumcised, and he too was a Greek.)

Acts 16, 1-3. 'Paul wanted to take him (Timothy) along on the journey, so he circumcised him because of the Jews who lived in that area, for they all knew that his father was a Greek.'

(We have rarely seen something as hypocritical as this in the Holy Bible and this was certainly not inspired by the Holy Spirit. And by whom Timothy was compelled to be circumcised? By the hypocrite, by Paul and according to this Paul; 'Christ,' will be of no value at all to Timothy. How sad this is.)

Galatians 6, 13. 'Not even those who are circumcised obey the Law.'

(Paul knew it, for he was circumcised himself and so was Timothy. We all know now also that Paul was not observing the Law of God, and he was teaching others to do the same. But when comes to the others; this was their problems, not Paul's; so why did he even mention that? See Paul in;)

Philippians 3, 4-6. 'Though I (Paul) myself have reasons for such confidence. If anyone else thinks he has reasons to put confidence in the flesh, I have more; circumcised on the eighth day, of the people of Israel, of the tribe of Benjamin, a Hebrew of Hebrews; in regard of the Law, a Pharisee; as for zeal, persecuting the Church; (killing the Jesus' disciples) as for legalistic (the Law) righteousness, faultless.'

(The Law of God that says: 'You shall not kill.' Here is the rest of;)

Galatians 6, 13. 'Yet they (the Jesus' apostles) want you to be circumcised that they may boast about your flesh.'

(But what was the real reason for Paul to circumcise Timothy? The apostles wanted for other people to be able to say before God; 'We too Lord are your people.' Let us suppose that God will say to all uncircumcised men born after he made his covenant with Abraham: 'I don't know you.'

Galatians 6, 14-15. 'May I never boast except in the cross of our Lord Jesus Christ, through which the world has been crucified to me, and I to the world.'

(Although, Paul has already said boasting about his weakness, which is written in Corinthians. And besides, if the world was crucified; it would be dead and so would be Paul and all of his abominations.)

2 Corinthians 11, 30. 'If I must boast, I will boast about the things that show my weakness.'

See also 2 Corinthians 12, 9. 'Therefore I will boast all the more gladly about my weaknesses.'

'Neither circumcisions nor incircumcision means anything; what counts is a new creation.'

(Then why Paul mouthed so much to prevent men to be circumcised, if that meant nothing to him? The circumcision has indeed, made a man a new creation by making him respecting the covenant God made with him. And as far as I know, neither the world nor Paul was crucified, but Jesus, the Messiah was; these were not Paul or the false Christ. And if circumcision or incircumcision meant nothing for Paul; it did and it does for all the Jews of this world, for the people of God, it does for God and for all of his children. And if circumcision meant nothing for Paul, then why was that such a big deal for him that he wanted to eliminate all of those who practiced it? This was except himself, of course.

Galatians 6, 16-17. 'Peace and mercy to all who follow this rule, even to the Israel of God.'

(It is evident that we are getting at the end of Paul's letter, because the tone has changed a lot. Never in his life Paul would have asked peace for Israel; he who hated it and also its people and the Jews with passion.

'Finally, let no one cause me trouble, for I bear on my body the marks of Jesus.'

(Would this be Jesus, who would allow your right eye to be blinded and your right arm to be completely withered, Paul? This was done by God, because you, Paul, you are the worthless shepherd and you deserved what you received.

And you my readers, who are reading these lines and to better understand; please go read again;)

Zechariah 11, 17. '"Woe to the worthless shepherd, who deserts the flock! May the sword strike his arm and his right eye! May his arm be completely withered, his right eye totally blinded!"'

(And this letter from Paul ended the same way it was started, with the writing of someone for whom the disciples were brothers and not children and for whom the name of the Messiah was respected.)

Galatians 6, 18. 'The grace of our Lord Jesus Christ be with your spirit, brothers. Amen!'

Chapter 9

I finally got through Galatians, but I must admit it; this was not easy at all. This was through Jesus' messages, especially from this one here that comes next and one from God I received in a dream that my eye were opened, and I thank God with all of my heart.)

See Matthew 24, 15. 'Therefore, when you see the abomination that causes desolation, which was spoken of through Daniel the prophet—standing in the holy place—(in the Bible) let the <u>reader</u> understand.'

(I have repeated it many times, but this will be never enough, because this is through reading carefully all of the Jesus' messages, from the true Messiah that we can distinguish the wheat from the weeds, the truth from the lies.

Even if it is painful sometimes, even very desolating; it is also very comforting to know what to do and mainly whom to put out of our life and in turn to be sure that we are with the good guide, with the one who leads us in the truth and to God.

God said it Himself that He is the God of the circumcised, but it is clear that Paul didn't want any part of them and he didn't want his disciples to be part of them either.

See Genesis 17, 7-13. 'I (God) will establish my covenant as an everlasting covenant between Me and you and your descendants after you for the generations to come, to be your God and the God of your descendants after you. The whole land of Canaan where you are now an alien, I will give as an everlasting possession to you and your descendants after you; and I (God) will be their God."

(God is the God of the circumcised.)

'Then God said to Abraham, "As for you, you must keep my covenant, you and your descendant after you for the generations to come. This is my covenant with you and your descendants after you, the covenant you are to keep: Every male among you shall be circumcised. You are to undergo circumcision, and it will be the sign of the covenant between Me and you. For the generations to come every male among you who is eight days old must be circumcised, including those born in your household or bought with money from a foreigner—those who are not your offspring. (Either they are Jews or pagans.) Whether born in your household or bought with your money, they must be circumcised. My covenant in your flesh is to be an everlasting covenant.'

(I myself often wondered why the Son of Man, the Messiah, asked his angels not to pull out the weeds from the wheat and I got a few answers since, but the main reason I think is in what is next.

Matthew 4, 4. 'Jesus answered, "It is written: 'Man does not live on bread alone, but on <u>every word</u> that comes from the mouth of God.'

(Neither Jesus nor God wanted that even a single word from the mouth of God be lost. The Messiah knew very well that Satan would use some of God's words to seduce and to mislead people and this is exactly what the devil did.

But the word of God, either it is spread out by a Jesus' disciple or by one of Jesus' enemies disguised as an angel of heaven; it remains still a word of God. And just like Jesus said it; every word that comes from the mouth of God is nourishing for the soul of the human being.

His words are nourishing and I am satiated as a Jesus' disciple and I try to do what he has prescribed.

Of course I have experienced desolation for seeing so many abominations in the holy place, in the Holy Scriptures, but fortunately; Jesus had warned me ahead of time. There are a lot of warnings from the Messiah and this in just about everyone of his parables he spoke to us about his kingdom, the kingdom of heaven. This is the kingdom of heaven that only Matthew mentioned in his gospel. This doesn't mean that there is no truth somewhere else, because according to Jesus; there is some truth just about everywhere, but we have to pay attention to what or how we read. We have to be vigilant.

'Seek and you will find.'

'You will recognize the tree by its fruits.'

'Many are invited, but few are chosen.'

'There are the weeds and the wheat.'

'He is a murderer and a liar from the beginning.'

'Watch out that no one deceives you.'

'Don't let anyone deceive you in any way.'

'Let the reader pay attention when he reads.'

(And many more!

What helped me the most I think was the fact that I knew Jesus' messages, the messages of the true Messiah, because that all and everything that is against him mislead and scatter.

One out of three of Adam and Eve children was a liar and a murderer. One third of God's created angels have revolted against Him and those are the ones who are leading the war to God's children on earth. They are trying to seduce them by all kind of evil tricks and using the words of God is one of their main trumps.

The Messiah knew it, and it is against them that he warned us. But of course, this was in the interest of the sons of the devil to say that everything that is written in the Holy Bible was all inspired by the Holy Spirit and that it contains only the truth. But it is also true that there are also lies in it, that there are weeds, and that Satan disguised as an angel of heaven is also in there. If this was not the case, the Messiah wouldn't have had to give us all of those warnings, especially this one; 'May the reader be careful when he reads.'

This means then that the traps are in the Holy Book, they are in the Scriptures and that is the abomination that causes desolation.

This is what I have seen and I could not keep quiet about it nor keep it to myself. This is why I want to share it with the rest of the world that need this badly.

God wanted to share his creation with all men and He has always used men to accomplish that. He used Adam and Eve to populate the earth. He used Noah and his family to save a part of the population and to continue filling the earth. He used Abraham, Isaac and Jacob to establish his people, his first born in Israel. He used Joseph to save his people from the famine. He used Moses to deliver his people from the servitude in Egypt. He used David to establish a permanent king over his people. He used Jesus to proclaim justice to all the nations. God is using me to warn all the nations that this is their last chance to turn to Him before the end of the age, and I am very happy to serve Him.)

See again Matthew 24, 14. 'And this gospel of the kingdom (of heaven that I preach) will be preached in the whole world as a testimony to all nations, and then the end will come.'

(The enemies of Israel are God's enemies.)

See Zechariah 12, 9. 'On that day I (God) will set out to destroy all the nations that attack Jerusalem.'

(So, you better watch out Palestine, Iran, Syria, Russia, Turkey and all the others who hate the Jews, because your destiny is already marked in the book of the truth.

As for my own person, I have already mentioned it that Jesus had one traitor out of twelve and if I am lucky; I will have one faithful out of twelve.

When comes to the rest of the New Testament; most of it was written by Paul and company. Just remember that none of Jesus' apostles and none of Jesus' disciples have spoken about the Messiah by just saying: 'In Christ, by Christ, for Christ,' and so on, but Paul has done it many times. I counted 257 times where Paul has done that. There is no one who has respect for the queen Elisabeth would call her; 'Beth,' and yet, in my opinion, she is not as important as the Messiah is.

We can see the truth in the writings of James and in Jude, a mixture in 1, 2, 3 of John, the Jesus' brothers. There is a huge mixture of truth and lies in 1 and 2 Peter, but Peter is not to blame for that. This means that we have to be very careful as we read them and remember what I wrote a bit earlier about those who have just wrote, 'Christ,' while speaking about the Messiah.

We also know that Satan is a great imitator and just like God has put his words in the mouth of a prophet like Moses, raised up among his brothers in Israel, as it is written in Deuteronomy 18, 18; Satan too has put his lying words in the mouth of Peter. And he did this more than once. We have seen it at the beginning of the Acts and we have seen it also in;)

Matthew 16, 23. '"Get behind me, Satan! You are a stumbling block to me; you do not have in mind the things of God, but the things of men."'

(We can see it again in 1 Peter; which is for the most the way of Paul to speak and to write. This is not Peter who wrote from Babylon, but Paul and it is not Peter who wrote this way either.)

See 1 Peter 5, 13-14. 'She (the church) who is in <u>Babylon</u>, chosen together with you, sends you her greetings and so does <u>my son Mark</u>. Greet one another with a kiss of love. Peace to all of you who are in <u>Christ</u>.'

(The church of Babylon was and is one of Paul's churches, and remember that this was Paul who had the habit to call his disciples his children, but Peter was told they were all brothers among them. Remember also this message from the Messiah to his apostles written in;)

Matthew 10, 5-6. 'Do not go among the Gentiles or enter any town of the Samaritans. Go rather to the lost sheep of Israel.'

(And you can be sure of one thing; this is that the Jesus' apostles obeyed him and Peter even more, for he is the one who carried the keys of the kingdom of heaven.

This is not Peter either, who has written this, but Paul, I am sure of it.)

2 Peter 3, 15-16. 'Bear in mind that our Lord's patience means salvation (which is false) just as our dear brother Paul also wrote with the wisdom that God gave him. He writes the same way in all his letters, speaking in them of these matters. His letters contain some things that are hard to understand,'

(These are the lies, the contradictions and mainly the abominations.)

'Which ignorant and unstable people (like myself) distort, as they do the other Scriptures, to their own destruction.'

(Paul knew that one day or another someone would discover his ruses and have the courage to speak about them. But don't worry for me, because I don't give a damn about Satan's threats, even if he wants me to go the hell. By telling the truth, no matter what it is and how painful it is; I have God's approbation and blessing, because He is the One who asked me to do it. More than that; without is request, I wouldn't have wanted to do it and I couldn't do it either.

See that Peter's ways to speak about our Master is much different than Paul's ways in;)

2 Peter 1, 14. 'Because I know that I will soon put it aside, as our Lord Jesus Christ has made clear to me.'

See also 2 Peter 1, 16. 'We did not follow cleverly invented stories (as Paul has often done it,) when we told you about the power and coming of our Lord Jesus Christ, but we were eyewitnesses of his Majesty.'

(No one calls his Majesty or his Master by his or her first name.

When I speak about respect from a disciple for the name of his Master; this is what we have just seen in 2 Peter 1, 14-16. There is the whole difference.

Speaking like Peter did is much different than speaking like the John of Paul did it in the Revelation and the words he put in the mouth of the false Christ who said this in;)

Revelation 3, 3. 'But if you do not wake up, I (false Christ) will come like a thief, and you will not know at what time I will come to you.'

(See now the difference from the mouth of Peter in;)

2 Peter 3, 10. 'But the day of the Lord will come like a thief.'

(The Lord and the day of the Lord are two very distinct things, to me anyway, but the Lord is not a thief and he won't act like one either. The one who acts like a thief is a thief, but Jesus is not one of them.

This John had repeated this lie in;)

Revelation 16, 15. 'Behold, I come like a thief!'

(The false prophets and the false Christs have preferred to say that the Lord is like a thief instead of saying he is like a benevolent employer.

See what the Messiah has really said in;)

Matthew 24, 42-44. 'Therefore keep watch, because you don't know on what day your Lord will come. But understand this: If the owner of the house had known at what time of night the thief was coming, he would have kept watch and would have not let his house be broken into. So you must also be ready, because the Son of Man will come at an hour you do not expect him.'

(Your soul must be worth more than all of your goods, because it is written: 'What good for someone to win the universe if he looses his soul?'

(See also Jesus in;)

Matthew 25, 13. 'Therefore keep watch, for you do not know the day or the hour.'

(To be a thief or to be like one is a qualification I would not attribute to God or to the Messiah. To be an animal, to be a Lamb is not something I would attribute to them neither.

But aren't we lucky, because the Messiah warned us? This is something that neither a thief nor an employer would do?

Paul has exaggerated his speaking about faith and many times by quoting Sarah and Abraham. We can find that mainly in Hebrews, but to him, this was at the detriment of the Law of God. 'It is by faith,' was he saying.

Take for example a man who is lost and he gets at a crossroad. He takes a left turn when he should have taken a right turn to make it to his destination. He had faith and he believed that the left turn was the right one to take, but that was a mistake. In this case here, it is not too bad, because he can always turn around and with a bit of luck find his way home. But it is way more serious when the faith leads someone into the abyss, because he can really be lost and forever.

Even faith in God is worthless without obeying the Law of God, without acts of love, of mercy, charity and forgiveness. This is what the Law of God is all about, as James, Jesus' brother showed us.

See James 2, 14-20. 'What good is it, my brothers, if a man claims to have faith but has no deeds? Can such a faith save him?' Suppose a brother or sister is without clothes and daily food. If one of you says to him, "Go, I wish you well keep warm and well fed," but does nothing about his physical needs, what good is it? In the same way, faith by itself, if it is not accompanied by action, is dead. But someone will say, "You have faith; I have deeds." Show me your faith without deeds, and I will show you my faith by what I do.

You believe that there is one God. Good! Even the demons (like Paul) believe that—and shudder. You foolish man, (Paul) do you want evidence that faith without deeds is worthless?'

(James too had faith and he knew the Law just as much as Paul knew it, but on top of it and contrary to Paul, James, just like the Jesus' apostles, has spent a lot of time near his brother Jesus. James, contrary to Paul, has learned to know the truth and he has learned how to preach it also.)

See James 2, 8-9. 'If you really keep the royal Law found in Scripture, "Love your neighbour as yourself," you are doing right. But if you show favouritism, you sin and are convicted by the Law as lawbreakers.'

(James could have had added this; 'that you believe in it or not! But I do.

Faith is very good, but only if it leads you to the truth. If faith leads you to the lie, then it is rather a curse to you, because then, it takes away from you any hope to be saved, just like Paul has done in what we can read in;)

Hebrews 6, 4-6. 'It is impossible for those who have been once enlightened, (like Jesus' apostles) who have tasted the heavenly gift, (like Jesus' apostles) who have shared in the Holy Spirit, (like the Jesus' apostles) who have tasted the goodness of the word of God and the power of the coming age, (like the Jesus' apostles) If they fall away, (like Jesus' apostles did) to be brought back to repentance, because, to their lost they are crucifying the Son of God all over again and subjecting him to public disgrace.'

(But these are not the Jesus' apostles, nor his disciples who are subjecting the Messiah to public disgrace; these are the sons of the devil, and if they cannot be brought to repentance, this is because they are too proud to repent, just like Paul who wrote this abomination.

To repent is to get rid of our sins, so don't waste any time, because we don't know the hour and neither the day when the Master will knock at the door and for all of us; this can be anytime. If we love God with all of our heart, our soul and mind; this becomes a very easy thing to do, just like to obey his Laws.

But on the other hand, if a person doesn't love God, then that person is against Him and against everything that comes from Him, just as it is writing in;)

2 Thessalonians 2, 4. 'He will oppose and he will exalt himself over everything that is called God or is worshipped, so that he sets himself in God's temple, proclaiming himself to be God.'

(Such a man is the Antichrist and he is the one I denounce in my writings, in all of my books, and if this demon is not Satan; he is for sure one of his followers. But one thing remains evident, he is a seducer, because millions, if not billions have followed him and still do.

This is a real disaster for the humanity. This is the reason why we have to hurry and that Jesus and I need the help of all of those who love God with all of their heart, to wake up the world that is caught in this devil's trap.

Satan has his helpers, many associates, many of his hell angels, many of his demons, who are at work constantly. Then the God's children have to get busy too and to start denouncing the liars, the lies and all and everything that contradict the Messiah, everything that contradicts the Jesus' messages. To denounce all and everything that is against God. Not to forget also that the reward that is coming from Satan is hell and the reward that will come from God is paradise, everlasting life.

I have a good warning though for all of those who will reach me in this gigantic deed for the service to God and this is not to go argue with those who want to suppress the truth by their wickedness, because they already know everything I talk about in this book. Those are working for Satan and they are not the ones you should try to save. Try to save those who don't know the truth, because they might just have a chance to receive and to accept it. But do it without forgetting that medicine is taken in small quantities. And we can't tell the beast that it is the beast without any risk, because it will destroy you as it has always done it. It is only a pleasure for the beast to kill God's children.

Many are scandalized to see so many crimes being committed by the Muslim terrorists. Don't forget that Christianity has done worse, it has committed more murders. The Messiah said it; 'Satan is a murderer from the beginning.'

Make sure you'll have a nice answer ready, when the Almighty will ask you; 'What have you done for Me? He who knows everything.

James Prince, a Jesus' disciple.

Printed in the United States
By Bookmasters

Printed in the United States
By Bookmasters